SPECTACULAR RHETORICS

# SPECTACULAR

*Next Wave:*
*New Directions in*
*Women's Studies*
A series edited by
Inderpal Grewal,
Caren Kaplan, and
Robyn Wiegman

# RHETORICS

HUMAN RIGHTS VISIONS, RECOGNITIONS, FEMINISMS

WENDY S. HESFORD

DUKE UNIVERSITY PRESS | DURHAM AND LONDON

Designed by April Leidig-Higgins

Typeset in Arno by Copperline Book Services, Inc.

Library of Congress Cataloging-in-Publication Data
appear on the last printed page of this book.

For my daughters,
Mia and Lou Fei Cariello

And in memory of my father,
David Hesford (1936–2010)

# CONTENTS

## ACKNOWLEDGMENTS

This book investigates how visual rhetoric has shaped the normative frameworks of international human rights law and advocacy, and how human rights principles are culturally translated into a visual vernacular that imagines Western audiences—generally American audiences—as moral viewers. To emphasize the rhetorical dimensions of human rights work is not to diminish or deny its material impetus or consequences, however. First and foremost, I acknowledge the individuals whose lives have become a part of a cultural production, human rights campaign, or scholarly pursuit such as this book represents. Though these cultural productions have kept me at a safe distance from the violence that many of the subjects represented have experienced, I want to acknowledge the suffering of those whose human rights have been violated and the courage of human rights defenders to speak out even when the risks are severe. Indeed, this safe and critical distance has enabled me to devote a significant portion of the last six years to better understanding the visual economy of human rights and to contemplating how scholars, activists, and artists (which are not mutually exclusive categories) respond to crises in ways that make the progressive potential of human rights imaginable for all.

In this book, I examine a number of cultural sites (film festivals, photographic exhibitions, and theater productions) that I have had the privilege to enter, given my institutional affiliations and research support. The Ohio State University (OSU), in Columbus, provided research and travel support through the Departments of English and Women's Studies, and the College of Humanities. I especially want to thank Valerie Lee for her unflinching support during her term as chair of the Department of English, and colleagues in English, comparative studies, and women's studies for their intellectual engagement and friendship. A special thanks to my colleagues in English—particularly Brenda Jo Brueggemann, Jim Fredal, Kay Halasek, Nan Johnson, Jim Phelan, and Amy Shuman—who devoted considerable time to reading portions of this manuscript at critical junctures, and whose interventions made this a better book. Thanks to colleagues in comparative studies, especially Julia Watson, Maurice Sanders, and Barry Shank, for opportunities to share work in progress. Thanks also to faculty and colleagues in administrative positions across the university for institutional support on this project in its many phases; particularly helpful were Valerie Lee, Richard Dutton, Ester Gottlieb, Sebastian Knowles, John Roberts, Debra Moddelmog, and Cathy Rakowski. The Department of English administrative staff also provided daily help on the details of research and writing. Thanks to Lynne Berry, Katherine O'Brien, Cheryl Frasch, and Carolyn Wilkins.

An interdisciplinary network of scholars at OSU has been especially significant in sustaining me, including participants in the Democracy and Culture project, OSU-WID (Women in Development), and the Moritz School of Law. Gratitude is due to many graduate students in English and women's studies, some of whom have moved on with their professional careers, for their inspiring work and critical engagement: Subho Chakravorty, Rebecca Dingo, Timothy Jensen, Amy Monticello, Ryan Omizo, Nancy Pine, Raili Roy, and Wendy Wolters Hinshaw. Thanks to undergraduate students at OSU in my Law and Literature and Rhetoric of Social Movements courses for their probing questions. Thanks to Theresa Kulbaga for collaborations and research assistance, and to Barney Latimer for his editorial assistance in preparing the manuscript during its final stage.

This project was also supported through a 2005 National Endowment for the Humanities summer fellowship to attend the Human Rights in an Era of Globalization seminar at Columbia University. Special thanks are due to Andrew Nathan for his leadership in the seminar, and to its participants—especially Stephanie Athey, Lisa Lynch, Angela Reyes, and Ben Olgin—for their critical exchanges. My 2007 stint as a visiting scholar at Columbia University's Center for the Study of Human Rights provided me with time to focus on several chapters, to interview representatives at New York–based human rights organizations, and to attend, yet once more, the Human Rights Watch International Film Festival. I have also benefited from the encouragement of Andrew Nathan, Bruce Robbins, Joseph Slaughter, and other colleagues at the center and elsewhere at Columbia, who met with me and offered important complications to my ideas. Scholars across the United States with whom I have shared portions of this work over the years and conversed in ways that were especially meaningful to this project include: Eleni Coundouriotis, Allen Feldman, Lindsey French, Leigh Gilmore, Inderpal Grewal, Daniel Gross, Andrew Herscher, Renata Kirin Jambresic, Ratna Kapur, Arabella Lyon, Steven Mailloux, Eileen Schell, and Sidonie Smith. Special thanks to my intellectual soul mate Wendy Kozol, with whom I have had the pleasure of collaborating over the last fifteen years. Her critical vision and probing questions have greatly influenced this work.

Thanks to audiences at Eugene Lang College and the New School of Social Research; Indiana University, in Bloomington; Miami University of Ohio; Oberlin College; Ohio State University, in Columbus; the Baldy Center for Law and Social Policy at the State University of New York, Buffalo; Syracuse University; the University of California, at Santa Barbara and Irvine; the University of Connecticut, in Storrs; the Rackham Human Rights Lecture Series and Sweetland Writing Center at the University of Michigan; and the University of Missouri, in Columbia, where I was invited to share my work in progress. Thanks also to those at conferences over the years for their warm reception and persistent questions, including participants at national conferences sponsored by the American Studies Association, Rhetoric Society for America, College Composition and Communication, and Modern Language Association, and at regional conferences such as the Human Rights Documentation Conference at Columbia University, the Feminist Rhetorics for Social Justice at Syracuse University, and the Women and War Conference, Human Rights Confronting Images and Testimonies Conference, and Amnesty International Conference, all at OSU.

Several human rights activists have also provided access to archival materials and media images, and given me interviews and critical feedback along the way. I am especially grateful to Sam Gregory at Witness, Andrea Holley and Carroll Bogert at Human Rights Watch, and Steve Ruhl and Zeke Johnson at Amnesty International. Thanks also to the artists featured in this book, especially Ursula Biemann and Melanie Friend, for interviews and generous responses to my queries.

At Duke University Press, the wisdom, patience, and guidance of Ken Wissoker enabled me to envision the book that my manuscript would become and to work hard to achieve that vision. Mandy Earley guided me with care through the submission and review phases. Rebecca Fowler guided me through the copyediting and production phases. I would also like to thank the copyeditor, Jeanne Ferris. Anonymous reviewers provided critical interventions at various points along the way, enabling me to better discern the book's aims, scope, and limits. My gratitude to Inderpal Grewal, Caren Kaplan, and Robyn Wiegman for making the publication of this book possible through the Next Wave: New Directions in Women's Studies series. Finally, thanks to my husband Matthew, and our two daughters, Mia and Lou Fei, for the creative and loving spaces you yield to me daily.

Chapters that were previously published are reprinted here with permission. They have all been revised and edited for this book. A shorter version of chapter 2 was first published in *TDR* 50, no. 3 (fall 2006): 29–41, and then in *Dramaturgy of the Real on the World Stage*, edited by Carol Martin (Basingstoke, England: Palgrave MacMillan, 2010). The Chinese version of chapter 2 appeared in *TDR China* 1, no. 1 (2007): 98–123. Chapter 3 was first published in *Biography* 27, no. 1 (winter 2004): 104–44. A shorter version of chapter 3 that emphasized pedagogical concerns appeared in *Teaching Rhetorica: Theory, Pedagogy, Practice*, edited by Kate Ronald and Joy Ritchie (Portsmouth, NH: Boynton/Cook, 2006). Chapter 4 was first published in *Just Advocacy? Women's Human Rights, Transnational Feminisms, and the Politics of Representation*, edited by Wendy Hesford and Wendy Kozol (New Brunswick, NJ: Rutgers University Press, 2005). A shorter version of chapter 4 was reprinted in *Ursula Biemann: Mission Reports; Artistic Practice in the Field—Video Works 1998–2008*, edited by Ursula Biemann and Jan-Erik Lundstrom (BildMuseet, Umea Universitet Sweden, 2008).

SPECTACULAR RHETORICS

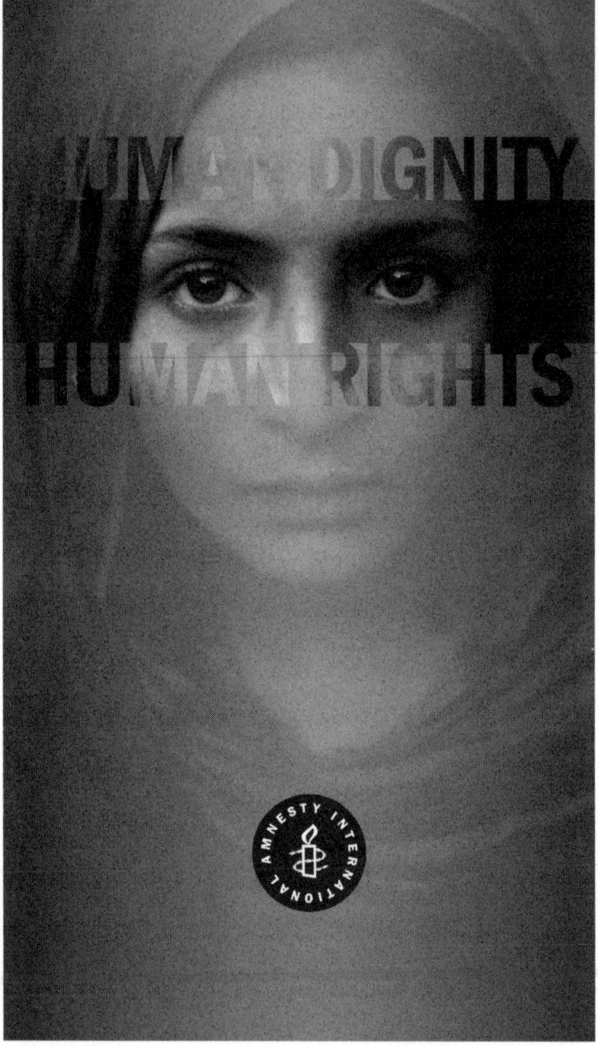
HUMAN DIGNITY
HUMAN RIGHTS
AMNESTY INTERNATIONAL

# Introduction

hose story do these eyes tell?

Amnesty International USA (AIUSA) launched its "Imagine" campaign in 2002 to inspire a new wave of global human rights activism.[1] On the cover of the campaign brochure, AIUSA features a photograph of an Afghan refugee, a girl in a green headscarf (fig. 1).[2] She lives in a refugee camp in Peshawar, Pakistan.[3] The phrase "human dignity, human rights," superimposed on her face, frames the girl's sea-green eyes. Diffused turquoise light radiates through the center of the image, drenching all but the horizontal band across her eyes. Her youth, beauty, and innocence are common signs of femininity and the gendering of sympathy in the American transnational human rights imaginary. The girl's direct yet vulnerable stare echoes the haunting gaze of another Afghan girl, who was featured on the cover of the June 1985 issue of *National Geographic* (fig. 2), a highly publicized and internationally circulated image, which has come to stand for the "troubled face of Afghanistan" (Cumbo 2002).[4] What normative assumptions about the conditions of social and legal recognition underwrite Americans' engagement with the image on the AIUSA brochure? What meaning does the image of the face of an Afghan girl refugee take on in the visual field of human rights advocacy?

The neutral background and closely cropped portrait aid the image's iconic function by isolating the girl from her material circumstances and constructing her (part for whole) as the archetypal Afghan refugee.[5] Although the United States, with its strict refugee laws, has granted asylum to few of the world's refugees,[6] the Afghan girl has become a symbol of Ameri-

(*Opposite*) 1. Cover of the brochure for Amnesty International USA's "Imagine" campaign. "Girl with Green Shawl," photograph by Steve McCurry, 2002. By permission of Magnum Photos.

2. Afghan girl at Nasir Bagh refugee camp, Peshawar, Pakistan, 1984. Photograph by Steve McCurry. By permission of Magnum Photos.

can charity and compassion—a representation that rests on the narrative configuration of the girl refugee as a deserving victim in need of rescue, and on the familiar dualism of tradition and modernity—intended to champion human rights within the framework of Western liberation. Specifically, *National Geographic*'s rescue narrative obfuscates the United States' role during Afghanistan's war with the Soviet Union in the 1980s, which included covertly channeling aid to some of the extremist Islamic groups with histories of gender violence and ties to the Taliban.

AIUSA's "Imagine" campaign brochure attempts to persuade the reader to support the campaign by activating the tacit knowledge, systems of belief, and "structures of feeling" (to use Raymond Williams's term) that guide social interaction and civic judgment in its targeted Western audience. The image of the Afghan girl is iconic in that it mediates the pervasive features and norms of the public that AIUSA seeks to address (Hariman and Lucaites 2007, 10). In contemporary, pluralistic societies, tacit knowledge is not nec-essarily shared, but the demand to imagine aimed at the American viewer frames the Afghan girl as an object of our feeling and sight. The blurring of all but the young girl's eyes graphically makes a burqa out of the more revealing *hijab* that she wears. That is, her head covering is made more con-servative than it actually is; the burqa is more in line with Talibanic require-ments than with dominant Middle Eastern cultural norms.[7] When read this way, the word *imagine* recasts the Western, Orientalist fantasy of imagining what is behind the veil as a project of imagining this girl with rights and dignity—a move that situates the young refugee in the normative frame-work of human rights internationalism and all its paradoxes. To account for these paradoxes, *Spectacular Rhetorics* calls for the critical engagement of the normative frameworks and narratives that underlie human rights law, shape the process of cultural and legal recognition, and delimit the pos-sible forms of public response to violence and injustice. The concerns at the heart of this project are how human rights discourse constructs humanity and its capacities through spectacular rhetorics, imagining technologies, and an ocular epistemology, and how the visual field of human rights in-ternationalism often functions as a site of power for and normative expres-sion of American nationalisms, cosmopolitanisms, and neoliberal global politics. AIUSA's media director, Steve Ruhl, indicates that the marketing team chose "Girl with Green Shawl" for its "Imagine" campaign because the photograph resonated with the more famous shot of the other Afghan girl (fig. 2). Her direct gaze at the camera, Ruhl explains of the campaign image (fig. 1), "is symbolic of the connections that Amnesty tries to encour-age everyone to forge through a shared mission to protect one another's rights."[8] Ruhl's description suggests a relation of mutual recognition—a reciprocity—that moves beyond masculinist, Orientalist representations of Afghan women and girls as distant and exotic others. Amnesty Inter-national's motive, however, may be incongruous with the historical asso-ciations and affects that the iconic image evokes in its targeted audience, which include a dialectical politics of recognition caught up in the logic and legacies of Western imperialism parading under the cloak of international humanitarianism and human rights advocacy and the projection of the

Afghan girl as a compelling object of identification.[9] Indeed, the genealogy of these struggles for recognition and reinscription can be tracked in the history of the development of human rights (see chapter 1).

In the context of the AIUSA "Imagine" campaign, the incorporation of the Afghan girl into the discourse of human rights is based on the simultaneous recognition of her universality (as a human being) and her difference (as a female child and a refugee). But the incorporative process can also reiterate social hierarchies, wherein the spectator is configured as the holder of rights and as their distributor to those who are unable to claim them independently. The attribution of the status of *National Geographic*'s picture of the Afghan girl as a human rights subject is achieved through the superimposition of the language of human rights on perceptions of the headscarf or veil, which Westerners typically view as emblems of the oppression of women and girls under Islam—a perception that ignores Muslim women's use of the veil in acts of resistance (Eisenstein 2004a, 170–71).[10]

These two photographs of Afghan girl refugees, then, as framed by *National Geographic* and AIUSA, do not tell the girls' story as much as they tell a story about the West as an "imagined community" (to use Benedict Anderson's term) that "inhabits the transnational zone of safety and construes human life in the zone of suffering as the West's 'other'" (Chouliaraki 2006, 10). To argue that the West finds its story in the images of Afghan girl refugees is not to suggest that these photographs offer just one intrinsic meaning, or that the images couldn't confer looking privileges on other viewers—including Afghan girls, who might see themselves in the images. Throughout this book, the term *West* denotes a historically and socially constructed category, a locus of power from which some nations have imposed values, norms, and narratives on other parts of the world. As Gillian Whitlock reminds us in *Soft Weapons*, "'The West' can only be defined relationally. It is not a geographic location but a locus of symbolic and grounded power relations emanating from the United States and Europe; there is no ground for identifying an essential 'Western' subject" (Whitlock 2007, 7). My use of *American* likewise refers to the discursive construct of the United States that symbolizes freedom and democracy yet is also a sign of imperial power (Grewal 2005, 8–9). *American* is not meant to imply that the

United States is a unilateral power, or that American nationalism is a stable construct.

Diverse political forces, technologies, and cultural expectations have kept the figure of the Afghan girl refugee in the public eye; its renewed topicality in the United States is linked, as Holly Edwards suggests, to its "resonance with core narratives of American political dominance" (Edwards 2007, 77). As Mark Reinhardt and Holly Edwards argue in *Beautiful Suffering*, "the life cycle of a formally generic, though aesthetically pleasing, portrait can reveal numerous agents and multiple beneficiaries of the traffic in pain" (2007, 10). Following the 2001 terrorist attacks on the United States, in a climate of invigorated American nationalism and anti-immigrant rhetoric, there was a renewed interest in the gendered icon of the Afghan girl. Representatives of the Bush administration invoked images of veiled Afghan women and girls to gather support for the War on Terror. In her radio address to the nation on 17 November 2001, first lady Laura Bush set in motion a gendered rescue narrative that situated the United States as a liberator and Afghan women and children as victims deserving to be rescued: "The brutal oppression of women is a central goal of the terrorists. . . . I hope Americans will join our family in working to insure that dignity and opportunity will be secured for all the women and children of Afghanistan."[11] The United States has used the language of gendered victimization to bolster support for post-9/11 military actions in Afghanistan and Iraq. Yet as the Bush administration invoked Afghan girl refugees to advocate for the U.S. invasion of Afghanistan, it depoliticized human rights through the broader moral rhetoric of human dignity—moving away from the priorities of human rights foreign policy during previous administrations (Mertus 2003, 371). The more amorphous *human dignity* replaced *human rights* as the policy term of choice—a rhetoric that complemented the administration's appeals to action grounded in humanitarian and faith-based initiatives rather than in international human rights law (ibid., 379).[12] The Feminist Majority Foundation was among the U.S.-based feminist organizations that capitalized on the missionary and humanitarian-intervention discourses of the U.S. government, discourses that reverberated after 9/11 and turned media attention away from punitive state laws and systemic human rights violations to the "celebratory media spectacle of unveiling [Afghan women] rampant in the U.S. media after the 'successful' invasion of Afghanistan" (Puar 2007, 7). This spectacle of veiled Muslim women is common in Western media, including liberal American feminist representations, where the veil is a symbol of gender apartheid.

Consider the power of the veil and the staged unveiling of Zoya, a representative of the Revolutionary Association of the Women of Afghanistan (RAWA), at New York City's Madison Square Garden in February 2001. Preceding a performance of Eve Ensler's *Vagina Monologues*, this staged liberation of the Muslim other, as Zoya reports in her book *Zoya's Story*, began with Oprah Winfrey reading Ensler's poem "Under the Burqa," which is based on Ensler's experience of traveling to Afghanistan and meeting with women living under Taliban rule. Ensler writes the poem in the voice of an Afghan woman, a vocalization that connects the poem's narrator and its subject through shared experiences of suffering. Zoya, who had been asked to wear her burqa, walked onto the stage. All the lights were off except for one aimed at the mesh in her burqa. "Slowly, very slowly," Zoya writes, "Oprah lifted the burqa off me and let it fall to the stage" (Zoya 2002, 211). A dual rhetoric of recognition was thereby staged between Zoya and the audience, a rhetoric that cast Zoya as a victim "awaiting liberation" rather than an "active agent in history" (Whitlock 2007, 53). To allow another's pain to "enter us," as Ensler writes in *Insecure at Last: Losing It in Our Security-Obsessed World*, where her poem was reprinted, "forces us to examine our own values, . . . insists that we be responsible for others, [and] compels us to act" (Ensler 2006, 18). Ensler may imagine solidarity as a byproduct of affective identification with another's pain, but, like Zoya's unveiling, identification in *Insecure at Last* validates her own presence. In this way, Ensler's imaginative identifications are a form of self-recognition.

The unveiling of Muslim women has been a flash point for feminist critiques of anti-imperialism in the 1980s and early 1990s. Readers might recall Chandra Talpade Mohanty's classic essay "Under Western Eyes" (first published in 1984), in which she highlights the inscription of power relations in Western feminist texts that codify assumptions about liberated Western women through the "production of the 'third world woman' as a singular monolithic subject" (Mohanty 1991, 51). Or, as Inderpal Grewal puts it, "the discourses of American nationalism produce female subjects who [see] themselves as 'free' in comparison to their 'sisters' in the developing world" (2005, 142). These attitudes are pervasive in the field of human rights, though they have not gone unchallenged. Yet while the unveiling at Madison Square Garden might be said to have reproduced a monolithic image of the "third world woman," the spectacular performance also provided an opportunity for an Afghan feminist activist to speak to an audience of thousands about the role of the United States and allied governments in arming the Taliban in the recent past (Mohanty 1991, 54). Competing motives animate the spectacle of Zoya's unveiling as a human rights subject, and they include the cultural politics of recognition—an identity-based politics of visibility—that dominated Western liberal feminism at the end of the twentieth century and that directed public attention away from the regressive politics and growth of global capitalism (Fraser 2005a, 299).

As Zoya's unveiling suggests, the human rights spectacle justifies the exercise of disciplinary power and, in its more optimistic formations, holds the potential for social intervention and contestation. Although the "mass media production of the spectacle of suffering," as the legal scholar Upendra Baxi suggests, "divest[s] it of any structural understanding of the production of suffering itself" (Baxi 2006, 155–56), the human rights spectacle is not fully allied with abusive power. Nor do human rights advocates pursue their work only by defying hegemonic structures; rather, the human rights spectacle is riddled with paradoxes and contradictions. I use the term *human rights spectacle* to refer to the incorporation of subjects (individuals, communities, nations) through imaging technologies and discourses of vision and violation into the normative frameworks of a human rights internationalism based on United Nations (UN) documents and treaties. The human rights spectacle, therefore, refers not to individual images, iconic or otherwise, but to social and rhetorical processes of incorporation and recognition mediated by visual representation and the ocular epistemology (see chapter 1) that underwrites the discourse of human rights. The term also encompasses appropriations of human suffering in activist, cultural, and legal contexts, as well as Western democratic nations' use of images to deflect attention from their own human rights violations by turning other nations into spectacles of violence (Chow 1991), mapping "the world in terms of spectator zones and sufferer zones" (Chouliaraki 2006, 83).

I am particularly interested in understanding how the human rights spectacle develops in and travels through the history of human rights as a sign of contradiction that is mediated by truth-telling genres and their contexts—and, more broadly, how human rights principles are culturally translated into a vernacular that imagines audiences, particularly Western audiences, as moral subjects of sight. I have coined the term *spectacular rhetoric* to highlight the visual rhetoric of human rights, of which the spectacle is only a part, and to accommodate audiovisual and mixed-media forms and rhetorical techniques, such as *ekphrasis* (to bring before the eyes), that are used in speech and writing to convey experiences of vision. I therefore aim to integrate the visual into, rather than set it against, textual approaches and to scrutinize the objectivist model of visual evidence—seeing is believing—foundational to contemporary human rights politics. Images may be more immediate and memorable than words at the sensory level, but, like all texts, images acquire social value and symbolic overtones from larger frames of reference. Although we are witnessing the democratization of tools for imaging human rights violations (cellphones, YouTube), the sociopolitical impact and meaning of images depend on the "discourses that articulate them" (Kellner quoted in Zelizer 2000, 8). Correspondingly, I use *spectacular* in the book's title both in its broadest sense, to signify sensational representations and the exhibition of a specified character (the common definition), and, more narrowly, to refer to discourses of vision, modes of visibility (the means or medium through which something is viewed or regarded), and the distribution of visual capital in human rights politics.

Attending to the distribution of visual capital requires understanding the visual field of human rights differently, as a visual economy. As David Campbell argues, "the idea of a visual economy makes clear that the visual field is both made possible by and productive of relations of power, and that these power relations bear at least some relationship to wider social and political structures which are themselves associated with transnational relations of exchange in which images are commodities" (2007, 361). The methodological implications of such a view demand not only that we look at the iconography of images, which "depends on intertextuality for its interpretive power" (Rose 2001, 149), but also that we understand the rhetorical intertextuality of images in "networks of materials, technologies, institutions, markets, social spaces, affects, cultural histories and political contexts" (Campbell 2007, 361).[13] Transnational networks and technologies have extended the moral discourse of a UN-based human rights internationalism to a number of regions around the world. Not surprisingly, this discourse has been incorporated into the powerful imaginary of neoliberalism and its "promises of rights," which, as Grewal has noted, are "believed to be achievable through the workings of market capitalism" (2005, 124). Yet neoliberal political rationalities, economic policies, and governance have also reified the disjuncture "between the global diffusion of the idea of universal human rights and the social, political, and economic conditions necessary for their effective realization" (McGrew 1998, 196). Thus, to focus on the visual economy of human rights is to examine the potential of neoliberal politics and human rights politics to jointly incorporate victim subjects into social relations that support the logic of a global morality market that privileges Westerners as world citizens. Finally, the concept of the visual economy of human rights suggests that we highlight the visual performance of the social field (see Mitchell 2002, 171) to better understand how visualization makes certain social practices and relations, as well as identity categories, possible (Campbell 2007, 361). This focus on the performative parallels my study's emphasis on how spectacular rhetoric activates certain cultural and national narratives and social and political relations, consolidates identities through the politics of recognition, and configures material relations of power and difference to produce and ultimately to govern human rights subjects. In the case-study chapters that follow, I demonstrate how spectacular texts and contexts project identifications onto audiences and how human rights subjects are represented as possessing certain identities.

## Intercontextuality and the Transnational Human Rights Imaginary

Implicit to this study is a view of rhetoric as forms of social-symbolic communication through which identities, social relations, and relations of power are articulated and through which human subjects are incorporated into systems of value.[14] Steven Mailloux suggests that a rhetorical analytic that questions relations of power must investigate "the political effectivity of trope, argument, and narrative in culture" (2006, 40).[15] *Spectacular*

*Rhetorics* approaches the political effectiveness of rhetoric in terms of how, when, and why certain tropes, arguments, and narratives gain momentum among rhetorical publics. In other words, my focus is not on whether a rhetorical act persuades a particular individual but on how its contextualization defines the parameters of the public's engagement with key human rights issues.

To grasp how human rights texts and contexts acquire symbolic importance and to understand the systems of belief and interpretive themes that they come to represent, we must challenge the hierarchical dichotomy of texts and contexts, which privileges social contexts as real and subordinates texts as abstractions. "Context does not simply exist as a prelinguistic reality that language faithfully describes," as Lloyd Kramer notes (1989, 114). In other words, we need to recognize the "textuality of the 'historical field'" (116) — or, as Dominick LaCapra puts it, "Context itself is a text of sorts" (1983, 95–96). Moreover, rhetorical acts create contexts, project imagined publics, and establish communities: "The writer/speaker is not just a responder to context, but a performer of context, defining situations, identifying relationships and goals" (Li 2009, 93). To analyze why an image and the meanings attributed to it are persuasive, culturally resonant, and politically viable at any given historical moment, or *kairos*, is to consider the texts and contexts with which it is entangled — to read intercontextually.[16] My use of the term *intercontextual* is meant to foreground both the textual and contextual dimensions of representational practices. An intercontextual analytic also complicates analytics that focus solely on scale (such as nation-to-nation analyses) by foregrounding how meaning is produced, materialized, and experienced between and among multiple, ever-shifting contexts. Intercontextuality is a key element of a rhetorical analytic that seeks to understand how arguments and images travel across cultural and national borders, and how symbols and symbolic practices are appropriated, translated, and historicized. An intercontextual analytic, however, does not invalidate geopolitical categories, especially given the mobilization of categories such as the West and non-West in the field of human rights internationalism by both its proponents and adversaries. The methodological challenge of understanding the convergence of contending nationalisms that drives contemporary human rights politics, as this study demonstrates, is not a problem of scale, but a matter of articulating the "technologies of interactivity and the relativity of contexts" (Appadurai 1996, 178). I am, therefore, as interested in how contexts shape human rights discourse as I am in how human rights discourse generates context. In *Modernity at Large*, Arjun Appadurai argues that the relationship between the cultural and economic dimensions of global politics is not "a simple one way street" (41). In my study, the discourse of human rights internationalism must be understood as "punctuated, interrogated, and domesticated" by the discourses of American nationalism and neoliberalism, creating convergences and disjunctures of discourse that affect material practices across contexts (10).

My rhetorical approach to intercontextuality can be traced to Mikhail Bakhtin's notion of *heteroglossia*, a polyphony of voices, identities, and positions and their negotiation of power and control.[17] Bakhtin's dialogic theory of language enables us to critically examine texts, including images, as multivocal rhetorical performances that arise out of specific historical and social contexts and in relation to specific discursive practices, instead of seeing either texts or contexts as discrete or isolated entities. To read intercontextually is to identify in a composition or performance the internal references to other texts or rhetorical acts, to become reflexive about the social codes and habits of interpretation that shape the composition or performance's meaning and that it enacts, and to comprehend how texts are formed by the institutions and material contexts that produce them and through which they circulate.[18] As Jacques Rancière puts it in *The Future of the Image*, "images . . . are not primarily manifestations of the properties of a certain technical medium, but operations: relations between a whole and parts; between a visibility and a power of signification and affect associated with it; between expectations and what happens to meet them" (2007c, 3). Just as the spectacle is intercontextual, spectators are intercorporeal; they cannot be conceived of outside a web of interrelations and discourses of which they are a living part (Holquist 1990).

International human rights politics is saturated with images, and advocates, policymakers, scholars, and news media are alert to their power. Yet the study of human rights has not grasped the rhetorical intercontextuality of the spectacle of suffering, or how international human rights law itself "establish[es] visibilities and police[s] invisibilities, stereotypes, power relations, the ability to know and to verify" (Rogoff 2000, 20). Attending to the structures of visibility and invisibility that define the moral discourse of human rights as it is inflected by and targeted for Western audiences requires viewing persuasion, or rhetoric, more broadly—as a practice of making and remaking social and political relations and incorporating subjects into discursive formations and regimes of truth. In *The Archaeology of Knowledge*, Foucault suggests: "Whenever one . . . can define a regularity (an order, correlations, positions and functionings), . . . we are dealing with a discursive formation" (1972, 38). For Foucault, discourse—specialized forms of knowledge and the institutions through which that knowledge circulates—may be a form of discipline, but discursive formations are not deterministic. As Gillian Rose notes, they do not "impose rules for thought and behavior on a pre-existing human agent. Instead, human subjects are produced through discourse" (2000, 137).

Human rights can be considered a discourse of public persuasion that envisions certain scenes of rhetorical address and normative notions of subject formation (see chapter 1). As Rachel Riedner and Kevin Mahoney point out: "This is not persuasion in the classical sense of rhetoric, but persuasion as a mode of authoritative discourse . . . enacted materially, on bodies, practices, subjectivities, cultures, and communities" (2008, 10). From this perspective, materiality cannot be separated from the symbolic meanings that are vested in it. *Spectacular Rhetorics* pays particular attention to how human rights discourses, structured by visual constructs of recognition, become entangled with systems of identification (gender, race, class, ethnicity, nationality, ability, and sexuality) and how normative identity registers join visual technologies to produce the world citizen of human rights internationalism. Pheng Cheah claims that the fundamental axiom of human rights instrumentality is "the human being, who is capable of rationality, is free and possesses dignity, and therefore is a bearer of inviolable rights" (2006, 4). The rhetorical intercontextual perspective that I bring to this study complicates this axiom in its account of "the construction of the identity of self and other [that] takes place always against the monologue of legal subjection" (Douzinas 2002, 386). In several of the case studies in this book, we see the link between social and civil recognition and ideological subjection, and we see cultural productions in which this link is imagined in ways that seek a reciprocal recognition, often construed through the rhetorical construct of witnessing. Although bearing witness is construed as an alternative to passive spectatorship, it is not immune to historical, material, or rhetorical forces, nor should it be immune from critical interrogation. For instance, Zoya's participation in her own unveiling may be read as a performance of a dialectical process of recognition to which she knowingly subjects herself in order to establish a rhetorical platform from which to speak. If we view recognition processes as staged scenes of address, as Zoya's performance suggests, we come to see how certain bodies—but not others—have benefited from human rights internationalism and the dialectical politics of recognition inherent to it.

Mounting my argument as a feminist rhetorician, I am interested in intersecting identity markers. Yet I am also aware of the methodological risks of using intersectional identity paradigms as an analytic tool, especially given disciplinary protocols and conventions that compartmentalize normative identity registers and uphold static notions of the subject even while analyzing coordinates. As Jasbir Puar notes: "No matter how intersectional our models of subjectivity, no matter how attuned to locational politics of space, place, and scale, these formulations may still limit us if they presume the automatic primacy and singularity of the disciplinary subject and its identitarian interpellation" (206). Puar admonishes feminist scholars to shift our emphasis from an intersectional model of identity—which, she argues, runs the risk of "collud[ing] with the disciplinary apparatus of the state" (212)—to a model of assemblage that would let us approach gender, race, and sexuality not as "parameters of identity" but "as *events*" (211).[19] Puar's attention to the "performative aspects of identification" (21) echoes my own call for a rhetorical approach to human rights subjectivity, identity, and agency. Puar comes closest to a rhetorical, dialogic analytic in *Terrorist Assemblages* when she notes that "intersectional identities and assemblages must remain as *interlocutors* in tension" (213; emphasis added). *Spectacular Rhetorics* draws greater attention to these tensions among interlocutors to deepen our understanding of the rhetorical intercontextuality of the American transnational human rights imaginary.[20] As Mary Poovey notes more broadly, following Charles Taylor, "a social imaginary is not simply a theory developed by specialists. Instead it is at least partly generated by ordinary people for use in everyday life, and it reveals itself in stories, myths, and commonplaces as well as theoretical narratives . . . a social imaginary is not simply descriptive; it also has a normative or prescriptive function, which guides the evaluation of practices as well as the practices themselves" (Poovey 2002, 131). Although the imaginary transcends topical spaces, recognizing the imaginary's normative and prescriptive functions is an essential part of understanding "the context of action" (C. Taylor 2002, 110). I opt to describe the human rights imaginary as transnational, rather than global, to draw attention to the ongoing relevance of nation-states and nationalisms in human rights politics, and in the visual as a locus of power in present and past configurations of globalization. The transnational human rights imaginary is neither a static entity nor a totalizing global discourse; rather, it is a differentially available discursive formation in which human rights subjects are constituted and connected through technologies and rationalities, and through which relations between individuals and nation-states, between corporations and the state, and between state and nonstate actors are negotiated.[21]

Human rights discourse is produced by and distributed through formal human rights networks that monitor and adjudicate human rights crimes (the UN and nongovernmental organizations) and through informal domains of human rights advocacy (grass-roots activism and cultural productions). This study focuses primarily on the translation of human rights internationalism, based on UN documents and treaties, into cultural forms that target Western—chiefly American—audiences. The spectacular rhetorics at the heart of this study therefore represent circuits of transnational media in which the discourses of human rights internationalism, and its particular American inflections, are circulating. Strict legal definitions of human rights are the most actionable, but cultural translations and enactments shape the perception and application of legally based human rights discourses. Indeed, the diversity of cultural forms through which human rights internationalism is articulated and the range of cultural spaces that it occupies suggest that a rhetorical analytic that stresses intercontextual practices is necessary to understand how human rights and the spectacle of suffering acquire meaning and social value.

## The Spectacle of Human Rights: Dominance and Difference

My use of the term *human rights spectacle* takes as its point of departure Guy Debord's argument in his influential manifesto *The Society of the Spectacle*, first published in 1967, in which he claimed that the "spectacle is not a collection of images; rather it is a social relationship between people that is mediated by images" (1994, sec. 4). But I part ways with Debord when he argues that "the spectacle is the existing order's *uninterrupted* discourse about itself" (24, emphasis added), as well as "the moment when the commodity has attained the *total occupation* of social life" (42, emphasis added). For Debord, the spectacle was a tool of pacification—a "permanent opium war" (44). Debord and the Situationist International (SI), a group of avant-garde Marxist revolutionaries active from 1957 to 1972, viewed the spectacle as a symptom of an increasingly media-saturated world. Influenced by theorists associated with the Frankfurt School, whose conception of a "totally administered" (Horkheimer and Adorno [1948] 1972) or "one-dimensional" society (Marcuse 1964) paralleled their own, the SI theorists claimed that capital had perfected itself through the overproduction of material and symbolic goods and through the state's management of consumer obedience (Rasmussen 2006, 10).

Members of the SI were indebted to Karl Marx's trenchant analysis of capital, but they supplemented the Marxian emphasis on class struggle by focusing on cultural transformations—namely, the collapse of art and everyday life—with an eye toward overcoming forms of separation and depoliticization associated with the spectacle in bureaucratic communist and capitalist societies (Best and Kellner 1999, 131). To counter alienation propelled by the spectacle, the SI developed the *dérive,* aimless wandering through the city, and *détournement* the idea of a "turning aside," an ironic "rearrangement of pre-existing elements" (Knabb 1981, 45). Together these strategies led to the creation of situations that were meant to engage spectators in "a moment of life concretely and deliberately constructed by the collective organization of a unitary ambiance and a game of events" (ibid.). Debord and the SI construed diversion, or détournement, as a response to a totalizing spectacle. Yet Debord was skeptical, even pessimistic, about the political potential of art and cultural formations in the battle against the spectacle in advanced capitalism (Rasmussen 2006, 12): "wherever representation takes on independent existence," he wrote, "the spectacle reestablishes its rule" (Debord 1994, 17). Scholars from a range of disciplines have challenged the monolithic and determinist conceptions of the spectacle that emerged in SI political theory and the simplistic "'hypodermic needle' models that assumed that individuals are merely injected with ideology" (Best and Kellner 1999, 142). As Rancière asks in his incisive critique of the partition of the sensible that underlies the spectacle theorized by the SI: "Why identify 'looking' with 'passivity' if not by the presupposition that looking means looking at the image or the appearance, that it means being separated from the reality that is always behind the image?" (2007b, 277). "Emancipation starts," Rancière insists, and I concur, "when we dismiss the opposition between looking and acting and understand that the distribution of the visible itself is part of the configuration of domination and subjection. It starts when we realize that looking is also an action that confirms or modifies that distribution, and that 'interpreting the world' is already a means of transforming it, or reconfiguring it" (ibid.).

The logic of spectacularity as a site of dominant power may be to arrest the public's gaze—to discipline, display, and isolate the subject. However, as Jonathan Crary observes, "attention, as a constellation of texts and practices, is much more than a question of the gaze, of looking, of the subject only as a [passive] spectator" (1999, 2). To understand the spectacle, Crary suggests, is not to focus primarily on the act of looking at images, but rather to consider "the construction of the conditions that individuate, immobilize, and separate subjects, even within a world in which mobility and circulation are ubiquitous" (74). Like Crary, I do not aim to isolate the spectacle or to collapse all visuality into the spectacle. To understand the spectacular culture of contemporary human rights politics requires a methodology that emphasizes the materiality of rhetoric and the distribution of visual capital, as well as recognizing representations that have a spectacular quality but that may suspend or refocus our perception (3). This viewpoint runs against the grain of arguments that visual practices threaten deliberative exchange and literate rationality. Although the spectacle may function as a form of domination, it need not be sutured to a theory of the image as a totality or as isolated from the word. Therefore, rather than flatten out the image, I highlight the rhetorical intercontextuality of images and their meanings and approach the human rights spectacle as a rhetorical phenomenon through which differently empowered social constituencies negotiate the authority of representation. Furthermore, I argue that spectacular rhetorics and the contradictions that they stage are emblematic of the political and ethical struggles with which human rights advocates and scholars are engaged. Lest readers think that *Spectacular Rhetorics* is simply a celebration of the legacy of détournement in human rights politics, I expose the intellectual fissures in human rights discourses that, like the discourses of SI political theory, are a product of an entrenched nostalgia for the supposedly real outside discourse, and I offer a critique of authenticity and its deployment, strategic or otherwise.[22]

Extensive scholarly work exists on the spectacle and the disciplinary politics of visibility, especially with regard to colonial representations of cultural difference and to scientific discourses on criminality, deviance, illness, disability, and the control of sexuality.[23] Specular and panoptic logics have long been used to classify differences of ability, race, gender, and ethnicity and to discriminate on the basis of these visual differences construed as corporeal essences. For centuries, visual technologies have been used to control populations. Pain and torture have long been properties of the visual economy of truth and justice: the ancient Greek legal system associated the violence of interrogation—namely, the torture of slaves—with the reproduction of truth (DuBois 1991, 47).[24] As Foucault notes in *Discipline and Punish,* in the sixteenth and seventeenth centuries the spectacle (e.g., the public execution, the scene at the scaffold) was the primary method of penal legislation. In the eighteenth century, he argues, surveillance began to replace the spectacle and the public force of the sovereign's power with "a mechanism that coerce[d] by means of observation" (1975, 170). Foucault based his model of compulsory visibility on the panopticon, an architectural form that was "capable of making all visible . . . , a faceless gaze that transformed the whole social body into a field of perception: thousands of eyes posted everywhere" (214).

Yet Foucault's claim that the public spectacle has shifted to a more covert system of surveillance erases the continuity of sexist, racist, and nationalist state violence around the globe, including the public spectacle of torture in European and American colonies, where it was inflicted on indigenous peoples in the name of the sovereign (James 1998, 24–25). Joy James reveals the limitations of the metanarrative of *Discipline and Punish* for understanding the history of the spectacle of racist violence in the United States, including the inscription of torture onto the black body and the specter of lynching, as well as the history of racialized terror in U.S. foreign policy (24). Countering Foucault's argument in *Discipline and Punish* that modern societies are now so thoroughly disciplined that they do not need the spectacle, Page DuBois notes that torture is a global spectacle, a production not necessarily of truth but of "broken bodies and psyches, both for local and international consumption" (1991, 155). Furthermore, specular and panoptic logics often conspire. The Ku Klux Klan's terror spectacle, as Robyn Wiegman points out, "functioned within a panoptic logic, as the perpetrators of dismemberment and murder were ritually veiled and acted not in the service of a lone sovereign but for a non-homogenized, known-but-never-individuated, power" (1995, 39). After the terrorist attacks against the United States on 11 September 2001, the terror spectacle and panoptic mechanisms of power have coalesced once again, as I discuss in chapter 2, as the U.S. government curtails its citizens' civil rights and relinquishes international human rights law governing the treatment of detainees. Tracing how specular and panoptic logics are mobilized by governments to harden ideological support for the curtailment of rights and for both humanitarian and military interventions is as important now as it ever has been.

Spectacular rhetoric is not newly nomadic. But what Crary calls the spectacular architecture of globalization has taken on specific characteristics in the late twentieth century and early twenty-first (1999, 74), largely through transnational circuits, the diffusion of media, and technologically altered time-space configurations, which include the construction of virtual realities and digital activism that bring distant human rights and humanitarian crises into an interactive personal space. Digital human rights activism takes on a host of forms, including letter-writing campaigns and petitions. Amnesty International's 2007 virtual campaign to close down the U.S. Guantánamo Bay prison exemplifies human rights activists' use of the spectacle as social commentary. As each supporter signs the "Tear It Down" petition, one more pixel in the image of the prison on the AI website is replaced with the signer's name, dismantling the human rights spectacle pixel by pixel. "Once 500,000 people have expressed their determination to end this human rights disgrace," Amnesty International says, "our image of Guantánamo-style injustice will disappear."[25] To dismantle Guantánamo one pixel at a time is to provide an imaginary that opposes the spectacle of state power by harnessing the potentially subversive force of the deconstructive spectacle for human rights activism.

Human rights crises and activism often coalesce around the spectacle of suffering but the visual field of human rights does not form a monolithic rhetoric. The spectacle is open to cooptation and containment, but it can also serve as an occasion to challenge, exploit, or at the very least rupture the objectifying gaze, as Amnesty International's "Tear It Down" campaign and Zoya's address to an audience of thousands at Madison Square Garden illustrate. Thus, I argue that instead of thinking about the spectacle as a narcotic, we need to understand it as heterogeneous and as a rhetorically dialogic process that is nevertheless subsumed within repetitive forms. Truth-telling genres are the most ardent hosts of the human rights spectacle. That is, human rights subjects emerge through the genres, contexts, and technologies—legal, literary, social, and ecclesiastical—of truth telling. But I am less interested in posing questions of genre than in examining the ways in which deployments of spectacular rhetoric advance political, cultural, and moral agendas. My aim is to understand the visual rhetoric of human rights in which truth-telling genres (e.g., photojournalism, testimonials, documentary cinema and theater, editorials, ethnography, and academic scholarship) are significant components but not exclusive considerations. My attention therefore is not directed toward whether truth-telling practices adhere to or break their genres' conventions, but rather toward how truth-telling genres and the contexts they generate support the specular and increasingly panoptic culture of U.S. internationalism and its regulation of human rights subjects.

Consider, for instance, the issue of access and the hierarchy of recognition staged by the Genocide Prevention Mapping Initiative, Crisis in Darfur, developed at the United States Holocaust Memorial Museum in collaboration with the Google Corporation, which uses high-resolution satellite images to watch over Darfur's most vulnerable villages. Google's involvement with the project has raised questions about the intertwining of human rights, corporate culture, and digital technology, in that the project privileges the interface of Google Earth, a private company, as the mechanism for the distribution of information about Darfur (Parks 2008, 18). Moreover, because of U.S. export controls and economic sanctions against Sudan, the Sudanese themselves cannot access the projects using Google Earth technology (20).

In contrast to scholars who treat the spectacle itself as a genre, or who attribute to it the status of antinarrative, I demonstrate that no genre is immune to the spectacular, and that the spectacle is at the core of human rights narratology. Framing human rights as an optic that disciplines as well as empowers drives the analysis of the cases in this book. *Spectacular Rhetorics* draws together the insights of scholars from a range of fields, most prominently rhetorical studies, American studies, visual culture studies, trauma studies, and postcolonial and feminist legal studies—in particular, scholars who focus on the representational politics of truth telling as it intersects with the imperatives of contemporary globalization and human rights. The book takes part in the transnational feminist project to the extent that it seeks to demonstrate the interarticulations (to use Grewal's term) of cultural, national, and transnational discourses in contemporary human rights politics and advocacy. Transnational feminists' critique of the prominence within the human rights project of Western-centric cosmopolitan epistemologies that romanticize travel and engagement with the women and children of the so-called third world also constitutes part of this book's argument, as it seeks to draw attention to contrasting feminist ideas about the productive possibilities and limitations of human rights internationalism staged by and for Western audiences. *Spectacular Rhetorics* does not strive or pretend, however, to represent any of these fields in its entirety; rather, it operates as a mechanism of critical dialogue, orchestrated in the form of rhetorical criticism.

## Structure of the Book

The title of this book purposely highlights visual aspects of persuasion. But *spectacular rhetoric* is not limited to visual media. Rather, the term encompasses the discourses of vision and modes of visuality that structure international human rights law and advocacy, as well as their history. Al-though the book emphasizes visual and audiovisual media and dramatic performances, several expository works that engage the human rights spec-tacle are interwoven with the cinematic, photographic, and theatrical. Each chapter might be viewed as a rhetorical case study presenting a group of spectacular cultural artifacts that point to a prominent human rights cause (torture and unlawful detention, ethnic genocide and rape warfare, migra-tion and the trafficking of women and children, the global sex trade and child labor) of the late twentieth century and early twenty-first, and that deal with different aspects of victimization and the controversies over its representation. The studies are intended not to represent an exhaustive sur-vey but to highlight examples of how international human rights law and cultural practices work together to create sites of political engagement and creative intervention. Finally, by foregrounding cultural forms of engage-ment and the convergences of human rights internationalism and American nationalism, I seek to respond to the growing interest among humanities scholars in human rights, to contribute to the emerging field of transna-tional American rhetorical studies, and to counter the common assumption that legal approaches are the only politically viable means of taking action against human rights violations by both state and nonstate actors. As Sally Engle Merry argues in *Human Rights and Gender Violence*, "Human rights law is itself primarily a cultural system. Its limited enforcement mecha-nisms mean that the impact of human rights is a *matter of persuasion* rather than force, of cultural transformation rather than coercive change" (2001, 16; emphasis added).

Studying the cultural translation of human rights principles into a visual vernacular for Western consumption will help us understand the public's readiness (or lack thereof) for deliberations and policies predicated on human rights principles. Moreover, by attending to the intercontextuality of cultural and law-based human rights discourses, we are better able to grasp how the suffering body becomes sutured to the spectacle and incor-porated into the visual economy of human rights. The thematic constella-tion of texts and contexts that define the critical parameters of each case-study chapter enables the rhetorical methodology that drives the project and its investigation of human rights as a regime of seeing and enforced attentiveness. The juxtaposition of texts and contexts also enables certain theoretical conversations. In other words, text selection is itself a critical apparatus. The cultural works that are most insistent about viewing the spectacle as a rhetorical process are those that draw attention to the ethical regimes of seeing and, therefore, are reflexively intercontextual.

But why focus on the spectacle at all, especially at a time when one of the world's most powerful nations—the United States—is engaged in two wars? Aren't there more pressing political and rhetorical considerations than the visual politics of human rights, especially when we consider the perilous conditions and consequences of war? But to frame the question in either-or terms is to presume that cultural representation and political action are fundamentally separate rather than interdependent. Given that the "visuality of war remains profoundly undemocratic," as Nicholas Mirzoeff notes, the issues of who has the power to represent whom and which events are rendered visible or invisible are profoundly important (2006, 23). Consider that embedded journalists in Iraq were allowed to see only a hundred of the twenty thousand bombing raids on Iraq (Mirzoeff 2005, 175), or ponder the fact that increased media censorship and limits on Internet and cellphone access accompanied the Burmese regime's violent repression of peaceful demonstrators in September 2007, and the Iranian regime's crackdown in June 2009 after the contested reelection of President Mahmoud Ahmadinejad. As Marina Warner points out, "the character of our representations matters most urgently. . . . The images we circulate have the power to lead events, not only [to] report them; the new technical media have altered experience and become interwoven with consciousness itself" (2005).

Methodologically, each case study approaches human rights representations as sites of material and ideological struggle over meaning. Each therefore oscillates between the internal features that distinguish rhetorical acts and contexts and the relation of these acts and contexts to other discourses and material formations. Together these critical moves constitute an intercontextual, or relational, analytic. Each chapter moves from an analysis of spectacular rhetorics that both solidify social-identity categories and scenes of coerced and forced recognition to an examination of interventions or transformations of the spectacle that challenge hierarchical social relations and the fixity of identity categories, and yet endow the human rights subject with agency. To highlight configurations of agency is not to retreat to static notions of subjectivity or modernist notions of the autonomous subject, however. Rather, a relational approach attends to the dispersion of rhetorical agency and the "articulated networks that connect speakers and hearers in multiple, sometimes contradictory ways" (Wells 2003, 1). In contrast to theories of agency that replicate the hierarchy of subject and other/object, or that imagine agency in some wild zone outside culture and discourse, *Spectacular Rhetorics* does not presuppose "a universal category of acts—such as resistance—outside of the ethical and political conditions within which such acts acquire their particular meaning" (Mahmood 2004, 9). Instead of romanticizing resistance or conflating it with agency— because agency may be complicit with dominance—*Spectacular Rhetorics* invites the reader to explore agency as an interarticulation of discursive and material formations of texts and contexts. Each case-study chapter looks at how human rights advocates, scholars, and governmental and nongovernmental organizations mobilize discourses of vision (spectacle, recognition, identification, and witnessing) and engage in visibility politics through cultural representations of human rights violations. The sequence of texts and contexts illustrates in each case study how the social, political, and legal—namely, the evidentiary—demands of truth telling shape the human rights spectacle and its instrumentality and, conversely, how the human rights spectacle is made to exert pressure on truth-telling conventions to achieve political effects and to manipulate affect. Reading across texts and contexts enables us to better understand the ideological work that spectacular rhetorics perform, and how they both contain and expand public engagement with human rights issues. *Spectacular Rhetorics* therefore does not simply denounce the pervasiveness of the spectacle in human rights politics; it seizes the spectacle's moral ambiguities and contradictions to engage them critically.

Chapter 1, "Human Rights Visions and Recognitions," establishes a close analogy between the modes of visuality and the discourses of vision, including the ocular epistemology, that characterize the history of human rights in Western moral philosophy, social theory, and aesthetics. This chapter presents the development of human rights internationalism as a history of selective and differential visibility and examines the tension between human rights' aesthetic ideology—with its implicitly universalist theory of recognition, largely underwritten by a discourse of trauma and subjection—and the enactment of human rights as a form of social criticism. I argue that theories of subjectivity and agency predicated on the Hegelian master-slave dialectic corral human rights subjects and advocates into an endless struggle in which the attribution of recognition reinforces the very identity categories that human rights claims contest. Finally, I consider the possibilities of a differentiated politics of recognition and of a human rights discourse that moves beyond an identity-based paradigm. This chapter sets the stage for my analysis of the cases that follow by showing how the discourses of human rights internationalism—rooted in Western notions of subjectivity, agency, and personality development—limit the parameters for ethical engagement. I argue that in order for publics to open themselves to the pain of others and to rectify social injustices, human rights advocates and scholars need to offer a different epistemology from those that, as Veena Das puts it, "provide the cover to engage in voyeurism" (2007, 211).

Chapter 2, "Staging Terror Spectacles," builds on the preceding chapter by exploring the connection between the discourses of vision and modes of visuality that structure the convergence of American nationalism and human rights internationalism in the age of the War on Terror. Specifically, this chapter establishes a correspondence between the terror spectacle and the human rights spectacle, both of which organize perception around the experience of shock and propel the identification of history as trauma—a metanarrative that is problematic insofar as it detracts attention from the scenarios of power that structure history. I argue that in the context of the U.S. War on Terror, the terror spectacle enacts an intimate collusion between the traumatized self and the terrorized nation that is predicated on the consumption of corporeal difference. The texts and contexts I consider include the 2004 *Inconvenient Evidence* exhibit at the International Center for Photography in New York City; Rory Kennedy's 2007 documentary film, *Ghosts of Abu Ghraib*; and Victoria Brittain and Gillian Slovo's 2004 documentary play, *Guantánamo: "Honor Bound to Defend Freedom."* This chapter foregrounds the dialectical politics of recognition and stereotypical representations that characterize the resurgence of American nationalism and Islamic fundamentalism in the age of the War on Terror, and efforts by human rights activists, scholars, and artists to counter these representations.

Chapter 3, "Witnessing Rape Warfare: Suspending the Spectacle," throws the limiting politics of identification and recognition at the core of human rights internationalism into greater relief by highlighting how the pain of subjugated identities are entrenched in representations of rape warfare as a human rights violation. The chapter centers on the visual mediation of women's testimonies about the trauma of rape warfare and ethnic violence in the former Yugoslavia and the transnational witnesses they construe. Human rights documentaries seek to create a rhetorical space of intersubjectivity, of bearing witness, and in so doing to trouble the dialectic between self and other/object. Yet, as I argue in my analysis of feminist representations of rape warfare, human rights scholars and advocates alike must account for the ruptures in identification and for the histories of nationalism, militarization, and inequalities of citizenship that structure spectatorship. Chapter 3 also examines cultural depictions of rape warfare that refuse spectacular icons of victimization and instead engage the paradoxes of representation by foregrounding the dynamics of absence and presence involved in becoming a witness—depictions that further trouble the dialectical theories of recognition that typically underwrite human rights appeals. Among the documentary films I consider here are Mandy Jacobson and Karmen Jelincic's *Calling the Ghosts: A Story about Rape, War, and Women* (1996) and Midge Mackenzie's *The Sky: A Silent Witness* (1995). I also examine a photo-testimonial exhibit by Melanie Friend, *Homes and Gardens/Documenting the Invisible: Images from Kosovo* (1996); a photograph from Ron Haviv's *Blood and Honey: A Balkan War Journal* (2000); and several essays by Catharine A. MacKinnon.

Chapter 4, "Global Sex Work, Victim Identities, and Cybersexualities," considers the strategic use of victim narratives in contemporary anti-trafficking video campaigns produced by nongovernmental women's rights organizations and by an independent feminist filmmaker. This chapter builds on chapter 3 by urging human rights scholars and advocates to stop focusing on the binary identity categories of victim and agent that structure human rights internationalism's politics of recognition and to consider identity as a field of rhetorical and material action. Such a shift creates a new way to think through the opportunity structures and exigencies that affect the mobility, marketability, and visualization of certain identifications and narratives associated with female bodies and sexuality, and to imagine a differentiated politics of recognition that accounts for both coerced and chosen transnational movements and for multiple, shifting identities. This chapter considers the documentary videos *Bought and Sold: An Investigative Documentary about the International Trade in Women* (1997), directed by Gillian Caldwell and Steven Galster as part of the Global Survival Network; the Coalition against Trafficking in Women's campaign video *So Deep A Violence: Prostitution, Trafficking, and the Global Sex Industry* (2000); and two experimental videos by Ursula Biemann, *Remote Sensing* (2001b) and *Writing Desire* (2001c).

Chapter 5, "Spectacular Childhoods: Sentimentality and the Politics of (In)visibility" circles back to issues at the heart of this introduction, including the emphasis on the convergence of human rights and humanitarian discourses in representing non-Western women and their children as sympathetic objects of feeling and sight for Western audiences. In chapter 5, I turn from women's to children's human rights and further develop the link between the concept of agency and structures of recognition—here, as it pertains to representations of "endangered" children. Human rights and humanitarian campaigns have long construed children as symbolically appealing and as passive victims. Recent children's human rights campaigns, however, attempt to leave the rhetoric of childhood innocence and salvation behind and to emphasize children's self-determination and sense of justice. Acknowledging children's status as persons and political subjects further troubles the normative politics of recognition that underwrites human rights internationalism and the history of human rights law. Chapter 5 takes up the issue of children's agency as it pertains to the UN Convention on the Rights of the Child; representations of child prostitution in the U.S. news media; *Modern Babylon?*, Heather Montgomery's 2001 feminist ethnographic study of child prostitution in Thailand; and two documentary films—Zana Briski and Ross Kauffman's 2004 *Born into Brothels*, which centers on the experiences of children growing up in one of Calcutta's red-light districts, and Tareque and Catherine Masud's *A Kind of Childhood*

(2007), about the struggles of children working in Dhaka, Bangladesh. A central concern of this chapter is how the spectacle of childhood innocence and the transformation of the child from object (property) to agent (rights-bearing subject) deflect attention from or draw it to the social and economic conditions that shape children's lives. This chapter calls into question moral universalism and its elevation of the depoliticized victim in children's human rights law, demonstrating the potentially subversive elements of children's agency when the substance of that universalism is not innocence, but children's sense of familial and social responsibility. Finally, the chapter contemplates the mediator's role in fomenting hierarchical scenes of suffering and recognition, prefiguring my call for greater collaboration between human rights activists, artists, and scholars in investigating how the axes of ethical engagement are regulated through the often convergent discourses of humanitarianism and human rights internationalism.

As a scholar and educator working in the United States, I share with human rights activists a profound frustration that the War on Terror has hijacked the imperatives of the international human rights movement. The proliferation of systematic human rights violations by nation-states in the name of humanitarian military intervention, liberation, or democracy makes me, and many others, cautious about the progressive potential of international human rights discourse and law. Nevertheless, in the book's conclusion, I join many others in advocating a commitment to human rights and to the cultural forms that imagine its productive possibilities.

# CHAPTER ONE

# Human Rights Visions and Recognitions

uman rights defenders fight for international recognition and visibility in a global marketplace that tends to recast structural inequalities, social injustices, and state violence as scenes of individual trauma and victimization. Yet human rights advocates and scholars have not sufficiently considered what the status of visibility is in human rights advocacy, or how the moral vision of human rights internationalism becomes entangled with global capitalism and hierarchical structures of recognition and visual technologies to produce and regulate human rights subjects. Although visualism is implicated in the debates that have long occupied human rights scholars, such as debates over universality and cultural relativism, the field's embrace of an ocular epistemology (the seeing-is-believing paradigm) that heightens the salience of normative scenes of social and civic recognition (or misrecognition) warrants greater scrutiny. To gauge the political and ethical quandaries that shape human rights appeals and the entangled discourses of humanitarianism, global capitalism, and human rights, we need to investigate the underlying faith in vision and a dialectical politics of recognition, a faith manifested in our engagement with human rights subjects and the discourse about them.

The goals of this chapter are fourfold: (1) to interrogate the cultural and ideological work of spectacular rhetorics in perpetuating a dialectical politics of recognition, underwritten by trauma and subjection, in the history of human rights and its professedly egalitarian imaginary; (2) to explore the tension between humanitarian sensibilities and the enactment of human rights as a form of social criticism, particularly as that tension is manifested in scenes of suffering; (3) to complicate the ocular epistemology and seeing-is-believing paradigm of human rights advocacy by approaching spectatorship and witnessing as historically contingent rhetorical acts; and (4) to deliberate the potential of a differentiated politics of recognition or models of ethical exchange that move beyond recognition. Together these critical forays provide a new vantage point from which to engage the human rights paradox of an exclusive universality, as well as the rhetorical force of the visual field in the perpetuation of the normative assumptions to which human rights internationalism is tethered.

## Human Rights Struggles for Recognition

It is . . . an ongoing task of human rights to reconceive the human when
it finds that its putative universality does not have universal reach.
—Judith Butler, *Precarious Life*

The history of human rights can be told as a history of selective and differential visibility, which has positioned certain bodies, populations, and nations as objects of recognition and granted others the power and means to look and to confer recognition. As this history suggests, struggles for recognition are also struggles for visibility. Kelly Oliver, a philosopher and social theorist, argues that "recognition is a matter of seeing. The stakes are precisely the unseen in vision—the process through which something is seen or not seen" (2001, 158).[1] Invoking visual metaphors to characterize empowerment (as visibility) and disempowerment (as invisibility), Upendra Baxi, a legal scholar, points out that, in effect, "the hegemonic function of rights language, in the service of *governance* . . . consisted of making whole groups of people socially and politically invisible" (2006, 46).[2] Here Baxi refers to the "modern" human rights paradigm and European modernity, which were characterized by the logic of exclusion, and the tradition of rights talk and the philosophy of natural law that emerged from the American and French revolutions (42). Both the European liberal tradition of thought and the criteria of individuation associated with Enlightenment rationality privileged the capacity to reason as the criterion for what it meant to be "human" (44). Only those viewed as possessing the "capacity for *reason* and autonomous moral *will*" were accorded the status of "fully" human beings; slaves, colonized peoples, indigenous peoples, women, children, and the "insane," marked as other and therefore as not fully human, were by definition not "considered worthy of being bearers of human rights" (ibid.). At the same time that the capacity to reason was differentially applied, so too was the dispersal of compassion. Western liberal philosophy of the late eighteenth century linked modern moral identity to the capacity to sympathize with distant others across boundaries of race, class, religion, gender, and nation—an attribute associated with the development of humanitarianism, and the secular universalism of liberal humanism (Hunt 2007; Nussbaum 1998; and Rorty 1993). Although humanitarianism emphasizes the alleviation of suffering and human rights focuses on the legal defense of violated rights, the two movements are not easily disentangled. Both share intellectual origins in liberal political philosophy and natural law thinking of the eighteenth century. In recent years, human rights and humanitarian law have again converged, both in their shift away from the state as the bearer of rights and toward individual victims and in their representation of distant scenes of suffering characterized by the projection of a hierarchy of victimhood, recognition, and action (Wilson and Brown 2009, 5–6).

Baxi highlights the contrast between the modern human rights paradigm, with its exclusionary criteria, and the contemporary paradigm, which, he contends, is based on principles of inclusion (2006, 46). The contemporary paradigm refers to rights specified in international law in the period following the Second World War.[3] No longer exclusively at the service of imperial conquests, as Baxi claims, the contemporary human rights principle of radical self-determination took precedence in the recognition of the equal worth of all human beings (46). According to Baxi, the contemporary human rights paradigm should not be seen as separate from the struggles for self-determination and national independence among European colonies or the social movements of the post–cold war era, which included civil rights, women's rights, indigenous rights, gay rights, refugee rights, and, more recently, disability rights. Sociopolitical struggles and national liberation movements, however, as Reza Afshari (2007) maintains, have had only a modest impact on the evolution of the concept of human rights as interdependent and indivisible.[4] Single-cause movements contributed to the creation of a culture of public engagement, but they did not first and foremost draw attention to the interdependence of human rights. It was only when single-cause movements began to articulate interconnections among causes that the idea of universal human rights took hold (34–35). Yet like Afshari, Baxi is careful to point out the paradoxes of contemporary human rights, including their fragmented universality, which can be seen through the contradictory role of the capitalist state, a site that both "negotiate[s] conflicts between different factions of capital" and reconciles "antagonism[s] between labour and capital" (2006, 38). Baxi's efforts to pluralize the history of human rights are both celebratory and discerning. Though his inclusion/exclusion heuristic has limitations, Baxi rightly points out that the authorship of human rights expanded in the contemporary period—an authorship "marked by intense negotiation between the practitioners of human rights activism and of human repression" (47).

Aware of the political struggles against Western imperialism by excluded groups in both Western and non-Western contexts, postcolonial and feminist scholars have taken issue with the notion that human rights are inherently "Western values" (Narayan 1998, 97). Gayatri Spivak argues that the very notion of "human rights" implies a corresponding doer of "wrongs"—usually in the global south (2003, 169). She maintains that it is "disingenuous to call human rights Eurocentric. This is not only because, in the global South, the domestic human rights workers are, by and large, the descendants of the colonial subject, often culturally positioned against Eurocentrism. It is also because, internationally, the role of the new diasporic is strong, and the diasporic in the metropolis stands for 'diversity' 'against eurocentrism'" (171). Makau Mutua, a professor of law and the director of the Human Rights Center at the State University of New York, Buffalo, has been a strident critic of the Eurocentricity of the history of human rights and the contradictions that drive the international human rights project (2001, 203). Given that human rights norms are identified with political democracy, the rights that have been privileged are those "that strengthen, legitimize, and export the liberal democratic state to non-Western societies" (Mutua 2001, 215). Thus, despite the professed egalitarian imaginary of human rights, non-Western sociocultural practices have been its prime targets; the "messianic ethos" of human rights is pitched to "help those who cannot help themselves" (231). Preeminent among historical accounts of human rights are patrimonial narratives of human rights traditions as "gifts of the west to the rest" (Baxi 2006, xiii). The inability of the United States to recognize its own violations of human rights— American nationalist rhetoric often assumes that all violations take place elsewhere—is a classic example of this messianic ethos. The scene of recognition, wrapped in American internationalist gift-giving rhetoric, appears to enable mutual recognition, but this scene often does little more than consummate an unequal exchange.[5] "Although the human rights movement is located within the historical continuum of Eurocentrism as a civilizing mission, and therefore as an attack on non-European cultures," Mutua argues, "it is critical to note that it was European, and not non-European, atrocities that gave rise to it" (2001, 210).[6]

The Universal Declaration of Human Rights (UDHR) was framed as a direct response to the incontrovertible evidence of Nazi atrocities—the witnessing of "barbarous acts which have outraged the conscience of mankind" (preamble). Echoing the sentiment of the UDHR, Michael Ignatieff, the present leader of the Liberal Party in Canada, argues that the "human rights instruments created after 1945 were not a triumphant expression of European imperial self-confidence but a war-weary generation's reflection on European nihilism and its consequences" (2001, 4). In *Human Rights, Inc.*, the comparative studies scholar Joseph Slaughter similarly argues that the UDHR tacitly acknowledges the failures of the Enlightenment, which the spectacular horrors of the Second World War and the Holocaust made evident, but that it also "recuperates from the natural law tradition . . . the promise of Enlightenment still to come" (2007, 15). The UDHR unleashes a teleological narrative that converts the violence of genocide into "an instrument of historical reason"—the rationality of the law (Žižek 2005, 1).

## The Universal Declaration and the Paradoxes of Recognition

The UDHR and its formation of the universal human body articulate the theories of recognition and personhood at the root of these paradoxes, and the separation between the International Covenant on Economic, Social, and Cultural Rights (ICESCR) and the International Covenant on Civil and Political Rights (ICCPR) demonstrates the gap between the economic and political dimensions of justice that continues to afflict human rights advocacy. With the ICCPR and the ICESCR, both of which were adopted by the UN in 1966 and entered into force in 1976, the UDHR, adopted by the UN General Assembly on 10 December 1948, constitutes the core of international human rights law. The three documents are collectively referred to as the International Bill of Human Rights. Representatives from industrialized Western nations and Eastern/emerging economic nations were involved in drafting parts of the UDHR.[7] While the discursive construct of a single "conscience of mankind" may have erased the differences—ideological, cultural, religious, and so on—that marked the creation and signing of the declaration, many of the participants from non-Western countries, like Charles Malik of Lebanon and P. C. Chang of the Republic of China, had been educated in the West and were well versed in Western philosophical traditions.

Notwithstanding a UN General Assembly declaration that the two groups of rights should remain "interconnected and interdependent,"[8] the covenants were split in response to pressures from the West. The conflicts over the framing of the UDHR and the two covenants illuminate the tensions among the leading powers and their competing national interests. Whereas Western members sought a nonbinding resolution that emphasized civil and political rights, third world and Eastern bloc members fought for the inclusion of economic, social, and cultural rights. The debates stretched over two decades, amid cold war antagonisms, decolonization movements, and shifting power balances in the UN, including on the UN Human Rights Commission, which was dominated by Western members well into the 1960s. After the inclusion of newly independent third world countries (sixteen African countries joined the UN in 1960) and the formation of the nonaligned movement, however, the Human Rights Commission shifted its focus to issues of racism and colonialism, as illustrated by the passage of the Declaration on the Granting of Independence to Colonial Countries and Peoples in 1960 and the International Convention on the Elimination of All Forms of Racial Discrimination in 1965 (Koshy 1999, 6–7). These developments responded to the insufficiency of the UDHR and put into play a differentiated politics of recognition in human rights arguments that moved beyond philosophical universalism and its transcendence of the particularistic. A provisional universalism emerged, which was framed through the identity-based discourse of cultural difference.

Prior to the Second World War, only states, not individuals, had rights in international law. However, the UDHR recognized the rights of individuals regardless of status: "Everyone is entitled to all the rights and freedoms set forth in this Declaration, without distinction of any kind, such as race, colour, sex, language, religion, political or other opinion, national or social origin, property, birth or other status" (article 2). Although the declaration has no binding juridical power, its emphasis on universal individuality empowers citizens to protest against state abuse (Cubilié 2005, 29). Foundational to the UDHR is the idea that all members of the "human family" have a "natural" tendency toward nonviolence (33). Article 1 states: "All human beings are born free and equal in dignity and rights. They are endowed with reason and conscience and should act toward one another in a spirit of brotherhood." But, as the scholar and UN consultant Anne Cubilié points out, the declaration "erases struggles over what, if anything differentiates one person from another from the moment they are born" (2005, 33), as well as the repressive cultural and state structures and state violence predicated on such differences and often justified on their basis (31). In other words, the universal body defined in the declaration renders certain bodies and scenes of subjection visible, and others invisible (30).

Cultural theorists of citizenship, the nation-state, and global civil society (Benhabib 2004 and 2006; Berlant 1997; Bernstein and Naples 2010; Grewal and Kaplan 1996, 2001; Lister 2003; Ong 1999; Puar 2007; and others) have argued that even as the universal body imagined in nationalism is abstracted, it refers to a specific kind of body (white, male, heterosexual, and propertied). The universal appeal of a human rights internationalism based on UN documents and treaties involves another paradoxical particularity: the distance between the articulation of universal rights and their sociopolitical recognition. For instance, although article 1 of the UDHR accords human rights to all human beings, these rights must be publicly claimed. The UDHR confers universal subjecthood upon every human being, but it implies that this identification—the incorporation of the subject into the regime of rights and citizenship—has yet to be attained. Indeed, the visualization of suffering, or the human rights spectacle, is often meant to trigger this sought-after incorporation. First, the declaration assumes an a priori universal subject that both preexists and comes into being—that, in Slaughter's words, "becom[es] what [it] already is by right" (2006, 1415). It is particularly important to consider this narrative of personhood because human rights law essentially makes its appeal through the recognition of personhood, which, as this study shows, is dependent on hierarchical structures of suffering and the visualization of social injustices as scenes of individual trauma and victimization—including the depiction of the nation as victim, as seen in the discourse surrounding the U.S. War on Terror.

Second, human rights law offers the promise of international citizenship, yet it relies on nation-states and national citizenship for recognition. In its debt to unitary notions of the nation-state, international human rights law depends on the "dual existence of the subject as both internationally and nationally obligated; as well as the foundational nature of the state for human rights language and intervention/prevention" (Cubilié 2005, 21). In other words, international human rights law places the promise of international citizenship in the hands of nation-states. Similarly, human rights media may try to attract the attention of a transnational witnessing public by designating the nation-state as a protector, even while depicting the state as the violator of human rights.[9] If national sovereignty is the legitimating ground for visibility in the juridical field of human rights, then we have to ask: What happens to the rights of stateless subjects (Cubilié 2005, 21), and how are stateless subjects depicted in both legal and culturally based human rights representations?

Although the UDHR recognizes various state formations, as Cubilié notes, the declaration nevertheless assumes that people live within state structures and therefore does not address stateless persons, such as refugees (2005, 34).[10] Here we see the dialectics of the universal and particular and of international and national formations, as well as how the figure of the refugee—as Hannah Arendt observed in *The Origins of Totalitarianism* (1978)—throws the ethics of recognition and the relation between human rights and citizenship into crisis. Slavoj Žižek similarly observes that "the paradox is that one is deprived of human rights precisely when one is effectively, in one's social reality, reduced to a human being 'in general,' without citizenship, profession, etc., that is to say, precisely when one effectively becomes the ideal BEARER of 'universal human rights' (which belong to me 'independently of' my profession, sex, citizenship, religion, ethnic identity)" (2005, 4). People without national affiliation aren't always able to claim a selfhood defined by the parameters of human rights law. Clearly, in some cases, refugees do claim such a selfhood, but they often do so through the nation-state and its ideology of the "deserving" and "grateful" refugee, as we see in many of the political-asylum cases in the United States.[11] Although human rights scholars and advocates must account for the perpetual violence of nation-states and the disjuncture between human rights internationalism's appeal to universal recognition and nationalist formations of identity and citizenship, we also need to recognize the limits of antistatist configurations of internationalism by acknowledging how the power and machinery of nation-states can be mobilized to address injustices (Robbins 1999, 33–34).[12] To identify nationalist instantiations of human rights internationalism is not to capitulate to the abusive power of nation-states, or to deny the need for multilateral solutions, but to recognize, as Bruce Robbins puts it, that "as internationalism, reconciling itself to culture, acquires constituency, it also surrenders ideal purity. . . . And unlike internationalism in most of its versions, it cannot pretend that it is simply the antithesis of nationalism" (31). Yet, as the case-study chapters in this book demonstrate, internationalist and nationalist discourses often converge in the field of human rights to legitimize certain identities and social relations over others. Therefore, human rights scholars and activists need to address the disjuncture between human rights' universalist vision and the hierarchical scenes of suffering in which social and legal recognitions take place.

Human rights advocacy is largely about the process of making public the experience of those who, as the political theorist Wendy Brown puts it in another context, are "suffering the paradoxes of rights" (2002, 432). Or, as the legal scholar Jack Donnelly puts it, the ability to claim one's rights "distinguishes having a right from simply being the (rights-less) beneficiary of someone else's obligation. Paradoxically, then, 'having' a right is of most value precisely when one does not 'have' (the object of) the right—that is, when active respect or objective enjoyment is not forthcoming" (2003, 9). But we must ask: What are the properties of this process of making public? What happens when no rights exist—that is, when individuals are subject to inhuman repression and are not in a position to claim their rights? The French philosopher Jacques Rancière argues that, in such cases, "somebody else has to inherit their rights in order to enact them in their place" (2004, 308). This inheritance, however, in validating the agent's right to intervene on the victim's behalf also returns the "disused rights that had been sent to the rightless . . . back to the senders" (308–9). Thus we need to consider the hierarchies of recognition and the cultural narratives and structures that support them and the degree to which these hierarchies undermine the pursuit of social equality and justice.

Consider, for example, the historic gendering of the liberal public sphere —the realm of human rights—and the denial of political subjectivity to certain populations, including female victims of domestic violence. Article 12 of the UDHR, designed to protect individuals from the state, affirms that "no one shall be subjected to arbitrary interference with his privacy, family, home, or correspondence, nor to attacks upon his honor and reputation. Everyone has the right to protection of the law against such interference or attacks." In its replication of the private-public dichotomy, the declaration fails to acknowledge that a family, like any collective body, can be a viola- tor of human rights (Freedman 2007, 38), nor does it provide a framework for understanding violence associated with the private realm—such as do- mestic violence—as a human rights violation (Cubilié 2005, 31–32). Simi- larly, article 16, which states that men and women have the right to choose whom to marry and to have a family with, regardless of the other person's race, nationality, or religion (a reaction against Nazi racial marriage laws), singles out marriage as a protected category and sanctifies the heteronor- mative family as a private and safe space (36–37). Until recently, states have not been encouraged through international law to intervene in the private sphere. Gender-based violence, for instance, was not recognized as an in- ternational human rights issue until the 1990s, with the development of the 1993 UN Declaration of the Elimination of Violence against Women, the position of UN Special Rapporteur on Violence against Women, and the Statute of the International Criminal Court, which holds violence against women to be a punishable offense (see chapter 3). These legal activities and achievements not only entitled women who are abused by their husbands to protection from the state, but they also redefined gendered subjectivity and the interaction between the private sphere and the law by detaching, albeit temporarily, the individual from the familial structure in favor of a new relation to the state (Merry 2006, 187).

Among the successive human rights instruments characterized by their particularity—that is, forms of recognition that challenge the notion of the abstract universal subject of international human rights law—are the 1965 International Convention on the Elimination of All Forms of Racial Discrimination, the 1979 Convention on the Elimination of All Forms of Discrimination against Women, the 1981 Declaration on the Elimination of All Forms of Intolerance and of Discrimination Based on Religion or Belief, the 1989 International Labor Organization Convention Concerning Indigenous and Tribal Peoples in Independent Countries, and the 1990 Convention on the Rights of the Child.[13] However, some of these movements addressed by these documents have been subjected to the cultural imprints and biases of identity politics. The women's-rights-as-human-rights movement, for instance, has been criticized by some feminists—Cubilié (2005), M. Dutt (1998), Grewal (2005), Grewal and Kaplan (1996), Gunning (1998), and Hesford and Kozol (2005), among others—for prioritizing gender as its primary category of analysis, ignoring how gender interacts with other social markers (race, class, ethnicity, and so on), and framing its discourse around the spectacle of violence against women in non-Western cultures (for instance, female genital cutting, dowry burnings, and honor killings). At the heart of this human rights history, from the UDHR to the more specific conventions listed above, are the questions: Who counts as human, and who is included in the category as a bearer of human rights? What forces compel the norms of social recognition in the field of human rights? What is at stake in upholding or removing identification as a precondition for political action? To gauge the critical import of such questions to human rights past and future and, more specifically, to understand the visual economy of human rights internationalism and its American inflections, we need to examine the visual paradigm on which theories of recognition are based, and on which the formation of human rights subjectivity and agency rest.

## Recognition Scenes

Since the late twentieth century, there has been a renewed interest in theories of recognition among Western political philosophers and social theorists, especially in regard to the conceptualization of cultural identity and difference. Human rights scholars and activists often reconcile the universalism of human rights through the discourse of cultural particularity. Yet this critical reconciliation has not accounted for transnational or stateless subjects, who must navigate the volatile terrain of the global economy and shifting scenes of cultural and national recognition. To account for such subjects, we need a better understanding of the historical contingency, rhetorical exigency, and the fluidity of identities, and the complexities of social networks. The investigation of Western philosophical concepts of recognition, affiliation, and belonging are important to this study, as is the entanglement of the development of human rights and humanitarian law and discourse, because these concepts and entanglements delimit the parameters of Americans' engagement with human rights representations.

Paul Ricoeur identifies three phases in Western philosophy's engagement with the concept of recognition: recognition as identification, self-recognition, and mutual recognition.[14] Descartes' philosophy of judgment, indebted to rational psychology, exemplifies this first phase. Cartesian judgment, as Ricoeur summarizes, "keeps in reserve the concept of a transition between the two senses to recognize ... to grasp (an object) with the mind, through thought" and "to accept, take to be true (or take as such)" (2005, 36). Ricoeur attributes the emphasis on self-recognition within the second phase to Henri Bergson's reflexive psychology and his focus on the recognition of memories (18). The third phase, infused by Hegelian thought, refers to recognition in the context of the actualization of an individual's freedom. In the Hegelian tradition, "recognition designates an ideal reciprocal relation between subjects" (Fraser 2005b, 10)—but reciprocity is achieved through a violent battle in which the self must *supersede the other*" (Oliver 2001, 28). In his *Phenomenology of Spirit*, Hegel describes self-consciousness as a process of double-signification (Hegel [1807] 1994, 51). Similarly, in his *Philosophy of Mind* Hegel conceptualizes the dialectical origins of social subjectivity: "The fight of recognition is a life and death struggle: either self-consciousness imperils the other's life, and incurs a like peril for its own—but only peril, for either is no less bent on maintaining his life, as the existence of his freedom" ([1830] 1971 430–39).

Contemporary scholars working in the field of human rights—including Agamben (1998), Douzinas (2002), and Rancière (2004)—tend to draw on Hegel's philosophical account of the origins of self-consciousness as a struggle for recognition and on his thinking about the paradoxical dialectics of universalism and particularity. The legal scholar and philosopher Costa

[Margin handwritten notes:]
recog. as identification – see III (cover)
knows she exists
self recog – try to identify w/ person
mutual recog. – she understand & we
understand a commonness

Ricoeur

Douzinas notes that, for Hegel, "thought, consciousness and the spirit are active forces caught in a continuous struggle, in which the spirit fights its own alienation in the external world, recognizes objectified existence as its own partial realization, and returns to itself through its negation, acknowledging history as the process of its gradual realization" (2002, 380–81). Douzinas embraces "this dialogical construction of identity through the (mis)recognition of others" in his argument for the relevance of the Hegelian dialectic for human rights and, in so doing, differentiates himself from liberal philosophers—who, he argues, erase traces of otherness and glorify the individual as identical with itself (385). According to Douzinas, given that human rights law cannot finally deal with contingent, mutable subject positions—the action of legal rights is to extend abstract recognition to all—legal recognition (and, I would add, the historiographies of human rights framed by the binary construct of inclusion and exclusion) remains tied to the generality of certain identity positions and categories.

Douzinas argues that the differentiated characteristic—for instance, gender, race, ethnicity, sexuality, and disability—and the misrecognitions make the law both necessary and inadequate (402). He writes: "Human rights claims therefore involve a paradoxical dialectic between an impossible demand for universal equality, initially identified with the characteristics of western man, and an equally unrealizable claim to absolute difference" (400). This "paradoxical intertwining of identity, desire, and human rights," Douzinas claims, "is Hegel's lesson for postmodern jurisprudence" (405). Like Hegel's, Douzinas's formulation may help to explain "the existence of war and oppression," but, as Oliver suggests, "if *normalized* it makes it impossible to imagine peaceful compassionate relations with others across or through differences" (2001, 10).

To imagine reciprocal relations that do not reify the self-other hierarchy, or the construct of inclusion versus exclusion, which minimizes the complexity of social networks in the formation of forced and chosen identities, Oliver claims, requires that we turn to theories and practices that offer a differential politics of recognition or that move beyond recognition. In contrast to theories of subjectivity that replicate the hierarchy of the subject and the other or object, and that therefore remain caught in the trap of recognition and "logic of oppression that made [struggles for recognition]

necessary in the first place" (2001, 26–27), Oliver calls for a dialogic understanding of subjectivity as "response-ability" and "address-ability" (6).
She advocates a "relational subjectivity . . . not founded on [an originary]
trauma" (7) but grounded in the assumption that "otherness is always internal to subjectivity and encounters with others" (10): "Trauma is part of what
makes subjectivity othered, but it is not what makes subjectivity subjectivity" (7). One of the many problems with theories of subjectivity that are
linked to trauma and subjection, Oliver argues—correctly, in my view—
is that they do not provide a mechanism through which to "distinguish between becoming a subject and being oppressed, abused, or tortured" (65).

Yet what Oliver does not fully consider, which is essential to the development of the rhetorical method that this study advances, is how the social
and aesthetic mechanisms for and structures of emotion take hold within
a post-Hegelian model, or how the process of imagining "peaceful compassionate relations" is itself entangled with the normative principles of human
rights and sentimentality of liberal humanism. As we imagine alternatives
to the dialectical theories of recognition, then, we need to pay greater attention to the potential of alternative models to reify rather than unsettle the
figure of the Western cosmopolitan feeling for distant, non-Western others.
If the scaffold of compassionate cosmopolitanism collapses under the
weight of its contradictions in human rights practices and its personification of justice, as scholars on the cultural left such as Berlant (2004) and
K. Woodward (2004) suggest will be the case, we need to ask how we can
move beyond such contradictions in the creation of peaceful and just relations.

Contemporary critical theory is dominated by conceptions of subjectivity, identity, and agency tethered to a Hegelian notion of recognition,
wherein "relations with others are described as struggles for recognition"
(Oliver 2001, 4). According to Oliver, visual foundations of the struggle for
recognition are discernible in poststructuralist theory, where the "other
is the invisible, unspoken, nonexistent, the underside of the subject" (à la
Foucault and Butler), and in critical theory, where the other "confers recognition on us" (à la Honneth and Jürgen Habermas) or is "the one on whom
we confer recognition" (à la Taylor and Nancy Fraser) (5–6). Scholars envision various ways out of the ontological trap and dialectical deadlock of
Hegel's theory of subject formation as a warring struggle for recognition

response – response to her

address – she is a muslim girl

not just a trauma victim what her lesle is she whatmaker

and the compassion cosmopolitan antidote. Nancy Fraser is one of several prominent contemporary social theorists who examine the relation between theories of recognition and of social justice. Specifically, she explores how struggles for recognition and political agency are shaped by political institutions and their normative assumptions and rules of interaction. She challenges theories of recognition that isolate interpersonal relations and psychological development from larger social and political concerns and from the problem of representation—a critique she levels against both Charles Taylor and Axel Honneth. As Lois McNay points out, Taylor embraces a Hegelian notion of recognition, but his focus is on recognition as a form of intellectual judgment about the worth of an individual or group. In other words, Taylor's theory privileges those in a position to confer or withhold recognition. Honneth turns to theories of recognition to compensate for the marginalization in classical sociology of the role of emotions, moral indignation, and suffering as grounds of action. Drawing on object-relations theory, as practiced by Jessica Benjamin and Donald Winnicott, Honneth claims that the desire for recognition is fundamental to individual self-realization (McNay 2008, 275).

Critics argue that Honneth's conception of recognition subordinates social theory to moral psychology (Fraser 2003, 212). Honneth put it this way: "Even distribution injustices must be understood as the institutional expression of unjustified relations of recognition" (2003, 114).[15] McNay argues that Honneth's theory of social suffering as a universal impulse motivating political struggles does not account for the power relations that mediate emotions, including those caused by social suffering. McNay suggests that "the emotion of hope," for example, "does not arise spontaneously in individuals . . . but is crucially linked to a particular social position, most especially to the agent's objective ability to manipulate the potentialities of the present in order to realize some future project" (2008, 281). To frame agency solely in terms of the dynamics of recognition or misrecognition is to ignore how agency emerges as a "historically specific effect of a given configuration of power relations" and to uphold the "normative claim that recognition constitutes the universal structure of ethical life" (275).

Fraser is critical of the politics of recognition to the degree that it reifies collective identities, risks separatism, and "sanction[s] violations of

human rights and freez[es] the very antagonisms it purports to mediate"
(2003, 92). Insofar as the politics of recognition deflects attention from "ex-
acerbating economic inequality," it produces, she argues, the "problem of
displacement" (ibid.). To counter the potentially damaging effects of the
politics of recognition—which, she claims, dominated social organization movements and political activism in the late twentieth century and
which, as this study shows, dominates the discourse of human rights internationalism—Fraser calls for an integrated approach to justice that encompasses both redistribution and recognition (90). She defines her position
as "perspective dualism" and calls for the replacement of an identity model
of recognition with a status model that accounts for the relation between
maldistribution and misrecognition (93). Contra Honneth's conception of
recognition as "intact identity," Fraser conceptualizes recognition as "status
equality" (219).

In a clear move away from individualistic and interpersonal views of recognition, Fraser, like Douzinas, sees recognition as a matter of justice and
an issue of social status, which requires critical engagement with "socially
entrenched patterns of cultural value, of culturally defined categories of social actors" (Fraser 2003, 50). For Fraser, the means to "parity of participation" (30) does not lie in self or social recognition, but in the "possibility of
participating on a par with others in social interactivity" (31). Finally, her
notion of recognition is not limited to the articulation of group identities;
it also "encompasses the sort of deep restructuring of the symbolic order
that is associated with deconstruction" (96). But Fraser does not sufficiently
develop the deconstructive aspect of her argument, nor does she consider
the radical potential of a differentiated politics of recognition.

McNay is critical of Fraser's "'non-identarian' rendering of recognition,"
which leads Fraser "to abandon an experiential or interpretative perspective
that is associated with the idea of identity" (2008, 272). McNay turns to Pierre
Bourdieu's notion of *habitus*—the social and psychological dispositions that
define a subject's being—to mitigate the objectivism of Fraser's account and
to complicate Honneth's elemental understanding of the emotions. McNay
embraces aspects of Fraser's seminal work on recognition and redistribution in its materialist orientation (Fraser 2001, 2003), but she parts ways with
Fraser, as do I, in resurrecting the subjective dimensions of oppression and

*Handwritten margin notes:* Fraser - replaces an identity model of recognition with a status model — social context — recognize peoples' statuses in context with others

agency and a material-relational understanding of subjectivity that connects identities and emotions to social structures (McNay 2008, 287).

This relational account of subjectivity establishes the value of a rhetorical intercontextual approach for studying struggles for recognition in human rights history and advocacy. Moreover, we need to consider how identity is "performatively constituted" (Butler 1990, 25), including how individuals solidify generalized categories of identity or take up multiple, often contradictory, subject positions in human rights representations.[16] I invoke Butler here not to endorse the notion of identity as subordination. (She, like Honneth, Taylor, and Fraser, builds subjection, subordination, and oppression into the foundation of subjectivity.) Rather, I turn to Butler because she foregrounds the discursive conditions of social recognition that constitute subject formation (1993, 225). The subject, she argues, is "the linguistic occasion for the individual to achieve and reproduce intelligibility, the linguistic condition of its existence and agency" (1997, 11). Butler's emphasis on the power of signification in the formation of the subject would seem to support an understanding of subjectivity as dependent on "addressability," though, as Oliver points out, "it need not be conceived as subordinate to another" (2001, 88).[17]

In *Giving an Account of Oneself* (published after Oliver 2001), Butler explicitly links scenes of recognition to scenes of rhetorical address. She argues: "No account [of oneself] takes place outside the structure of address, even if the addressee remains implicit and unnamed, anonymous and unspecified" (2005, 36). Yet she also cautions against an overdetermined understanding of self-expression: "We cannot conclude that the 'I' is simply the effect or the instrument of some prior ethos or some field of conflicting and discontinuous norms" (7). Echoing Foucault's view of self-constitution as a relation to a regime of truth, Butler writes: "The regime of truth offers a framework for the scene of recognition, delineating who will qualify as a subject of recognition and offering available norms for the art of recognition. . . . This does not mean that a given regime of truth sets an invariable framework for recognition; it means only that it is in relation to this framework that recognition takes place or the norms that govern recognition are challenged and transformed" (22). For Butler, then, ethical critique emerges as a property of this "struggle with norms" (26).

As *Spectacular Rhetorics* shows, in order to reset the ethical parameters of our engagement with human rights representations of suffering, we need to call into question the normative frameworks that govern subject formation and the scenes of suffering, as well as the recognition scenes in human rights discourse. For example, as I note in chapter 3, in becoming legal subjects at the International Criminal Tribunal for the Former Yugoslavia, women who were victims of rape participated in the regulatory structures of international recognition. The women framed their experiences as both individual and as representative of a group, as the 1948 Convention on the Prevention and Punishment of the Crime of Genocide requires, and, at the same time, their testimonies recalibrated legal norms by challenging the heretofore gendered public-private distinction that governs legal recognition. The act of testifying before the tribunal created a post-Hegelian scene of recognition in the sense that the women risked the possibility of unrecognizability, and this possibility served as "a critical point of departure for the interrogation of available norms" (Butler 2005, 24). Baxi makes a similar point in his discussion of the contingency of human rights subjects, when he notes: "The bearer of universal human rights is . . . no individual human being or community with a pre-posited 'essence' but a being born with a right to invent practices of identification, contest identities pre-formed by tradition, and the power to negotiate subversive subject-positions. . . . [T]he bearers of human rights remain *contingent persons*" (2006, 149). What would it mean to approach human rights advocacy and scholarship from such a perspective? What would we gain by redefining the parameters of our ethical engagement with human rights representations, including scenes of suffering, as scenes of rhetorical address?

Legal personhood is established on the basis of its violation, which in part explains the prominence of images of individual suffering in juridical contexts. Visual identification with a suffering other is also the prominent rhetorical scene of address in human rights campaigns. The presumption is that if one can imagine oneself in another's place, then one will (1) recognize the other as a human rights subject; (2) identify with the other through an awareness of one's own vulnerability; and (3) be moved to act on his or her behalf. Baxi claims: "To give language to pain, to experience the pain of the Other inside you, remains the task, always, of human rights narratology" (2006, 159). If the future of human rights is dependent on one's identification with suffering others, as Baxi suggests—a debatable proposition —then our challenge as human rights scholars and advocates is to recognize when identification fails, and when it risks obscuring the subjectivity of the other.[18] Victim identifications may make distant human rights violations visible and, in some cases, provide an opportunity for the disenfranchised to represent themselves, but the limitations of victim-based politics, as I have suggested throughout, are profound. Victimization rhetoric invites interventions and protectionist remedies that can obscure structural inequalities and economic injustices, and that therefore ultimately undermine the promotion of human rights. When personal stories are used "to tell of structural effects," as Lauren Berlant puts it, they risk deflecting attention from "a scene of pain that must be soothed politically" (1998, 641). Berlant draws a distinction here between what Luc Boltanski refers to as the "politics of pity" and the "politics of justice" (1999, 5). The "politics of pity" conflates the language of humanitarianism and human rights by positioning the other as the recipient of the gift of rights distributed by the powerful. Cultural theorists like Berlant argue that we need to consider the possibility of a future human rights politics that moves beyond the rhetoric of identification and self-recognition in its acknowledgment of the differences that cannot be transcended, but that may become a source of solidarity.

The feminist social theorist Iris Young engages the problem of identification and argues that "it is neither possible nor morally desirable for persons engaged in moral interaction to adopt one another's standpoint" (1997, 39). She proposes an "asymmetrical reciprocity"—a rhetorical process that, in Oliver's words, "involves listening with an openness that allows us to get 'out of ourselves'" (2001, 55). Lilie Chouliaraki calls for an understanding of the constitutive social function of representational acts in "bring[ing] into existence the identities that they appear to be merely representing" (2006, 203). Thus we might ask: What would human rights representations look like if subjectivity and agency were not construed in terms of a punitive struggle for recognition? What if humanity were not seen as something that can be given or taken away?

## Beyond Recognition

The legal and cultural theorist Samera Esmeir asks us to consider these questions and how "human rights law . . . claims jurisdiction over the declaration of this [dehumanized] status" (2006, 1545). Tracing the affinities between contemporary human rights law and late-nineteenth-century colonial law, Esmeir exposes human rights logics and operations of juridical humanity. For instance, UN human rights campaigns, until recently, have focused on peoples "thought to be dehumanized by their regimes and awaiting the promise of humanization by international human rights campaigns and legal reforms" (1546). It is precisely the configuration of a priori absence—the absence of humanity—that is at stake. Esmeir argues that the declaration of subjects as dehumanized "reproduces violence's power" by not providing identification other than that of victim (1549). Classifications such as "dehumanized" and "victim" grant certain protections, but Esmeir urges us to question the "idea that humanity is a matter of endowment, declaration, or recognition" (1549), and instead to work toward "the forging of concrete alliances with human beings who await not our *recognition* but our *participation* in their struggles" (1545, emphasis added).[19]

At stake here is the formation of political alliances based not on a communitarian ethos—the imagined identifications with a community to which one already belongs—but a rhetoric that challenges the "narcissism of pity" and the symbolic bias in transnational news flows toward hierarchical forms of global intimacy based on the relative proximity of spectators to scenes of suffering (Chouliaraki 2006, 209). Chouliaraki calls for a cosmopolitanism predicated on impersonal action, which she associates with Hannah Arendt's 1958) notion of the public, and "relationships of responsibility and commitment with the 'other' without asking for reciprocity or control over the outcome of action" (201). Similarly, and contra the Hegelian dialectic, Oliver advances a model of subjectivity based on an ethics of witnessing, which, she argues, results in neither "the assimilation of all differences into sameness or the alienation, exclusion, or abjection of all difference" (2001, 12).

Witnessing has both juridical connotations (as in eyewitness testimony) and religious connotations (as in bearing witness to something beyond recognition). For Oliver, this "double meaning of witnessing is the heart of subjectivity" (2001, 16). She elaborates: "Subjectivity is founded on the ability to respond to, and address, others" (15). She therefore reformulates vision as a connecting rather than an alienating sense, as part of a system of sensation and perception (12). Oliver insists that theories of recognition that subscribe to notions of vision as an alienating force conflate the pathology of racism and oppression with the normal process of becoming a subject (169). Frantz Fanon makes a similar argument in *Black Skin, White Masks* (1967) when he claims that the oppressed do not seek recognition from their oppressors but seek the power to create their own meaning, as Oliver observes (29). She notes: "The problem is not with vision per se, but with the particular notion of vision presupposed in theories of recognition and misrecognition" (11). Given human rights advocates' appeals to their targeted audiences to witness distant suffering and become involved in ameliorating it on the basis of what has been seen, it is instructive to consider Oliver's model as we contemplate how human rights representations constitute the witnessing publics they seek to engage. Unlike Martin Heidegger's ([1938] 1997) indictment of seeing as inseparable from visual objectification; Guy Debord's (1994) deterministic formulation of the commodity spectacle; feminist and postcolonial critiques, such as Trinh T. Minh-ha's (1989) of the link between vision and objectification; or Fredric Jameson's claim that "the visual is *essentially* pornographic" (1992, 1), the philosophy of vision that informs the representational practices of human rights public appeals, like Oliver's theory of witnessing, "bespeaks a more hopeful notion of vision" closer to that offered by the discourse of phenomenology (L. Allen 2009, 172). Phenomenology deconstructs the metaphysical narrative of subjectivity and breaks down the subject-object structure by locating the source of moral vision and ethical relations in the body of felt experience. In *The Visible and the Invisible* (published posthumously), Maurice Merleau-Ponty writes that "the seer and the visible reciprocate one another and we no longer know which sees and which is seen" (1968, 139). His moral vision is based on an understanding of intentionality as a form of reciprocity—a vision that shares some similarities with my emphasis on recognition as a scene of rhetorical address, but that diverges in its sublimation of how reciprocity is enabled and constrained by social hierarchies and power relations. In

*Phenomenology of Perception*, he writes: "The communication or comprehension of gestures comes about through the reciprocity of my intentions and the gestures of others, and my gestures and the intentions discernible in the conduct of other people. It is as if the other person's intentions inhabited my body and mine his" (1962, 185). As Levin notes, Merleau-Ponty believed that our awareness of this communicative intertwining of the "moral predispositions already inscribed in the flesh" could lead to a "heightened sense of justice" (Levin 2003, 217).

Emmanuel Lévinas is suspicious of vision as a paradigm of knowledge and truth—the "panoramic look" (1969, 220) that "totalizes the multiple" (292)—but he nonetheless proposes an ethical vision through his phenomenology of the face. Lévinas locates the other through the domain of appearance. The encounter with the face of the other calls forth a third party: the witness. In Lévinas, as Butler importantly points out, "'the Other' not only refers to the human other but acts as a place-holder for an infinite ethical relation" (2005, x). Levin aptly characterizes Lévinas's face-to-face encounter: "The face . . . is both the concrete other who is or could be facing me here and now, and also the abstract other, witness for humanity" (2003, 301). Lévinas refers to "the third party": "The presence of the face, the infinity of the other, is a destituteness, a presence of the third party (that is, the whole of humanity which looks at us) and a command. [The] third party, the whole of humanity, [is present] in the eyes that look at me" (213). For Lévinas, the face-to-face encounter breaks the objectifying gaze and moves beyond narcissistic recognition. In *Otherwise Than Being*, he writes: "To communicate is indeed to open oneself, but the openness is not complete if it is on the watch for recognition. It is complete not in the opening to the spectacle of or the recognition of the other, but in becoming a responsibility for him" (1981, 119). In the context of this study and its emphasis on representations of human rights violations, the third party might be understood as the projected and sought-after witness of human suffering—a witness, however, who, in seeking an ethical relation to the other, is caught up in a struggle with the norms of social and legal recognition. Although Lévinas upholds "an idealized dyadic structure of social life," as Butler observes, his attention to one's "primary susceptibility to the action and face of the other, [and to] the full ambivalence of an unwanted address," suggests that "responsibility is not a matter of cultivating a will, but of making use of an unwilled susceptibility as a resource for becoming responsive to the Other" (2005, 91).

Phenomenology paved the way for the idea of a moral gaze that was no longer ruled by the logic of the ego or subject but by the logic of alterity, and in this sense it triggered an advance in our understanding of the fundamental intersubjectivity of perception and of emotion. In the wake of contemporary critiques of presence (Derrida 1994) and the interrogation of the notion of a naturalized subject (Foucault 1997), however, phenomenology's transcendental ideal of the body as a bedrock of authentic experience has been replaced by poststructuralist accounts of the subject as an effect of discourse and of differential relations to others (Butler 1997 and 2005). Despite the prominence and persuasiveness of poststructuralist critiques, particularly in the humanities engagement with human rights (see the conclusion), Lori Allen argues, and I concur, that the aesthetic ideology underpinning the rhetorical work that images of suffering are expected to perform in human rights campaigns assumes that connections can be drawn irrespective of social hierarchies and structures of mediation (2009, 172). Like Allen, I view the process of recognition that the human rights spectacle is called on to activate as an inherently social and rhetorical process. This view contrasts with phenomenological orientations that posit an understanding of perception and emotion as prediscursive (Marks 2000, 144). The problem with the phenomenological aesthetic that underlies human rights advocacy, particularly advocacy directed at public engagement, is that it duplicates the inadequacies of legal and social recognition—the abstraction of the person—to which human rights claims are a response. That is, human rights representations of suffering subjects do not appeal to particularity or difference but to universality and sameness, although the appeal is initiated by difference. This tension between human rights aesthetic ideology—which is tied to a humanitarian sensibility and a phenomenological understanding of a shared, felt experience—and the enactment of human rights as a form of social criticism exposes the need for either a differentiated politics of recognition that is not based on a desired symmetry, or a move beyond recognition in human rights discourse. A rhetorical analytic, such as this study offers, enables us to approach scenes of suffering as scenes of recognition and rhetorical address, to understand how struggles for recognition and attachments to subjection, as well as the process of working through them or not, are mediated by historical contingencies and the imaging technologies through which these struggles are played out. To address the rhetorical dimensions of recognition is to complicate both Lévinas's face-to-face encounter and Oliver's theory of witnessing by acknowledging perception as a mediated act, and thereby unsettling the moral and legal visions of a human rights internationalism supported by an objectivist ocular epistemology.

## Mediation and Witnessing Publics

On his visit to the Yad Vashem Holocaust Memorial Museum in Jerusalem in July 2008, Barack Obama (then a senator from Illinois) wrote the following in the museum's guest book: "Let our children come here and know this history so that they can add their voices to proclaim never again."[20] The slogan "never again," which links the memory of the Holocaust to Jews and Israel, has come to signify both the evidentiary and commemorative power of bearing witness. The quest to remember crimes against humanity and to place human suffering in relation to a future that is free from systemic violations marks an advancement for human rights that is defined, in part, through an affective economy that transforms suffering into moral commentary. "Never again" imagines a progressive narrative of human rights history, which presumes that the more we uncover, witness, and remember, the more just our world will become. Yet, as we know, the post-Holocaust promise has been broken again and again, as the genocides in Cambodia, Rwanda, Bosnia, northern Iraq, and Darfur confirm. Every articulation of the slogan "never again," and its juxtaposition with images of suffering, puts forth "a sense of obligation to remember what one has seen and, in response to that haunting, to become involved in a story of rescue or amelioration" (Berlant 2004, 7). The Yad Vashem Holocaust Memorial Museum, like all public memorials, urges its visitors to witness its narration and display of historical events. Carrie Rentschler usefully elaborates: "Witnessing is a rhetorical act constituted by multiple levels of mediation: material artifacts, media texts, bodies, aesthetics, cultural and national politics, and so on" (2004, 298). A rhetorical approach to witnessing requires that we keep in view the scenes of recognition and address through which memory is constituted.

The moral vision of human rights law and advocacy evolved in conjunction with broader notions of truth telling and witnessing that developed in the latter half of the twentieth century. The methodological model of exposure—seeing is believing—and shaming tactics (Drinan 2001; Keenan 2004) that continue to dominate human rights advocacy and the means of public engagement with human rights internationalism in Western contexts, particularly the United States, shadow the history of modern Western moral philosophy and its ocular epistemology, as well as Holocaust studies and its belated witnessing of that genocide. As Barbie Zelizer notes, the truth value attributed to photographic realism as a tool for gathering empirical evidence of atrocities helped to legitimize photojournalism and to lift censorship restrictions during the Second World War. By the early 1940s, independent journalists and underground groups began to release images of mass graves and stacked corpses. But the photographic record, much of it produced by the Nazis, did not enter the public domain until after the war (1998, 45), which forestalled the public's ability to grasp the magnitude of the atrocities (40).

For many, the Nuremberg trials are the birthplace of the contemporary human rights movement, and the 1945 Agreement for the Prosecution and Punishment of the Major War Criminals of the European Axis is its birth certificate (Mutua 2001, 211). But it was the 1961–62 trial of Adolf Eichmann in Jerusalem, which broadcast to the world the testimonies of survivors of the Nazi genocide, that marked a turning point in the history of human rights representation through the symbolic power attributed to the transnational act of bearing witness. In contrast with the prosecutors at the Nuremberg trials, who sought to convict Nazi officials on the basis of material evidence (using the documentation of invoices, communications, and photographs), the chief prosecutor of Eichmann, Gideon Hausner, made the oral testimony of ninety Holocaust survivors the focus (225–26). As Sonali Chakravarti puts it, Hausner believed that "the testimony of victims could both (1) help convince the judges and the audience for the harshest punishment for Eichmann and (2) serve as a way to educate people about the Holocaust and also highlight the resiliency and strength of the Jewish people" (2008, 227). Historians confirm Hausner's expectation that media coverage of the trial would sharpen public awareness of the Holocaust and affirm Israel's sovereignty (Levy, Sznaider, and Oksiloff 2005, 105).[21] These trials also set an important precedent for future international tribunals and truth commissions, which, in part, cast witnessing as a process of resurrecting a nation and its sovereignty. In short, Holocaust studies has provided the dominant framework for understanding witnessing in the fields of human rights and the humanities, and psychoanalytic theories have become a prominent explanatory framework for understanding how survivors "work through" trauma and how Euro-American audiences engage representations of mass atrocity and human suffering.[22]

Shoshana Felman and Dori Laub's *Testimony* is among the foremost theoretical works on the relation between witnessing and secondary trauma. Felman and Laub's attention to trauma's reception acknowledges the dialogic nature of testimonial acts.[23] They argue that "the absence of an empathic listener, or more radically, the absence of an addressable other ... who can hear the anguish of one's memories and thus affirm and recognize their realness, annihilates the story" (1992, 68). In their foreword, they claim that "a textual testimony ... can *penetrate us like an actual life*" (2). "The specific task of the literary testimony," Felman writes, "is, in other words, to open up in that belated witness, which the reader now historically becomes, the imaginative capability of perceiving history ... in one's own body" (108). As Amy Hungerford notes, *Testimony* alternates between understanding the transmission of trauma as requiring a witness who has experienced something similar, and understanding that transmission as a process of sympathetic and imaginative identification (2001, 74). This vacillation suggests that "trauma ... exists in, and [can] be transmitted by, writing or speech" (75). Yet *Testimony* also reveals the distance between the traumatic event and its telling through its conceptualization of witnessing as translation. Felman argues that "translation, as opposed to confession ... becomes a metaphor for the historical necessity of bearing witness" (Felman and Laub 1992, 153). Paradoxically, for her, translation also becomes a metaphor for the failure to see—the impossibility of witnessing the original (159).[24]

To retain this sense of the impossibility of witnessing the original is to arrive at a place, as Rey Chow suggests, surprisingly close to Spivak's formulation of the untranslatability of subaltern discourse (1993, 35). Spivak urges critics to avoid resurrecting victims' voices in ways that replace those voices with their own, thereby neutralizing their untranslatability. She warns of the dangers of translation and its potential to reproduce hierarchical scenes of self-recognition (ibid). For Spivak (1988), like Butler (2005), ethical responsibility involves the acknowledgment of the limits of self-knowledge.

In her seminal work *The Body in Pain*, Elaine Scarry highlights the unsharability of pain. She argues that pain resists and shatters language (1985, 5). Nevertheless, she is devoted to understanding the rhetorical strategies that survivors, artists, activists, and practitioners employ to overcome pain's inexpressibility. Such strategies typically involve the use of "the language of 'agency'" (13). For instance, common expressions of pain include metaphors of pain as a weapon and as a wound—the experience of pain is the experience of "being acted upon" (16). Given the translation of pain and suffering into the language of agency and witnessing in human rights discourse, we might ask why we should hold on to the notion of its inexpressibility. The scholarly debate over the representability of pain, mass trauma, and genocide is most volatile within the interdisciplinary field of Holocaust studies or, more broadly, the comparative field of trauma studies. Some scholars, as Douglass and Vogler note, contest the notion that the Holocaust is an "inexplicable [and] horrible enigma" (Gottlieb quoted in Douglass and Vogler 2003, 29). First, as Douglass and Vogler argue, the notion that "an event defies all representation" is not an expression born after the Second World War; it is one of the "oldest tropes of Western writing, what Kant called the negative or non-presentation of the idea of horror in the sublime" (2003, 32). Second, to claim that the Holocaust is inexplicable is to foreclose an interrogation of the historical conditions that made it possible and of the rhetoric of the unspeakable itself (Mandel 2001, 228). Third, literary and cultural critics (Bennett and Kennedy 2003; Schaffer and Smith 2004) question the universal applicability of models like Felman and Laub's because they may not account for cultural forms of responding to cataclysmic events that are not grounded in Western perspectives on trauma. Finally, as the cultural anthropologist Veena Das reminds us, constructions of violence as unimaginable often reaffirm hierarchical boundaries between the "civilized" and "savage" (2007, 79), and therefore reproduce the very categories that human rights claims aim to contest. "If the process of naming the violence presents a challenge," as Das suggests, "it is because such naming has large political stakes, and not only because language falters in the face of violence" (205).

Feminist and postcolonial scholars in the fields of film, visual culture, and cultural studies (including Chow 1993; Kozol n.d.; Minh-ha 2005; Shohat 1998, 2006; Shohat and Stam 1994, 1999; and Zimmerman 2000) have demonstrated how looking constitutes and is constituted by power relations. Minh-ha has been particularly engaged with cinematic representations of "absent omnipresences of the dominant culture in our media practices" (2005, 17); she is concerned "with the visible presentation of invisibility itself" (153).[25] Likewise, Wendy Kozol urges us to situate acts of looking in relation to "historically produced discourses that structure differential sites of visibilities and invisibilities" (n.d., 5). She calls for a way of looking that acknowledges the histories of imperialism, militarization, and inequalities that structure witnessing, and the implication of those histories in the politics of domination (ibid). The question of how we, as human rights scholars and advocates, situate ourselves among a series of traumatic repetitions, Kozol suggests, calls for an understanding of witnessing as a historically contingent rhetorical act, which is implicated in and mediated by sociopolitical relations, discourses, and technologies.

Witnessing atrocity has come to mean not just the experience of the survivor but a more generalized mass-mediated experience, which, as this study shows, can function in ways that regenerate nationalist scenes of recognition and rhetorical address. Although the human rights media try to make their audience global witnesses to historical events and human suffering, in the hope that such an awareness will lead to action, images of atrocity may fulfill some people's voyeuristic pleasures. That is, "witnesses can also act complicitously in others' suffering by watching it without seeking to alleviate it, and they can empathize, or 'feel with,' others who suffer— an imagined form of affective participation" (Rentschler 2004, 298). Such claims attest to the transience of compassion. How (passive) spectators become (active) witnesses is an open question, which has elicited both idealistic and pessimistic responses in the field of human rights and in the humanities. "The act of bearing witness may no longer compel responsibility," Zelizer concedes (1998, 206). Susan Sontag issues a similar warning:

"Harrowing photographs do not inevitably lose their power to shock. But they are not much help if the task is to understand. Narratives can make us understand. Photographs do something else: they haunt us" (2003, 89). "Without a politically mobilizing news media, witnesses are left to 'feel' with little to no direction for how to act," Rentschler writes (2004, 300). Yes, photographs haunt. Looking may not compel responsibility. News media saturate the public in pathos. But, as I have suggested, looking is itself a rhetorically mediated act.

All modes of looking involve some level of interpretation or narration. Audiences draw on a host of historical associations, cultural narratives, structures of feeling and belief, and rhetorical expectations in their engagement with images as texts and their contexts. Therefore, instead of replicating the spectator-witness binary that has come to dominate critical accounts of the reception of visual representations of human suffering, we would advance the scholarly work of human rights, in particular in the humanities, by accounting for perception and witnessing as rhetorical and material phenomena. Such a view would also require us to frame the emotions that human rights images solicit as part of a visual economy of affect (S. Ahmed 2004, 121). As I suggest in the introduction, we might think of the sought-after imaginative identifications with the suffering other as part of an affective economy that transforms others into objects of feeling and sight. From this perspective, we would read certain emotions, as Gross advocates, "as markers of social distinction rather than just as expressions of a human nature essentially shared by all" (2004, 178). If we accept the notion that witnessing is part of an economy of affect, then we are prompted to consider how human rights media align audiences with the suffering other, the human rights organization, or the media themselves, and how these rhetorical alignments as scenes of address foster certain forms of recognition, engagement, and action.

The seeing-is-believing paradigm invests the human rights image with emotional appeal and enshrines it, as Abigail Solomon-Godeau puts it in another context, "as a humanist monument to the timeless struggle against adversity" (1991, 179). Moreover, this model presumes the power of the image to persuade (a narrow understanding of its rhetorical functions) instead of emphasizing the rhetorical and material power and the confluence of the discourses and apparatuses (organizations, corporations, governments, etc.) that deploy the image and that guarantee or hinder its circulation. Alternatively, to see the visual as a "structuring agent for a specified set of historical, social, and economic interests" (Pace 2003, 326)—the seeing-is-power model—is not to deny its evidentiary functions but rather to highlight the cultural and political work that human rights images perform.

Visual and audiovisual media are important features of contemporary human rights advocacy; organizations such as Witness, Video Activist Network, Just Vision, and Undercurrents provide handheld video cameras, portable editing equipment, and training in video technology for local human rights activists around the world.[26] Over the last decade, for example, amateur video has also played a key role in grass-roots campaigns, news media reports, and legal proceedings; in each context, it has corroborated evidence of human rights violations and counterbalanced official versions of a nation's human rights performance. Expository amateur video[27] played an important role in the trial of major leaders at the International Criminal Tribunal for the Former Yugoslavia, for example: video footage of a Serbian army invading a Bosnian Muslim town helped to convict General Radislav Krstić.[28] But visual evidence can be manipulated to serve contrary agendas. Following the June 2005 release of the video used in the tribunal, for example, a website issuing Serbian propaganda posted a story that falsely identified Bosnians as the perpetrators killing Serbs.[29]

And although visual evidence can focus a debate, it can also overwhelm deliberate arguments. Furthermore, in some instances visual exposure to violence fails to produce sustained attention or action, as in the case of the genocide in Rwanda or, more recently, the crisis in Darfur.[30]

The culture wars launched by conservatives in the United States in the 1980s over the content of federally funded art and humanities projects may have diminished, but independent media must constantly create "new ways to take ground in order to, quite literally, make public places" for the distribution of their work (Zimmerman 2000, 105). The relative lack of governmental financial support for independent nonfiction films, including films that focus on human rights, and reliance on private foundations exacerbates the challenges that human rights advocates and organizations face in getting their message and information out to a broad audience.[31] Moreover, human rights filmmakers rely on private foundations and are often pressured to some degree to conform to the foundation's political and social agenda. Similarly, to ensure their organizational survival, local NGOs are selective in the cases they take on and often conform to the mandates of major international NGOs and funding sources, and their normative assumptions and rules of interaction (38).[32] In other words, although technologies of visual representation such as the cellphone camera are becoming increasing available and affordable, and Internet platforms are also more available (although not all of these are unregulated) to communities around the globe, human rights appeals must nevertheless compete for attention in the international morality marketplace (Clifford 1992). An intercontextual rhetorical analytic, such as this study offers, can help us assess these contingencies and their political ramifications.

Human rights film festivals are becoming prominent public places for screening interrogative human rights documentaries and mounting photographic exhibitions of human rights images. Perhaps the most renowned of these is the Human Rights Watch Film Festival, an annual event in New York and London. The festival features a photographic exhibition and a series of documentary films about a range of human rights issues; filmmakers are invited to speak with audiences after the screenings. Each year, Human Rights Watch offers a Traveling Film Festival, which consists of a smaller number of films available to schools, colleges, universities, and community organizations. The packaging of these films includes pedagogical materials and resources available through the sponsoring organization's website and publication department. Additionally, human rights are packaged for public consumption and educational purposes through a variety of cultural forms and contexts, including literature and films, art installations and exhibitions, and documentary theater. Indeed, there is a subculture of human rights activism in the wake of the U.S. War on Terror in theatrical performances, one of which is considered in this study (see chapter 2).

Human rights organizations are also developing new social and technological relationships—imagining new witnessing publics—through online communities. Digitalization provides additional opportunities for collective social action and human rights education, but whether new media technologies and interfaces are better at enabling political action or creating an illusion of it remains an open question. Optimistic narratives about technological progress and its impact on the human rights movement obfuscate highly uneven media access and the manipulation of local and international coverage by repressive regimes. Thus, when we consider which global injustices mass media and human rights organizations make visible and which go unseen, we also need to acknowledge the gap between public knowledge and action—the knowledge paradox—and the status attributed to visual evidence in human rights politics.

As the independent scholar and filmmaker Meg McLagen reminds us, "the process of summoning witnessing publics" is complexly enabled and constrained not only by technology but also by a range of political and economic forces and agendas (2007, 312). To what degree, we might ask—as Baxi does—whether "contemporary" human rights is being supplanted by a "trade-related, market friendly human rights" paradigm (2006, 234). Specifically, we might ask in what ways human rights advocacy has become "subservient to a whole variety of logics and paralogics of homeland security and a 'global War on Terror'" (240–41). Pheng Cheah argues that "the very constitution of a subject entitled to rights invokes the violent capture of the disenfranchised by an institutional discourse that inseverably weaves them into the textile of global capitalism" (2006, 172). In the following chapter, I discuss these convergences by considering the spectacular impact of the U.S. War on Terror on international human rights politics; the scenarios of power and scenes of address that constitute the terror spectacle; and the cultural work that human rights advocacy, including the human rights spectacle, performs in reproducing and countering these formations of power. The human rights imaginary may be taxed by global capital and the discourses of national security, but we need not trade away our capacity to articulate both the injustices and justice that its vision for the world has created.

# CHAPTER TWO

# Staging Terror Spectacles

To build support for the U.S. War on Terror, the second Bush administration repeatedly invoked the spectacle of the terrorist attacks of 9/11 against the World Trade Center and the Pentagon. In so doing, the administration organized the war around the modalities of fear, trauma, and death and promoted a moralistic us-them divide.[1] In his 20 September 2001 address to the Congress and the nation, President Bush said: "Every nation in every region now has a decision to make: Either you are with us or you are with the terrorists." The characterization of the 9/11 attacks as an assault on Western civilization was also apparent in the Bush administration's implicit characterization of Arab detainees under U.S. jurisdiction as uncivilized, barbarian, and unlike us. The administration's resurgent nationalist discourse in the War on Terror and its disdain for both the United Nations and multilateral diplomacy extended to the national level the dialectic struggle for recognition, which typically refers to the formation of individual subjectivity as an antagonistic struggle between the self and the other (see chapter 1). In short, the administration deployed the terror spectacle in ways that scripted citizens of the United States as both victims of terrorism and agents of a newly imagined, ultranationalist state entrenched in stereotypical representations of the Muslim other and scenes of cultural subjection. If the visual repetition of the burning and collapse of the World Trade Center's twin towers on 11 September 2001 on television screens across the world codified perceptions of the terrorist threat and U.S. vulnerability, the Abu Ghraib photographs reclaimed dominance by transferring that fear, terror, and "vigilant visibility" onto the geopolitical body of "unlawful combatants" (Amoore 2007, 217). The Abu Ghraib snapshots that celebrate the sexual humiliation of Iraqi men at the hands of U.S. military personnel incorporate American viewers as participants in a neocolonial narrative about the inadequacy of Arab others. In assigning terrorist motives to all detainees, the Bush administration opened the door for the military police and military intelligence to bypass rules on the treatment of prisoners of war established by the Geneva Conventions and the 1984 UN Convention against Torture and Other Cruel, Inhuman or Degrading Treatment or Punishment, which the United States ratified in 1994, and to deny detainees rights to due process granted under habeas corpus. Moreover, like the interrogation dyad, wherein interrogation functions as an alibi for torture, the terror of the spectacle and the terrorist figure functioned as rationales for the Bush administration's curtailment of U.S. citizens' civil liberties and its disregard for international law.

The photographs of the abuse at Abu Ghraib, taken by U.S. soldiers, were first revealed on 28 April 2004, on CBS's *60 Minutes II*. They were then published in the 10 May *New Yorker* with an article by Seymour M. Hersh, which quoted from a secret report by Major General Antonio M. Taguba that detailed "sadistic, blatant, and wanton criminal abuses" at Abu Ghraib between October and December 2003 (quoted in Hersh 2004, 43). Before the release of the photographs, reports—some published by the U.S. military—had indicated that there was systematic abuse of prisoners in Iraq and Afghanistan.[2] Yet these reports did not capture the attention of the national media or the U.S. public until the release of the photographs. The wide circulation of the torture portraits on Internet sites and newspapers throughout the world not only exposed the violations but triggered at least eight major investigations, congressional hearings, thousands of pages of reports, the release of the U.S. Department of Defense files, and human rights activism across the globe. Whatever agenda the photographs are used to support—and there have been many—their prominence in public discourse as the face of the War on Terror illustrates how the spectacle can force contentious issues onto the public agenda and, as some scholars have argued, compound the "faith we put in the informative power of images" (Rodowick 2002, 22).

The mass circulation of the torture photographs may have undercut the Bush administration's tightly controlled visual strategies, which were used to sell the Iraq war to the American people as an act that would secure the U.S. homeland and bring democracy to the Iraqi people. These strategies included the suppression of images of Iraqi civilian casualties as well as the flag-draped coffins of dead American soldiers and the theatrical staging of the toppling of the statue of Saddam Hussein in the international media, not to mention President Bush's "mission accomplished" performance. But the Abu Ghraib torture images have not functioned solely to counter the controlled and antiseptic "shock and awe" military campaign, which visually displaced human suffering in its televised reports. In reaching beyond their target audience, the torture photographs have become the objects of a political contest, and opposing groups have projected onto them geopolitical identifications, denial narratives, and arguments for or against the war.[3] For example, the Bush administration refused to call what had taken place in prisons in Iraq and Afghanistan and at Guantánamo Bay torture. Instead, the administration—particularly in its early responses—construed the abuse depicted in the Abu Ghraib photographs as the exceptional acts of a few rogue soldiers. Such claims allowed the United States to adopt a rhetorical stance of critical and moral distance. If the images were to be seen as ordinary, as Susan Sontag provocatively suggested, they become us (2004, 26). But, as several critics have pointed out, the images *are* us, especially if we consider the abuses at Abu Ghraib as extensions of the violent preemptive strike on and the military occupation of Iraq under the stress of the insurgency (Danner 2004) and the transnational exportation of U.S. penal codes and their correlates: interrogation, punishment, and retribution (Michelle Brown 2005, 974). The images-are-us interpretation alludes to the collusion between the military and prison industries and points up the hypocrisy of the disavowal of the detainees' suffering and the moral unaccountability exhibited by the U.S. government based on "exclusionary conceptions of who is normatively human" (Butler 2004, xiv–xv).

Similarly, the spectacle of Saddam Hussein's capture played to the nationalist interests of the United States and shored up American exceptionalism by rendering invisible decades of U.S. support, especially its realpolitik encouragement of Hussein during the Iran-Iraq war. The legally expedient trial and execution of Hussein (for killing 148 Shiites in Dujail in the 1980s) bypassed a juridical process based on international human rights models that would have held Hussein accountable for the range of atrocities and war crimes he committed, and that would have been laboriously documented by human rights forensic investigators (B. Shapiro 2007, 5). The staged trial and execution, like the insidious Abu Ghraib torture-trophy photographs, revealed how national dramas and international relations are mediated by spectacular performances. The official videotape released after Hussein's execution provided a sanitized version of what was —as a cellphone video viewed by over four million Internet users later revealed—a far more dramatic judicial spectacle, or, as Bruce Shapiro put it, a "lynch party" (4). Clearly, the spectacle is a function of politics; it is highly rhetorical—that is, situational and performative (Taylor 1997, 29).

Guy Debord argues that "the spectacle is capital accumulated to the point where it becomes image" (1994, 23) and that late "capitalism had successfully employed an image industry to transform commodities into appearances and history into staged events" (25). The Abu Ghraib photographs, like the Hussein execution video, enact and record the terror spectacle. But the acts of violation at Abu Ghraib and their representation might also be read more broadly as an integrated spectacle, which Debord defines as the combination of the concentrated spectacle of authoritarianism and the diffused spectacle of globalization (2007, 8). The images of the abuses at Abu Ghraib reveal the integration of these two expressions of the spectacle and the induction of detainees into the U.S. military-industrial and prison-industrial complex, wherein the terror spectacle secures the operations of capital and the power of the nation-state even as the military is privatized through companies like Blackwater (which has changed its name to Xe). Thus the contemporary variant of the integrated spectacle within the War on Terror includes the concentrated spectacle of American exceptionalism and the diffused spectacle of the transnational exportation of the culture and economy of U.S. security and punishment.

Two discursive frames—predicated on the rules of evidence and causal logic, and linked to the truth-telling norms of documentary photography— have gained prominence in explanations of the abuses at Abu Ghraib (Michelle Brown 2005, 977). The first frame emphasizes individual actors and individual responsibility gone awry. From the individualistic perspective, which the Bush administration repeatedly endorsed, the American soldiers who perpetrated the abuses at Abu Ghraib are depicted "as 'in' but not 'of' the nation"; this perspective reinforces the operations of neoliberalism and racializes the embodiment of danger through the figure of the young Muslim man as a terrorist (ibid.). In contrast, the second frame—a systematic account—focuses on the links between the actions of individuals and the military order and thereby narrows human rights protections to those that culminate in patterns of abuse by the leadership (978). Michelle Brown exposes the limitations of these two frames and proposes a third—a transnational perspective, which centers on the cultural conditions and structural contexts that enable torture (979). She highlights the international implementation of U.S. penal technologies and the connections between the military war machine and the prison-industrial complex, and in this sense she also highlights their fundamental intercontextuality (974, 982). Building on Brown's analysis, in this chapter I investigate the gendered, racial, and sexual scenarios of power and recognition that constitute the links between the rhetorical politics of staging human rights spectacles and of staging terror.

Spectacular activist and cultural representations of the human rights violations at Abu Ghraib and Guantánamo provide a critical occasion to examine the rhetorical politics of staging empire (which includes the exportation of American penal culture) and the relation between the discourses of human rights internationalism, based on UN documents and treaties, and U.S. government practices of neoliberalism—a term that, in the wake of the U.S. occupation of Iraq, has come to mean a "radicalized capitalist imperialism that is increasingly tied to lawlessness and military action" (Ong 1999, 1). *Inconvenient Evidence*, a 2004 exhibit at the International Center for Photography in New York City, and Rory Kennedy's documentary film *Ghosts of Abu Ghraib* (2007) restage the terror spectacle in order to critique the war and, in the case of the documentary, to expose cultural and national scripts that U.S. officials invoked to rationalize the behavior and abusive actions of American soldiers. Victoria Brittain and Gillian Slovo's documentary play *Guantánamo: "Honor Bound to Defend Freedom"* (2004), in contrast, refuses the spectacular gesture in favor of an epistolary human rights rhetoric, which humanizes the detainees by imagining members of the audience as eavesdroppers and implicating them in the scene of violation that plays out as part of an ongoing geopolitical drama. That is, the play seeks to construe a reciprocal relation between detainees, with their families, and Western audiences. Although this chapter moves from an analysis of imbrications of spectacular rhetorics that solidify power relations by denying to the other the normative identity categories associated with human rights to an analysis of representations that enliven the subject with agency and humanity, it also considers the effectiveness of the normative categories of *human* and *inhuman* as they are deployed in cultural productions that aim to challenge hegemonic representations and the hierarchical scenes of recognition and nonrecognition common to the American nationalist discourse of the War on Terror.

## Inconvenient Evidence

Unlike the actual photographs from Abu Ghraib, icons derived from them are used by artists and activists as a form of social commentary. And again unlike the photographs themselves, strategic appropriations of the Abu Ghraib images at public protests in the United States and abroad have not been widely circulated in the Western media. However, the photograph of two people in Tehran walking past murals depicting the torture of Iraqi detainees at Abu Ghraib (fig. 3) was part of a larger exhibit titled *Inconvenient Evidence: Iraqi Prison Photographs from Abu Ghraib*, which ran at the International Center for Photography in the autumn of 2004.[4] The murals, created by an unidentified Iraqi artist, are based on the widely circulated photographs of an American solder holding an abused prisoner by a leash, and a hooded Iraqi detainee forced to stand on a box, with what appear to be electrodes attached to his body. The Farsi writing on the mural on the right reads: "Iraq today." The title of the exhibit cleverly refers to the "infidelity of photography" (Cadava 1997, 15), in that digital technology betrayed the superiority the U.S. War on Terror sought to inaugurate. In addition to sixteen prints of the torture photographs hung with pushpins (perhaps to highlight their amateur status and to generate an anti-aesthetic of witnessing), the exhibit included four framed images of citizens in the Middle East reacting to the Abu Ghraib photographs. These four images would seem to provide a counterdiscourse to the dominance and voyeurism of both the American media and the soldiers taking the photographs—an example of what the Debord and the Situationist International promoted as détourne-

3. An Iranian couple in Tehran walks past murals depicting the torture of Iraqi prisoners by U.S. soldiers at Abu Ghraib prison, near Baghdad, 1 June 2004. Photograph by Behrouz Mehri. By permission of Behrouz Mehri/AFP/Getty Images.

ment. But in the context of the United States and during its occupation of Iraq, the rhetorical function of these counterimages is far more ambiguous.

At the *Inconvenient Evidence* exhibit, visitors were directed through a claustrophobic gray gallery and past the sixteen infamous Abu Ghraib torture photographs before reaching the four critical images. The exhibit offered little guidance about how to read these four images or the contexts in which they originally appeared. For example, in the context of Tehran's urban landscape, the street murals recall the typology of mural propaganda and martyrdom cultivated during the Iran-Iraq war (Grigor 2002, 37). Because the murals appear along a public highway and are at eye level, they might also suggest a public reclamation of rhetorical space, rather than a message delivered from on high. The inscription "Iraq today" offers a commentary on changing relations between Iran and Iraq. On the one hand, the murals can be read as fostering empathy between Iranians and Iraqis along with a unified gaze directed against the United States. On the other hand, the mural might reinforce differences between Iraq and Iran, depicting Iraq as the weaker of the two nations because it is an occupied state. *Inconvenient Evidence* elides these distinctions, as well as regional ideological struggles, and ignores the connections between the abuses at Abu Ghraib and those within prisons in the United States.

*Inconvenient Evidence* sets the four critical images apart from the mass-produced and widely circulated torture prints. The act of framing the four critical images—in contrast to the torture prints—might be said to privilege them as art rather than as documentary evidence, a problematic binary that accepts the premise that art cannot be evidence and vice versa. The exhibit also might be said to set up a series of coexisting contrasts: between spectacle (torture prints) and social critique (the murals), between unethical and ethical representational practices, and between using the camera as an instrument of dominance and using it as moral witness. The murals draw our attention to how the spectacle is framed and imagines their viewers as participants in a critical interaction with the ultranationalist narratives and cultural logics on which the actions in the photographs are based. However, that the exhibition framed the photograph of the murals as art may enable some viewers to distance themselves from the acts they depict. That the torture photographs are displayed within an art institution, likewise, may contribute to their reception based on a set of stock cultural narratives and aesthetic visions. My concern, therefore, is not to reproduce binaries between art and evidence or to generate definitive interpretations of these spectacular images, but rather to recognize their multiple meanings and rhetorical functions, the identifications they have enabled, and the demands that confronting torture makes on the formal limits of representation. This multiplicity of meanings and identifications has been censored in post-9/11 U.S. public discourse, which has been dominated by the rhetoric of trauma (victimization) and retribution. The fact that the torture images function as both evidence and exploitation suggests a correspondence between the terror spectacle and the human rights spectacle, both of which direct our perception to trauma and the experience of shock. This correspondence is echoed in the scholarship on traumatic realism, which presumes the inevitable reproduction of the spectacle in cultural representations of and responses to human rights violations, and in scholarship on the spectacle, which argues that even satiric mimicry and parodic representations risk being absorbed into the spectacular economy (Erickson 1992, 51).

What follows is an exploration of the inauguration of trauma as a defining parameter of history and resurgent American nationalism in what has come to be called the age of terror. Trauma may be considered an element of the spectacle to the degree that the spectacle elicits a traumatic response or retraumatizes victims, and that its creation constitutes an act of violence, as theorists such as Shoshana Felman and Dori Laub (1992) propose. Cathy Caruth characterizes the belatedness of trauma as the traumatic paradox: "What returns to haunt the victim is not only the reality of the violent event but also the reality of the way that its violence has not yet been fully known" (1996, 6). In other words, the "truth" of trauma lies in its belated address, in its repetition (63). But to frame history and spectacle as essentially traumatic is problematic insofar as the framework pathologizes perception in the public sphere and the compulsive repetition of trauma at cultural, national, and international levels, thereby detracting attention from the scenarios of power that structure history and trauma. The metanarrative of history as trauma has serious implications not only for how we understand terrorism, but also for how we frame our moral responses to its visuality.

Veena Das issues a similar warning to scholars in her questioning of the "notions of ghostly repetitions, spectral presences, and all those tropes that have become sedimented into our ordinary language from trauma theory" (2007, 205). The risk, she argues—and I concur with her—is that such tropes "have little to say on how violence is produced or lived with" (ibid.). To view the spectacle through the lens of trauma is to frame violence as recurrent and belated—a view with some level of prominence not only in cultural and critical theory, as the previous chapter suggests, but also, as the *Inconvenient Evidence* exhibit illustrates, among cultural productions that seek to advance a human rights agenda. I turn to the scholarship on trauma and traumatic realism in order to highlight the limitations of trauma as an explanatory frame for understanding history and spectacle—both the terror spectacle and the human rights spectacle—within the context of the War on Terror.

The U.S. occupation of Iraq has been viewed by some commentators and critics as traumatic repetition or, more specifically, the compulsive repetition of trauma as retribution: the United States, a nation traumatized by 9/11, invades and occupies another terrorized country (in this case, a country terrorized by Saddam Hussein). Paradoxically, trauma, which is most often represented as a break in narrative coherence, becomes history's metanarrative. As I argue in an earlier work, trauma is not straightforwardly referential but is translated through cultural discourses and disciplinary frames (Hesford 2001, 25). In classic psychoanalytic theory, trauma is signified as feminine, as an unrepresentable yet persistent defining negativity (26–27). Similarly, the Americans who photographed the torture and sexual humiliation of Iraqi detainees at Abu Ghraib engaged in the emasculation of the detainees, who emerged as powerless in the face of the camera. Yet framing terrorist acts and political and cultural responses to such acts through the rhetoric of trauma is a concession to certain habits of recognition that, in the long run, may condemn to failure efforts toward more peaceful and just resolutions. For example, for the United States to turn the 9/11 terror spectacle into a national trauma narrative enables it to construe itself as a victim nation and thereby to distance itself from implication in the circumstances out of which the terrorist acts may have arisen.

Dominick LaCapra contemplates the limitations of understanding history as "essentially traumatic" (2001, x). Among the problems with the conflation of history with trauma are the "indiscriminate generalization of the category of survivor" (xi) and the "appropriation of particular traumas by those who did not experience them" (65), both of which may lead to a lack of historical distinctions. Identifications are also reduced to what are considered to be founding traumas, which become the basis of identity for an individual or group (23). LaCapra is likewise critical of false redemption narratives, but he nevertheless seeks strategies (compositional and political) to use in working through the trauma (103). He proposes that empathetic unsettlement" is one way to counteract "the endless repetition of the past or being compulsively implicated in trauma" (153). Unlike a stance of full identification, wherein the self and other are construed as fused, empathetic unsettlement recognizes and respects the alterity of the other (27)—a position that resonates with Lévinas' face-to-face encounter (see chapter 1). LaCapra does not provide a distinct methodology for achieving such an awareness; instead, he warns against turning empathetic unsettlement into a routine methodology or style that "enacts compulsive repetition, including the compulsively repetitive turn to the aporia, paradox, or impasse" (47), a rhetorical pattern prominent in post-9/11 theories about the terrorist attacks and their spectacularity.[5]

Like LaCapra's conception of empathetic unsettlement, traumatic realism represents "an attempt to produce the traumatic event as an object of knowledge . . . and thus transform its readers [or viewers] so that they are forced to acknowledge their relationship to posttraumatic culture" (Rothberg 2000, 103). A hallmark of Holocaust studies, traumatic realism refers to "the activation of traumatic repetition," including at the level of technique (Feldman 2005, 215). Traumatic realism succeeds in capturing the simultaneous resistance of trauma to transparent symbolism and the cultural fascination with, and historical demands for, trauma's documentation (Rothberg 2000, 276). Indeed, the torture-trophy shots might be read as a visualization of the traumatic real. The decorative frame on the murals, however, ruptures the traumatic repetition by drawing attention to the theatricality of torture and its spectacular representation. Brian Wallis, director of the International Center for Photography and curator of the *Inconvenient Evidence* exhibit, characterizes the torture prints as "monstrous propaganda photographs, intended to assert cultural dominance locally and to restore racial and political hierarchies globally" (2004, 4). In the exhibition's text that accompanied the photographs, Wallis indicates that one of the exhibit's goals is to remember Abu Ghraib in order to counter the Bush administration's efforts to suppress this "inconvenient evidence and to disguise its original motives" (ibid.). Yes, the torture images have functioned as propaganda. But to characterize them solely as "monstrous propaganda" is to reinforce their status as aberrations in a way that colludes with the administration's early responses to the photographs as examples of individual irresponsibility, a representation that aimed to exempt the United States of any responsibility in the violent inscription of the torture spectacle onto the body of the other.

Technological reproducibility, as Eduardo Cadava proposes, "does not mean 'the return of the same.' What returns is the movement through which something other is inscribed within the same" (1997, 31). Like Bruce Robbins, I propose that we engage a sense of history based not on a trauma so great and absolute that time cannot be allowed to touch it, but as a memory for-

ever jostling for space and priority among other, competing memories"
(1998a, 9). From this perspective, the mural artist's strategic reproduction
of the spectacle would not be seen as a post-traumatic acting out but instead as the "repetition of alterity" (Cadava 1997, 31). Ultimately, what *Inconvenient Evidence* shows—and this is its pedagogical value as a cultural
production—is the intercontextuality of the terror spectacle and the human
rights spectacle as they take on different meanings and evolve through materially bound rhetorical publics. The street murals in Tehran reproduce the
terror spectacle, but they do so as part of their social critique of the reach of
U.S. power. In this way, the murals bring into greater visibility the imperial
powers of American nationalism and the politics of recognition in the staging of spectacles. More broadly, the *Inconvenient Evidence* exhibit displays
the rhetorical intercontextuality of the Abu Ghraib torture images, whose
meaning depends on the discourses and contexts that enunciate them. For
example, in certain contexts, the terror spectacle is transformed into a human
rights spectacle—that is, the Abu Ghraib images also function as a form of
critical commentary on the spectacle of violence and exhibitionism.

Like the murals and their iconic references, the hooded figure has been
appropriated and parodied by artists, protesters for human rights, and antiwar demonstrators around the world, as well as in fake iPod advertisements
(fig. 4). Figure 4 is one of a series of guerrilla posters that popped up in
major cities, most notably Los Angeles, in 2004. The West Coast versions
were designed by the art-activist group Forkscrew Graphics.

The iconic figure of the hooded detainee standing on a box with wires
attached to his body invokes a classic torture pose known to interrogation experts as "the Vietnam" (Puar 2007 102).[6] The fact that this image
has achieved iconic status can be attributed to a number of cultural and
historical factors. First, the image preserves the anonymity of the body of
the victim and "incriminates the viewer less than some of the more pornographic images." Second, the hooded image "radiates a distressing mys-
tique," which "harks back to the white hoods of the Ku Klux Klan" (104).
Third, the hooded and cloaked body resembles another iconic image, "that
of the oppressed Muslim woman in her burqa, covered head to toe in black
and in need of rescue." Additionally, Jasbir Puar argues: "It is plausible that
this image of 'the Vietnam' resonates as yet another missionary project

iRaq

10,000 Iraqis killed. 773 US soldiers dead.

4. An image from Forkscrew Graphics's iRaq series, yellow version, 2004. By permission of Forkscrew Graphics.

in the making." But she suggests that there is an even more ominous reason why the photograph has such an impact: "the Vietnam" is traceless as a form of torture, leaving no visible marks. Puar writes: "The only evidence of the Vietnam comes in the form of the photograph. Its mass multiplication and mutations may speak to the need to document and inscribe into history and our optic memories that which otherwise leaves no visual proof" (104).

Among all of the Abu Ghraib torture images, it is this one, the least sexually explicit image, that has been the most widely reproduced (Puar 2007, 102). In a mural on a street in Baghdad, an Iraqi artist ironically fused the Statue of Liberty and the photograph of the hooded detainee, highlighting the conjoining of executioner and victim. In Barcelona, on the eve of the first anniversary of the publication of the torture photographs, members of Amnesty International wearing hoods and shackles staged a protest against the mistreatment of Abu Ghraib prisoners by the U.S. military. On 9 February 2005 outside the Supreme Court in Washington, D.C., an activist dressed as the hooded Iraqi detainee protested the appointment of Alberto Gonzales as U.S. Attorney General. On 10 May 2004 in Gaza City, a photograph depicting the abuse of an Iraqi prisoner at Abu Ghraib was attached to a gravestone at the Commonwealth Military Cemetery, where vandals with axes and shovels desecrated thirty-two graves of soldiers killed in the First World War. On 7 December 2007, Amnesty International USA took out a full-page ad in the *New York Times*, which featured the classical female figure of justice wearing a black hood and holding a scale in one hand and a sword in the other; the ad urged readers to insist that the Supreme Court overturn the Military Commissions Act of 2006, which made it lawful to hold suspects indefinitely without charge or trial. Activist repetitions of iconic torture images such as these illustrate the critical appropriation of the terror spectacle and suggest that the circulation of the torture images countered the political paralysis that is often managed by the visual. Finally, such repetitions, like the *Inconvenient Evidence* exhibit, propose the interdependence between shock experiences and accumulated knowledge, suggesting that we can't have critique without spectacle (Benjamin 1986). Or can we?

In *Picture Theory*, W. J. T. Mitchell addresses the risk of reproducing the spectacle as part of a social critique. Most relevant to this discussion is his analysis of Malek Alloula's *The Colonial Harem* (1986), a photographic essay about European fantasies and "Orientalist" lust as represented by French colonial postcards of Algerian women. Alloula's textual commentary refutes the "predatory colonial gaze" of the images (Mitchell 1994, 309). But, as Mitchell notes, in reproducing the pornographic images of colonized Algerian women, *The Colonial Harem* collaborates in the French consumption of the very "staged fantasy of exotic sexuality and unveiling" that it intends to critique. Alloula's motive may have been to "reverse the pornographic process" (310). Not content with suppositions about motive, however, Mitchell turns to the reception of the images: "Can an American observer . . . see these photographs as anything more than quaint, archaic pornography, hauntingly beautiful relics of a lost colonial era?" He claims that the photographs "assert their independence and equality, looking at us as they collaborate in the undoing of the colonial gaze" (312). But by what means are we to understand our implication in the visual apparatus and economy of colonialism and technologies of war? How can we look and yet refuse to collaborate in the spectacle's repetition?

Both Rothberg (2000) and LaCapra (2001) put their faith in the process of self-reflexivity in working through traumatic repetition. But the self-referential rhetoric of the torture-trophy shots suggests the intimate collusion of certain forms of self-referentiality in the creation of the neocolonial spectacle. This collusion requires us to question our fidelity to self-referentiality, and to turn our attention to the rhetorical deployment of reflexive codes in order to discern the degree to which such codes prompt an interrogation of the spectacle or simply mobilize reflexivity as part of the technical instrumentality of dominance. Whereas Rothberg and LaCapra both endorse a judicious use of trauma in illuminating the complexity of events and their representation, my interest lies in understanding the gendered, racial, and sexual imaginaries that structure the history-as-trauma metanarrative itself, particularly as this narrative inflects human rights discourses in the age of the War on Terror, and their interface with imperial configurations of the other as an embodied spectacle. To represent human rights violations in terms of traumatic repetition and history-as-trauma is to problematically implicate audiences in an imagined pathological public sphere, with limited recognition of the imperatives that such an emphasis represses. Fidelity to the history-as-trauma concept likewise often circumvents an analysis of the conditions that enable its repetition. Such representational practices can operate, as they have in the discourse on the War on Terror, as a form of narcissistic nationalism. Edward Said warned two decades ago that "the terrorism craze is dangerous because it consolidates the immense, unrestrained pseudopatriotic narcissism we are nourishing" (1988, 158).

## Ghostly Publics

*Ghosts of Abu Ghraib*, a documentary by Rory Kennedy about the torture of Iraqi detainees by American soldiers at the Abu Ghraib prison and the links between the actions of individuals and those higher up the chain of command, confirms the social significance of the terror spectacle by revealing the causal narratives and imperial fantasies attached to it.[7] Although there are many documentaries about Iraq and the U.S. War on Terror, I turn specifically to *Ghosts* because it highlights the national compulsions, structural conditions, and instrumentality attached to the imperial configuration of the other as embodied spectacle. I use the term *embodied spectacle* to refer to the violent inscription of imperial fantasy-themes onto the body of the other and the term *fantasy* not to signify a falsehood but to highlight a shared "rhetorical vision" (Foss 1996, 125), in this case a "mythological nationalism" (Giroux 2007, 18).[8] The terror spectacle, in this case, attracts fantasy-themes that sustain American exceptionalism—a nationalism predicated on a moralistic us-them divide and a politics of nonrecognition.

The military police and intelligence officers interviewed shared a rhetorical vision based on the increasingly narrow definition of torture put into effect by the Bush administration after 9/11 (as revealed in memos from the Office of Legal Counsel and the Justice Department) and protected by the Military Commissions Act.[9] Several of the military personnel interviewed diffused their authority—casting themselves as actors without agency—by both invoking these narrow definitions of torture and alluding to orders from higher authorities to soften up the detainees. The opening sequence of Kennedy's documentary reinforces the character of the obedient soldier with footage of the 1961 experiment by Stanley Milgram, a psychologist at Yale University, who tested the willingness of volunteers to inflict pain on another person when asked to do so as part of an obedience study. Milgram's study revealed that the majority of participants, although not all of them, agreed to inflict the highest level of electric shock on an audible but invisible subject in the next room (in fact, an actor who made sounds of pain after each unreal shock) when prodded by the experimenter. Milgram justified the increase in levels and infliction of pain by telling the volunteer subjects that "the experiment require[d] that [they] continue."

Although the film draws a clear link between the individual actions of guards and military leaders by emphasizing the Bush administration's casting of detainees as "unlawful combatants," many of the military personnel involved in the Abu Ghraib scandal refer to the setting and its history as contributing to the conditions that enabled the abuses to occur. These justifications demonstrate the intercontextuality of torture: the Abu Ghraib prison is construed by the military personnel as a property with a haunting past, and as a structure of feeling that calls forth certain ghostly actions.

The word *ghosts* in the documentary's title refers not only to a "ghost de-tainee," Manadel al-Jamadi, tortured to death by U.S. agents at the prison, but also to those killed at the site during Saddam Hussein's reign. As Sam Provance, a military intelligence officer featured in the film, puts it: "You knew the history, . . . You felt that it was a haunted place. . . . At night time there's certain hallways you wouldn't want to go down by yourself 'cause you're afraid there might be a ghost . . . and you knew it was really pissed off. . . . *Apocalypse Now* meets *The Shining*, except that this is real and you are in the middle of it." As the camera pans down a long, dark hallway spotted with celebratory murals of Saddam Hussein, we hear Roman Krol, another intelligence officer, speak: "I heard that there were almost 30,000 people executed . . . under Saddam's regime. . . . The place was horrible. There were wild dogs running around digging up human bodies." The camera then hovers over a large hole in the floor with a noose hanging above it. Javal Davis, a guard, says: "There was a place inside the prison like the death chamber. . . . They'd hang eighty, a hundred people a day. . . . In our barracks there was [sic] two ovens, incinerators for bodies. . . . Where are we living at? How many lost souls are walking around here?"

The "ghosts" of Abu Ghraib—the victims who died at the prison site in Saddam Hussein's regime and the U.S. occupation, the victims of 9/11, and the haunting photographs of Abu Ghraib—are presented as having trauma-tized the U.S. national psyche. When the soldiers are in the place of terror, they are both terrified and act "terribly"—a capitulation to the pathology of war. In increments, "the spectre of terrorism forc[ed] the West to ter-rorize itself" (Baudrillard 2002, 81): protorture policies, disregard for the 1984 Convention against Torture and Other Cruel, Inhuman or Degrading Treatment or Punishment, the Geneva Conventions, withdrawal of civil liberties, and exemptions from protections of the U.S. Constitution. *Ghosts* presents the link between the traumatized self and the terrorized state and the implicit dismissal of human rights principles and conventions. "This place turned me into a monster," Javal Davis says. He continues: "You can go from being a docile jolly guy and you go to Abu Ghraib, and you become a robot." Sabrina Harman speaks directly about the adaptive function of repetition. "Something in your brain clicks," she says, "everything you see is normal. You'll go crazy if you don't adapt to what you're seeing." In *Ghosts*, individual stories accumulate, creating a narrative that moves beyond individual pathologies—pathology of the rogue soldier—to groupthink. Several of the U.S. military police and guards interviewed in *Ghosts* identify the haunting violations and the ghosts of Saddam Hussein's regime or the prison itself as the psychological trigger for their torture of the detainees.

Retributive explanations also characterize the American soldiers' representation of their actions—a discursive frame that emerged just hours after the attacks on 9/11, when President Bush addressed Americans from Barksdale Air Force Base in Louisiana and declared: "Make no mistake: The United States will hunt down and punish those responsible for these cowardly acts." Alluding to 9/11, Javal Davis, who is featured in the documentary, says: "It made me feel like we have to do something . . . someone has to pay. We can't let two buildings get blown up and not do anything about it." Until this point, the documentary generates evidence, turning memory into archive. But this rhetorical aim is undermined by scenes which highlight the coexistence of archive (evidence) and repertoire (practice) (Taylor 2003, 19). Here ghostly evidence animates the acts of torture.

In one scene in the documentary, an unidentified American soldier enacts a mock attack on a dummy made of a stuffed jacket and helmet. Simulating an interrogation scene, the soldier kicks and beats the dummy and yells: "Oh, you don't want to say anything!" In the background, two other American soldiers laugh. With no clear set of guidelines for engagement and no other clear way to legitimize their guarding of thousands of civilians, including young children, the violent role-playing might be read as a stress reaction, a displacement of the soldiers' sense of powerlessness and confusion onto the imagined other—the performance of yet another scenario involving a hierarchy of self and other or object. Similar to the torture rituals captured photographically, here the soldiers "reacquire, if only in an allegorical idiom, their former sense of mastery and command in a situation that is rapidly lurching beyond their grasp" (Feldman 2004a, 5). Adrenaline overrides mindfulness. Prior to the role-playing scene, an unidentified American soldier videotaped at close range chants a rap. The rap is clearly a complaint: "Which way to go, I honestly don't know. . . . My mind is a basement. Do I actually have a choice on my placement? Do I really have a voice in my displacement?" Interspersed with the footage of the rapper are full-screen reproductions of the torture photographs and several images that show U.S. soldiers in the roles of military guard and humiliated detainee. Sabrina Harman handcuffs herself to a cell; a hooded soldier waves thumbs-up; and Private First Class Lynndie England and Charles A. Graner simulate fellatio. At the end of the rap, another soldier speaks directly to the camera: "Abu Ghetto." "Ghetto Abu," another replies. The juxtaposition of the rap song with the role-playing scene evokes dominant critiques of rap as a genre that celebrates male violence. However, the performance of the rap in a film that goes to great lengths to humanize the soldiers suggests that the rap, like the role-playing, may mitigate the soldiers' lack of control and hopelessness. The film imports a set of values associated with the rap genre to highlight the duress of soldiers in a battle zone and to draw a parallel between their situation and those of socially and economically disenfranchised people in the United States. Although *Ghosts* does not highlight the socioeconomic characteristics of the soldiers involved in the abuses at Abu Ghraib, these military personnel do share similar work experiences and lower-class status (Michelle Brown 2005, 982). Embedded within the violent role-playing is a form of self-critique. The dummy in the helmet is meant to signify the other—the disembodied and objectified enemy. But because the helmet is an American one, the violent display seems like a self-inflicted trauma—a potentially contentious reading, but one that nevertheless opens up new ways to think about the terror spectacle as a tautological and deadly performance. Below I explore how the terror spectacle enacts intimate collusions between the traumatized self and the terrorized state, and between war and vision, which are predicated on the consumption of corporeal difference.

## Staging American Empire and the Erotics of Global Power

The Abu Ghraib images of sexual abuse exemplify how the terror spectacle functions as a form of national recognition through negative differentiation. The trophy shots in particular imply audience identification with the perpetrators' straight visual vernacular and thereby incorporate the viewers as participants in a neocolonial and heterosexist narrative about the sexual deviance of Middle Eastern others (Mirzoeff 2006, 26). But how, we might ask, does the participation of female military guards and clerks (Lynndie

England was a military clerk) as taunts and torturers reinforce or unsettle such identifications? How have women been integrated into the American nationalist and imperial masculinist spectacle that is the U.S. War on Terror? How have critics interpreted the gendered import of the prison abuses and their representation, and what are the strengths and limits of such interpretations for understanding the terror spectacle and its rhetorical intercontextuality?

One response has been a widespread indictment of feminism as a cultural force capable of unleashing torture and pornography. Rochelle Gurstein reads England's acts of violation against male detainees as evidence of the "coercive and brutalizing nature of the pornographic imagination" (2005, 4).[10] Gurstein views England as "the fruit of equal-opportunity feminism" (ibid.), and likens the image of England holding a leash around the neck of an Iraqi detainee to high-style fashion shots, which she implies is a form of mainstream pornography. Gurstein is not alone in interpreting women's involvement in sexual masquerades and violations against male detainees as a referendum on feminism. Linda Chavez, president of the Center for Equal Opportunity, argued that the photographs were evidence of the "sexual tension" fueled by "the new sex-integrated military" (2005). George Neumayr, a columnist for the *American Spectator*, went so far as to say that England's actions are "a cultural outgrowth of a feminist culture which encourages female barbarians" (2004). Even the best-selling author and feminist Barbara Ehrenreich (2004) got caught in the backlash when she claimed that the Abu Ghraib photographs led her to abandon assumptions about women's moral superiority, a stance that she uncritically attributed to feminism. Like several prominent American feminists, Mary Ann Tétreault (2006) argued it is the photographic act that renders the images pornographic. Hence, the collusion between torture and pornography lies in the visualization of objectification. Kelly Oliver, whose work is discussed in chapter 1, makes a similar point when she notes that "pornographic seeing itself is symptomatic of a particular rhetoric of vision—a rhetoric produced in conjunction with an economy of property" (2001, 156). In contrast to Fredric Jameson's claim that "the visual is *essentially* pornographic" (1992, 1), however, Oliver suggests that "it is not the visual itself that is pornographic but indeed our thinking about the visual, our conceptions of what it is to see" (2001, 157).

However, it is Nicholas Mirzoeff, a scholar of visual culture, who most clearly engages the limitations of interpretations that foreground the Abu Ghraib photographs as pornographic. The torture photographs interface with pornography in "making sexuality into visuality" (2006, 26), he acknowledges. But the photographs and the actions they depict are not about "consensual pleasure, fantasy, or desire," they are about "enforced sodomy" (28). He continues: "Enforced sodomy is a ritual of American masculinity in all its disciplinary institutions from the prison, to the armed forces, to the church and the school" (34). Moreover, Mirzoeff interprets the representation of enforced sodomy as "a spectral return," a haunting repetition of the rhetoric of imperialism in the era of slavery, in which the other "Africans and Jews alike were represented as sodomitical" (30–31). He reveals how the colonial imaginary and heternormativity are raced, gendered, and sexualized (26). The participation of female soldiers as torturers and as sexual taunts—or "thong teases," as the *New York Times* columnist Maureen Dowd described them (2007)—thus secures the imperial fantasy of the heterosexual, white nation. Melaine Richter-Montpetit similarly argues that the images enact a "heterosexed, racialized and gendered script . . . grounded in the war on terror and its hegemonic 'save civilization itself' national fantasy"—a fantasy predicated on American exceptionalism (2007, 41). Puar elaborates on how the discourse of Muslim hetero- and homosexualities work in tandem with the discourse of American sexual exceptionalism in the War on Terror (2007, xxiv). "The Orient, once conceived in Foucault's *ars erotica* and Said's deconstructive work as the place of original release, unfettered sin," Puar points out, "now symbolizes the space of repression and perversion, and the site of freedom has been relocated to Western identity" (94). The construction of brown men as effeminate seems to Zillah Eisenstein to be exemplary of acts of sexualized racism and homophobia within military culture (2004b, 4). Within that culture, she argues, women function as gender decoys, a distraction that keeps masculinized gender in its place (1). Eisenstein also notes the public invisibility of images of sexual violations against women in the War on Terror, an absence that likewise supports the narrative decoy: "Females are present to cover over the misogyny of building empire" (3). Unlike several critics, however, Puar questions the political astuteness of designating acts of torture as gay sex acts (87).

If instead of characterizing the photographs as pornographic, we turn to the visual erotics of global power, our attention shifts to how the "imperial body . . . understands itself as acting within pornographic scenarios of power" (Mirzoeff 2006, 26). In highlighting "scenarios of power," Mirzoeff usefully shifts our attention from reading the images as pornographic to the context in which the images were produced, circulated, and received. They were produced in scenarios of power wherein the mistreatment of detainees was considered routine, as suggested by the circulation of abuse images via e-mail and their use as a screen saver in the prison's Internet cafe for military personnel (24).

Instead of interpreting the excesses of the War on Terror and its visualization as pornographic, I suggest that the visualization of excess and dominance is pornographic to the degree that it deflects attention away from human rights abuses and their deadly consequences, and toward the fulfillment of an erotic imperial fantasy. Finally, I would argue that the adoption of the pornographic gaze by commentators and academics has itself functioned as an interpretive decoy, which has further reduced tortured detainees to objects and has kept public attention focused on the visualization of sexuality instead of on the abusive acts of nonconsensual sex. While pornography certainly permeates military culture, and pornographic fantasies clearly play out through acts of torture, torture and pornography are not equivalent: participating in a pornographic masquerade need not yield a performance of torture.

Like the postcards of African American lynching victims that were widely and publicly circulated in the United States from the end of the Civil War to the civil rights era, the trophy shots, though not intended for mass viewing, created an occasion for the staging of white heterosexual dominance through the imposed homosexuality of the Arab other. Toni Perucci likewise points out that the public lynchings of African Americans similarly functioned not only as theatrical spectacles but also as expressions of violence in service to a racialized political economy (2005, 5). Whether camouflaged as a shock (traumatic experience) or as pornography "the performances of torture at Abu Ghraib, in their banal and celebratory enactment of violence, are simply the spectacular realization of the ubiquitous violence that neoliberalism produces globally" (14). Baudrillard suggests that despite the goal of terrorism to destabilize the global order, its "unintended effect [is] to consolidate that order" (2002 53); the Bush administration's withdrawn commitment to international law supports that view. However, what the spectacle of terrorism has achieved, Baudrillard provocatively claims, is the "collapse of image" upon which the global order relies: "The global system ... can function only if it can exchange itself for its own image, reflect itself like the towers in their twinness, find its equivalent in an ideal reference" (2002, 82–83). Instead of constructing individuals as either victims or perpetrators in an imagined pathological or ghostly global public that functions by exchanging one wound for another, *Guantánamo: "Honor Bound to Defend Freedom"* attempts to imagine individuals as global citizens, as participants in a transnational public guided by international laws and universal human rights principles—a system that likewise functions only if it finds its equivalent in another, if mutual recognition is achieved.

## Post-9/11 Documentary Theater and Testimony

Terrorism is now called "theatre" while we try to convince ourselves that
what happens on stage can have anything to do with the real terrorisms of
ruptured bodies and wounded minds.—Anthony Kubiak, *Stages of Terror*

*Guantánamo: "Honor Bound to Defend Freedom"* is a documentary play written by Victoria Brittain and Gillian Slovo, and directed by Nicolas Kent and Sacha Wares, that foregrounds the violation of prisoners' human rights at the U.S. Guantánamo Bay naval base in Cuba, under the Bush administration's post-9/11 policies.[11] *Guantánamo* was first staged in June 2004 at the Tricycle Theatre in London; it was restaged at the Culture Project in New York City in October 2004, just before the U.S. presidential election.[12] The play is based on written correspondence and testimony collected from released detainees and their family members, lawyers, and human rights workers, as well as information from news conferences, lectures, and publications. It draws on the aural tradition of courtroom drama in its presentation of conflicting viewpoints and narratives. Additionally *Guantánamo* turns evidence (archive) into embodied memory (repertoire); the actors create "what is outside the [written] archive—glances, body language" (Martin 2006, 11). Most of the play is presented as a direct address to the audience. At the Culture Project performance, which I attended, the staging was sparse, with detainees in orange jumpsuits in mesh prison cages or on narrow cots, some reading from the Qur'an. The set shifted minimally throughout the play, with detainees and their families at the front of the stage reading from personal letters to each other, and government officials and lawyers appearing behind a lectern or small desk to indicate shifts in point of view.

*Guantánamo's* straightforward exposition and legal appeals are a departure from the reproduction of the terror spectacle in the U.S. and international news media. In the play, characters' stories are presented to the audience in long, isolated stretches of verbatim readings from testimonies and letters. Although there is no direct action and character development is sparse, the individual documents accumulate and begin to create a polyphonic subjectivity, as the authors seek to cultivate within the audience a critical subjectivity and a sense of collective rhetorical witnessing. In this way, the play corresponds to Emily Mann's notion of the "theatre of testimony," moving away from the creation of a single protagonist and toward the creation of a communal voice that counters "official" truths (1997, 34).[13] Yet this imagined rhetorical community is no less ideologically and visually mediated. The play's sought-after collectivity is based on an imagined democratic public and the projection onto both the detainees and the audience of universal subjectivity and humanist principles of international human rights law, from which the Bush administration distanced itself in the War on Terror.

*Guantánamo* garnered excellent reviews and played to sell-out crowds in London; its popularity has been described, in part, as a "measure of the British public's strong opposition to the way London had supported Washington's war on terror," drawing on a long tradition of political theater in London (Riding 2004). Staging *Guantánamo* in the United States, however, posed several challenges. In a political climate framed by resurgent nationalism and moral dualities ("you are either with us or against us"), and in which preemptive war is conflated with liberation and freedom, the *Inconvenient Evidence* exhibit, *Ghosts of Abu Ghraib*, and *Guantánamo* all risk being labeled unpatriotic. If *Inconvenient Evidence* reproduces U.S. dominance through traumatic repetition—an overdose of the antidote—

*Guantánamo* seeks to counter the imperial configuration of the other as embodied spectacle and pathology of recognition, to humanize detainees by providing a documentary stage for their life narratives.

*Guantánamo* removes the spectacular hood and attempts to contrast the construction of detainees as pathological. Although the play is structured by a convergence of human rights and humanitarian appeals, it is not premised on the narrative of a crisis, a victim, and a savior—the superior nation—that rescues the other. Rather, the Bush administration and the Coalition forces—representing the nation—are construed as the savages, and international human rights law as the potential savior. *Guantánamo's* turn to familial narratives and the genre of letter writing in an effort to make the terror spectacle problematic is not to imply that life narratives are pure, authentic, or unmediated. They are no less mediated by or vulnerable to the commonplaces that enable the human rights spectacle. For instance, life narratives struggle with and risk reductive victimization identifications. *Guantánamo* presents the detainees—that is, those presumed to be innocent— as ordinary men with middle-class values and aspirations and, in one case, as a patriotic British citizen, an identification that would presumably appeal to the play's targeted audiences in Britain and the United States and enable the detainees' uncomplicated incorporation as rights-bearing subjects in a Western liberal and legal paradigm. As a case worker puts it in act 1, "I met the family [of Bisher al Rawi] and I got to know them as friends and it struck me that no way are they fanatical about anything. [What I learned about] Bisher was that, yes, he was reasonably devout but he's the sort of guy that can sleep for England—he used to sleep through morning prayers" (Brittain and Slovo 2004, 19).

*Guantánamo* focuses on the detention of four men: Jamal al-Harith, Moazzam Begg, and the brothers Wahab and Bisher al-Rawi—all British citizens who were picked up in Pakistan, Afghanistan, and Gambia as "enemy combatants" and detained as terrorist suspects. At one point in the play, we also meet—through his letters and his father's testimony—Ruhel Ahmed, one of three U.K. detainees known as the "Tipton Three."[14] Wahab al-Rawi was released after nearly a month of detention and interrogation, while the others ended up at Guantánamo Bay. In March 2004, after approximately two and a half years in detention without legal representation—

and without knowing why they were being held—two of the detainees, Jamal al-Harith and Ruhel Ahmed, were released and returned home. Moazzam Begg and Bisher al-Rawi, along with two others we learn about at the end of the play, remained at Guantánamo Bay.[15] Moazzam Begg was finally released in January 2005, Bisher al-Rawi in August 2007.

Guantánamo is framed by human rights arguments and humanitarian appeals, and it is oriented toward a juridical resolution informed by human rights principles and international humanitarian law. The play opens with a lecture given by the United Kingdom's Lord Justice Steyn on 23 November 2003, in which he decries the United States for overextending its reach and adopting "measures infringing human rights in ways that are wholly disproportionate to the crisis" (Brittain and Slovo 2004, 5). In the opening scene, the authors try to get the audience to identify with the detainees, through rational and ethical appeals to the juridical process, legal and moral principles, and the burden of testimonial evidence. Guantánamo frames the detainees' oral accounts and written correspondence as evidence of the denial of due process, positioning the audience as belated witnesses or jurors. These accounts, along with those of lawyers and human rights workers, are an indictment of the Bush administration's handling of the War on Terror and the ethical implications of designating the detainees as "enemy combatants," instead of as prisoners of war protected by international laws governing their treatment.[16] This is not to say that the testimonies do not also have an emotional appeal. The authors attempt to mobilize the viewers' empathy and to activate the affective economy of human rights through the mechanism of the testimonial letter (see Berlant 2001, 42), namely the letters between detainees and their family members. In contrast to the display of torture photographs in the Inconvenient Evidence exhibit and the detailed testimonies of several Iraqi prisoners about their abuse featured in Ghosts of Abu Ghraib, the written correspondence in Guantánamo humanizes the detainees by establishing their individual subjectivities and ordinary lives prior to their detention. Moreover, in contrast to the humanization of U.S. soldiers in Ghosts, which is achieved through references to the haunted prison and the specter of Saddam Hussein, Guantánamo abstracts individual perpetrators. At the same time, the silence of potentially less innocent detainees (who pace in their cells onstage) echoes official responses to international terrorism ("we do not negotiate with terrorists") and, as Ryan Claycomb suggests, reflects what he claims is the play's "dystopian approach to theatrical space" and the rhetorical choice of "diatribe over dialogue" (2007, 2).

Yes, documentary theater runs the risk of didactics and diatribe, but it can also critically enact such risks. In *Guantánamo*, for instance, the testimonial letters implicate audiences by expanding the imagined rhetorical space of reception—the circle of recognition—and situating playgoers as eavesdroppers on private, familial conversations, while simultaneously situating the audience as interlopers. From his cell, Moazzam Begg reads aloud a letter addressed to his father:

> I received your message and am glad to hear all is well with you and the family. It is nearing a complete year since I have been in custody and I believe ... that there has been a gross violation of my human rights, particularly to that right of freedom and innocence until proven guilty. After all this time I still don't know what crime I am supposed to have committed for which not only I, but my wife and children, should continually suffer as a result. I am in a state of desperation and am beginning to lose the fight against depression and hopelessness. Whilst I do not at all complain about my personal treatments, conditions are such that I have not seen the sun, sky, moon ... for nearly a year! (Brittain and Slovo 2004, 55–56)

Corresponding to the assertion made in trauma studies that trauma "must be testified to, in a struggle shared between a speaker and listener" (Felman and Laub 1992, 16), audience members are cast as participants in the identification of the detainees as victims of human rights abuses and the transformation of their status as human rights subjects. In *Guantánamo*, this relationship is further complicated by the fact that many of the supposedly private letters were never received by the addressees or were censored. Making these more or less private documents public personalizes nonparticularized and anonymous audiences as belated witnesses, implicating them in the action as imagined global citizen-subjects of a human rights internationalism based on UN treaties and discourses. In this way, the play creates an imaginative zone in which the appeal to human rights can be made without reproducing either the terror spectacle or the human rights spectacle of victimization. We in the audience are witnesses to the life histories and the inner lives of the prisoners and their families, rather than witnesses to the spectacular display of dominance or suffering. The men emerge as husbands, fathers, and sons, and imperialist constructions of race, gender, and sexuality are countered and framed by familial appeals.

Within psychoanalysis and trauma theory, oral testimony is given the value of accumulated knowledge when it positions the listener as enabling the victim to work through trauma (Felman and Laub 1992, 58). However, *Guantánamo* is not so much about individual detainees working through trauma as it is about making British and American national audiences realize how the detainees and their families tried to work through the bureaucratic and ideological maze of detainment and international redistribution within the context of the War on Terror, and empathize with the detainees as human rights subjects. The play uses epistolary rhetoric to prompt (or simulate) mutual recognition. The testimonial letters serve as counterpoints to the dehumanization of detainees at Guantánamo by guards and by political figures such as U.S. Secretary of Defense Donald Rumsfeld, who is featured in the play. Rumsfeld claims:

> Anybody who has looked at the training manuals for the al-Qaeda . . . and how they were trained to kill civilians—and anybody who saw what happened to the Afghani soldiers who were guarding the al-Qaeda in Pakistan when a number were killed by al-Qaeda using their bare hands—has to recognize that these are among the most dangerous, best-trained vicious killers on the face of the earth . . . and that means that the people taking care of the detainees and managing their transfer have to be just exceedingly careful for two reasons. One, for their own protection, but also so these people don't get loose back out on the street and kill more people. (Brittain and Slovo 2004, 34)

The convergence of humanitarian and national security rhetoric seen here was prevalent in the Bush administration's discourse on Guantánamo, in its justifications for the invasions of Afghanistan and later Iraq, and, more generally, in its homeland security rhetoric.[17] The administration's self-serving use of the concepts of dignity and providence in place of human rights norms, its adoption of unilateralism over multilateralism, and its embrace of American exceptionalism, as I suggested earlier (see the introduction) represented a shift in priorities from those of previous administrations (Mertus 2003).

In contrast, *Guantánamo* seeks to humanize the detainees by enabling audience identification with them through the invocation of familial correspondence, human rights norms, and the figure of Tom Clark, who is a British citizen and reporter, not a detainee. Act 2 begins with a monologue, taken from the playwrights' interview with Clark, about the irony of his sister's death in the terrorist attacks on New York on 9/11. He says: "Obviously her loss was the most sad thing, but of all the things peripheral to it, of all the injustices and wrongs [at Guantánamo Bay], the fact that she actually did care about the things that led some people to think that was a smart thing to do, some sort of clever stunt . . . that really upset me" (Brittain and Slovo 2004, 28–29). Clark contemplates Guantánamo Bay, indicating that his sister "would have been incensed." "But then," he notes, commenting on the symbiotic relationship between terrorism and the media spectacle, she "was incinerated publicly, live on television, for an hour and forty minutes." He continues:

Let's say for the sake of argument that among those detained at Guantánamo Bay are some of the people who led to her death—who murdered her essentially—that's a little difficult for me to, you know, it's difficult for me to say it was a bad thing that they were there. . . . Part of me wants to say it's completely fine. Another part of me [wants to understand why] have they been detained so long. . . . I'm furious at the length of detention of these people, furious because those who are innocent have lost three years of their life, much as I lost, as I've been living in a sort of private hell since my sister was murdered, and although at least I've been able to recover and get over it and deal with, and still sort of have my life, they've had theirs taken away. . . . [T]hey deserve all of our sympathies and all of our efforts to sort of make sure they do actually get the justice that they deserve. (Brittain and Slovo 2004, 45–46)

Clark references the spectacle of terror not as a ground for revenge but as the basis for truth telling, justice, and human rights. He is presented as someone working through trauma at the interpersonal, intercultural, and international level. The rhetorical aim of his testimony is to reach out to audiences, particularly American and British audiences, to do the same. Although his struggle between grief at his sister's death and outrage over the events at Guantánamo does not necessarily humanize the detainees—the struggle primarily humanizes him—his testimony does prompt Western audiences to consider themselves as actors (not simply victims) in this geopolitical drama. One of the standards often used to judge political theater is whether a performance enables "empathetic unsettlement," to return to LaCapra's term, among its audience—that is, whether the audience is shaken out of complacency. Empathetic unsettlement contrasts with projective identification (or fusion with the other) insofar as it recognizes and respects the other and does not compel or authorize one "to speak in the other's voice or take the other's place, for example, as a surrogate victim or perpetrator" (LaCapra 2001, 27). The play attempts to create a space of critical witnessing, or empathetic unsettlement, through the visual idiom of the stage set, alternating front and back lighting, and the juxtaposition of varied rhetorical acts (criticism of the war and testimonials) and contexts (lecture hall, courtroom, prison cells, press conferences).[18]

If audience identification with the white male figure of Tom Clark is a key rhetorical strategy for humanizing the detainees, *Guantánamo* optimistically presumes that the testimonies of Arab detainees will be perceived as credible by Western audiences, a questionable assumption given the various national strategies of denial in the United States—including the denial of detainees' status as international prisoners of war—as well as a national climate of fear and culture of revenge and incarceration. While critics, and to a certain extent the play itself, imagine audiences as a "consensual community of citizen-spectators," such a notion ignores how actual audiences negotiate and contest imagined geopolitical identifications and grapple with the complexities of spectatorship (Reinelt 1998, 286). American audiences, for instance, may feel that the play unequivocally positions them within the space of imprisonment as guilty parties—a position that does not necessarily enable dialogue but may foster reflective stasis (Claycomb, 2007, 1). Despite the play's goal of situating both detainees and audiences as global citizen-subjects through its staged epistolary rhetoric and humanitarian and human rights appeals, the stage set itself and its positioning of the prison cells on the periphery suggest an all-encompassing nationalist rhetorical space and a more confined transnational human rights imaginary. In its focus on four detainees who are portrayed as innocent, and by presenting other less clearly innocent detainees without giving them voice, *Guantánamo* forecloses dialogue among the range of positions presented. As Claycomb puts it, "the play raises the spectre of terrorist violence; yet terrorism generally and terrorists specifically remain unperformable in the formal context of the play, even in a work that critiques the space in which terrorists may be detained" (2007, 2). But we should also entertain the possibility that *Guantánamo*'s refusal to give theatrical space to the terror spectacle represents its struggle with the formal limits of representation rather than its collusion with official responses to terrorism.

Guantánamo Bay represents an ambiguous geopolitical space that "conflates bay and base as though no distinction exists between Cuban geography and United States military rule" (A. Kaplan 2004, 12). It is as if Guantánamo is on "an uncanny shadow of the homeland itself" (13). Throughout the performance, I imagined restaging this ambiguity by having actors emerge from and move among the audience, further blurring our positions and roles. Hence, the most powerful moment came at the play's end, when the audience realized that there would not be a curtain call: the actors would remain in their roles, onstage in their cages and on their cots. The audience hesitated, not sure of when or whether to clap, and then quietly exited the theater. The ending therefore undercut any sense of traditional catharsis that one might expect from drama. Had *Guantánamo* created this level of discomfort and implication, this unsettling and contradictory space, this spectacle of inaction, at intervals throughout the play, it may have more persuasively extended the circle of recognition and made audiences feel morally culpable for creating a more critical conversation about human rights violations in the War on Terror and resurgent American nationalisms and fundamentalisms it imagines.

Documentary theater and cinema, like documentary exhibitions, can provide cultural spaces for audiences to contemplate the ethical and moral questions raised by the repetition of trauma and the violation of human rights. In the context of an ongoing geopolitical drama and war without resolution, *Guantánamo* raises the possibility of the failure of epistolary rhetoric to travel beyond its target audience—as in the failure of detainees' letters to reach their addressees—and to mobilize progressive political action. Ultimately, *Ghosts* highlights the traumatic embodiment of history and truth. The question remains, however, as to whether these works ask audiences to do more than project "[them]selves into the scene of trauma" (Baer 2002, 182). *Inconvenient Evidence* and *Ghosts of Abu Ghraib* restage the terror spectacle to both critique the war and, in the case of *Ghosts*, to contextualize the abusive actions of American soldiers. *Guantánamo*, however, steps away from the recurrent spectacle of 9/11 and Abu Ghraib, attempting to engage the audience with a different kind of epistolary idiom and use of theatrical and narrative space. *Guantánamo*, *Ghosts*, and *Inconvenient Evidence* may not achieve the level of empathetic unsettlement that the current times demand—no single cultural work could—but they do perform an important function in urging audiences to question the culpability of nations in cultivating acts of torture and the degrading treatment of detainees under its jurisdiction. Each of these cultural productions in its own way demands public attention to the rhetorical visions that enable the terror spectacle and defiant practices of legal recognition and prompt audiences to contemplate the dire consequences of complicity.

# CHAPTER THREE

## Witnessing Rape Warfare: Suspending the Spectacle

In its inscription of will on the world, violence is a signifying
act, giving expression and authority to identity and will.
—Anne Norton, *Reflections on Political Identity*

The American feminist scholar, lawyer, and activist Catharine
MacKinnon (1993) argues that Serbian soldiers in a Serbian-
run concentration camp for Muslims and Croatians in Bosnia-
Herzegovina turned rape into pornography as a tool of genocide. MacKinnon's incorporation of pornography into the rape-as-genocide
schema reinforces her position that pornography is not an expression of free
speech but a material violation of women's rights. She constructs a fairly
simplistic causal relationship between the consumption of pornography
and the eroticization of torture. A "pornography saturated Yugoslavia,"
she claims, fueled the sexual atrocities in that genocide. Pornography was
a "motivator and instruction manual" (28). She describes the Serbian-run
detention centers as "rape theatres," where rape and torture were staged for
private viewing (29). She argues: "This is ethnic rape as an official policy of
war.... It is rape under orders.... It is rape as an instrument of forced exile.
... It is rape to be seen and heard by others, rape as spectacle.... It is rape as
genocide" (reprinted in 2006b, 145). MacKinnon's conception of rape warfare echoes arguments made by feminist activists who contend that rape is
used as a tool of patriarchal hegemony and as a mode of state and institutional repression, and that it is therefore a human rights violation (Bunch
1990, Thomas and Beasley 1993). However, MacKinnon downplays the role
of the state and state actors by positing that rape in the context of war is an
epiphenomenon of pornographic violence; in so doing, she imposes a causal
relationship between pornographic looking and nonconsensual enactments
of sexual violation.[1]

Another of the problems with MacKinnon's assertion that pornography was a driving force behind the wartime rapes by Serbs is that pornography was not widespread in socialist Yugoslavia but was confined mostly to urban areas and tourist sites (Žarkov 2007, 149). Moreover, the final report of the UN commission of experts, appointed in October 1992 by Secretary General Boutros Boutros-Ghali, included only one reference to a filmed rape (United Nations 1994, 58). Žarkov points out that MacKinnon based her argument about rape as spectacle on this one reference, the source of which was a claim that she herself had made in *Ms.* (2007, 150). Like most Westerners who covered the conflict in the former Yugoslavia—and rape warfare in particular—MacKinnon focused on Serbian men as rapists, de-emphasizing the rape of Serbian women and reserving the role of powerless and ashamed rape victim for Muslim women (148). "The absence of Serb women as visible victims of rape in international media and scholarly work may be due to one objective factor . . . few Serbs gave testimony" and neither officials of the former Yugoslavian government nor the Bosnian Serb leaders cooperated readily with the tribunal (ICTY)[2] (Žarkov 2007, 151). Nevertheless the UN commission documented "patterns of conduct" indicating that, "regardless of the ethnicity of the perpetrators or the victim, . . . some level of organization and group activity is required to carry out many of the alleged rapes and sexual assaults" (United Nations 1994, 13).

In her *Ms.* article, MacKinnon includes the testimonies of Croatian and Muslim women survivors, who attest to the horrendous conditions in the camps and the presence of pornographic materials, and who describe in vivid detail practices of torture and rape. One account describes a woman having to "remain kneeling" as she is raped and beaten. There is no sense of the woman as an individual—just someone "kneeling." Rhetorically, MacKinnon approximates the position of the victims to persuade audiences to act on their behalf. She expresses "shock, a clarifying jolt" (1993, 25) at descriptions of rape in Bosnia. Her article, however, places its readers in the position of voyeur in this "rape theater" (29) and licenses the pornographic gaze that she has worked so hard to criminalize. Accompanying the essay is an image of a soldier holding an assault weapon aimed out a window. On the wall next to the window is what looks like a picture from a pornographic magazine of a topless woman in a provocative pose. The caption reads: "Serbian soldier practicing his aim" (28). The visual absence of victims may combat the spectacle of gendered victimization (the article explicitly points out that survivors' names are withheld for their protection), but the pornographic image—if we are to interpret it through MacKinnon's critical lens—privileges the perpetrator's gaze and aligns viewers' eyes with his. From this vantage point, the pornographic image, as a backdrop to the soldier's cocked firearm, codes looking as an act of violence.

Within the context of MacKinnon's essay, the women's testimonies, which might otherwise be read as sites of possible change and agency, newly animate the spectacle of rape as pornography. In other words, the women's testimonials become carriers of multiple exploitations; they become rhetorical proofs, points of authenticity, and documentary evidence in the service of MacKinnon's antipornography argument. MacKinnon employs the particularities of rape warfare in Bosnia, as conveyed through the anonymous women's testimonies, to support a "universal" claim about pornography.[3] As the photograph of the soldier's cocked gun alongside the pornographic pinup makes clear, MacKinnon is more interested in linking human rights violations (in this case, rape warfare) to her antipornography stance than in exploring these women's testimonials for what they say about the complexities of women's victimization, cultural location, and agency. Furthermore, MacKinnon's conflation of rape, pornography, and prostitution —comparing rape warfare in Bosnia-Herzegovina with Linda Lovelace's coerced role in *Deep Throat* (1993, 25), comparing "ethnic rape" with brothels all over the world (26), and comparing snuff films with filmed torture scenes in Bosnia—creates a universalized misogyny (as pornography) at work worldwide.[4] MacKinnon's conception of global patriarchy reinforces, as Dubravka Žarkov argues, "the greatest of all gender distinctions, assuming, once again, the omnipotence of men and the absolute powerlessness of women" (2007, 176). In the recognition scenes that MacKinnon constructs, then, several spectacular discourses converge, including the objectifying visual rhetoric of the simulated perpetrator's pornographic gaze and the spectacle of female victimization generated by MacKinnon's antipornography argument of universal patriarchy and by the women's testimonies themselves. MacKinnon's conception of rape as spectacle exemplifies the pervasive visibility of women as rape victims in international news media and U.S. public discourse, and the emphasis in women's human rights campaigns on violence against women. Although rape victims' testimonies may

"argue with the very position of the spectator, undermining distance and passivity [associated with the spectacle] by creating an entirely new relational structure" (Zimmerman 2000, 63), speaking out is not necessarily followed by respect or recognition of agency. Thus we need to consider on what grounds this "new relational structure" is consummated, and the ethics of recognition that such structures put into place.[5]

International attention to the use of rape as a tactic of warfare intensified between 1991 and 1995, as reports emerged about the existence of camps in Bosnia-Herzegovina and Croatia where women were detained and raped repeatedly by Serbian soldiers. Along with the media coverage, persistent activism by women's organizations contributed to the establishment of the ICTY in May 1993. The ICTY produced its first indictment in August 1994, against a prison guard at the Serbian-run Omarska camps (case IT-94–1). Not until 1996, with the Foča case (IT-96–23), however, did the ICTY clearly define rape as torture.[6] The legal authorities belatedly recognized that rape becomes a war crime and an instrument of genocide when the perpetrators are understood to be acting on behalf of a state (or statelike entity) in the context of war; international law still has little to say, though, about rape and other forms of gender violence as a human rights violation outside the context of state actors.[7] The ICTY provides a discursive context for the increased visibility of gender violence, but in the context of legal proceedings, women's testimonies are often reduced to descriptions of body parts and the actions of the perpetrator (Žarkov 2007, 177). In other words, legal remedies may inadvertently perpetuate the most powerful icon in the violent production of gendered identities—the spectacle of female victimization (178)—and "resubordinate the subject . . . historically subjugated through [that] identity" (W. Brown 1995b, 202).

Human rights testimonies continue to play a key role in advancing the international human rights agenda. But we must ask: What kinds of witnesses do human rights testimonies construe? In what ways are the testimonies of rape victims turned into opportunistic spectacles for self-positioning or for political agendas?[8] If human rights images and testimonies aim to create a rhetorical space of intersubjectivity—of bearing witness—how can human rights activists and scholars account for ruptures in identification and crises in witnessing? Finally, if the incorporation of the subject into a human rights internationalism based on Western inflections of UN discourses is structured by an ethos of recognition of subjection and trauma, as I have suggested (see chapter 1), in what ways do women's testimonial acts become entrenched in the cultural politics of identity in their own subjection? And what is at stake, and for whom, in the disinvestment of an ethics of recognition grounded in identity-based claims and asymmetries of power?

In the remainder of this chapter, I examine three documentary videos (Midge Mackenzie's *The Sky: A Silent Witness* [1995], Mandy Jacobson and Karmen Jelincic's *Calling the Ghosts: A Story about Rape, War, and Women* [1996], and Marija Gajicki's *Vivisect* [2003]) and a photo-testimonial exhibition by Melanie Friend (*Homes and Gardens/Documenting the Invisible: Images from Kosovo* [1996]). These cultural works take on the spectacle of rape warfare by drawing attention to the mediated properties of witnessing and the commodification of women's testimonies on the global stage. I ask how the visualization of women's rape testimonies or its suspension reinforces the spectator-witness dichotomy and the truth-telling contract established by the inclusion of human rights testimony—and, conversely, how testimony responds to the repressive functions of the spectacle. I demonstrate that the international women's human rights movement provides a discursive space within which victims can speak, be spoken about, and be incorporated into the normative frames of juridical subjectivity, yet I also acknowledge that these normative frames can function in ways that reproduce asymmetries of power by entrenching the pain of subjugated identities in human rights politics. Finally, I am interested in representations that break down the prevailing principles and evidentiary protocols through the recalibration of the norms of international human rights law and its underlying principles of recognition.

## Crises of Witnessing

Shoshana Felman and Dori Laub observe that the twentieth century was marked by events that produced a "crisis within history which precisely cannot be articulated, witnessed in the given categories of history itself" (1992, xviii). Felman and Laub allude to ruptures in identification and the limitations of disciplinary conventions in understanding atrocity, and they point to how trauma may throw into crisis existing paradigms and patterns of communication. In terms of the reception of representations of trauma, scholars in memory and trauma studies have called for a critical stance of bearing witness, wherein the witness (listener or viewer) "does not take the place of the other" (Chun 2002, 158). Similarly, Ulrich Baer argues that "empathic identification can easily lead us to miss the inscription of trauma because the original subjects themselves did not register the experience in the fullness of its meaning" (2002, 13). Moreover, Baer suggests, "identificatory responses indulge the illusion that we might somehow be able to assimilate [atrocities such as] the Holocaust fully into our understanding" (177). Following Walter Benjamin, Baer claims that "unless viewers suspend their faith in the future, in the narrative of time-as-flux that turns the photographed scene into part of a longer story (whether melancholic or hopeful), they will misconstrue the violence of trauma as a mere error, a lapse from or aberration in the otherwise infallible program of history-as-progress" (181).

Baer turns to a postmodern theory of photography to resist restorative, triumphant, and redemptive narrative criticism. His intent is to wrestle photographic criticism "away from a narrative model of experienced time [and] to account for catastrophic events without turning them into a continuous story" (2002, 105). Baer uses the term *ungovernability* to describe the "breakdown of context that, in a structured analogy to trauma, is staged by every photograph" (11) and by the "structuring *absence* [that] defines . . . [traumatic] experiences" (12). Though aware that viewers project narratives onto photographs, and that images elicit narrative impulses, Baer is less interested in photographs' connotative dimensions than in how they "can capture the shrapnel of traumatic time" (7). Instead of pointing to a loss, Baer argues, "every photograph is radically exposed to a future unknown to its subjects." In other words, there is a trace of the ungovernable in every photograph. Trauma, like the past, is an unstable referent (107); so too is the photograph. Yet the ungovernable makes an appearance in Baer's *Spectral Evidence* through survivors' testimonies of memories triggered by photographs. Baer notes that photography can "provide special access to experiences that have remained unremembered yet cannot be forgotten" (7). These memory narratives create a sense of identification with and belonging to the image. In other words, traces of identification linger, and I argue that it is these traces, these wounds, to which the ungovernable is attached. Thus, I extend Baer's definition of the ungovernable "staged by every photograph" in my application of the concept to the modes of rhetorical witnessing enabled by human rights testimonies and their visualization.

I share Baer's view of the crisis of reference as one that highlights the inability of representation to capture—as in fix or make static—the truth. However, I am equally interested in understanding the value attributed to truth-telling discourses and their cultural and institutional contexts. The process of documenting human rights violations is paradoxical in that violence is often represented in order for it to be resisted. But are violent representations necessary for the construction of social and legal recognition? What forms of empathetic engagement are constituted as solutions to violence, and what are the limits of such forms? In responding to these questions, I use the term *crisis of witnessing* to refer to the risks of representing trauma and violence, to ruptures in identification, and to the impossibility of empathetic merging between witness and testifier—an impossibility that is aesthetically and politically staged in several of the works under consideration in this chapter.[9]

Critical works in life-writing studies—a category in which human rights testimony and the testimonial genre are often located—and feminist ethnography have engaged ungovernable crises of reference and witnessing primarily in terms of the mediated nature of the testimonial genre and through the editorial processes of collaboration and mediation.[10] Feminist critics have pointed to the problem of having the privileged speak for rather than with the oppressed, thereby establishing an authenticating presence, and to the equally problematic assumption that the subject can speak only for herself, a stance that ignores the intercontextuality of constructions of subjectivity and agency.[11] The emergent focus in feminist rhetorical studies, for example, on "how one gets heard" "locate[s] identification in discursive spaces of both commonalities and differences" (Ratcliffe 1999, 204) and "turns hearing (a reception process) into invention (a production process), thus complicating the reception/production opposition" (220). To echo Iain Chambers, rhetorical listening as theorized by Krista Ratcliffe significantly "abandon[s] a fixed (ad)vantage for a mobile and exposed politics of listening" and thereby recognizes multiple positionalities (Chambers

1996, 51). But how are we to understand this mobility? And for whom are these movements forced, coerced, or elected? To what extent does a mobile rhetoric of listening reflect a generalizing of otherness, which depends, in Edward Said's words, on a "flexible positional superiority" (1978, 7).

In order to better understand the sought-after rhetorical intersubjectivity of testimonial acts, including women's rape testimonies, I argue that we need to recognize the interdependence of witnessing (as a visual rhetorical act) and listening (as an auditory rhetorical act)—especially, but not only, when considering mixed-media representations. This chapter advances my earlier discussions of the need for a differentiated politics of recognition (a differential universalism) in its engagement of the paradoxes of representation involved in becoming a rhetorical witness of rape warfare as genocide and of the allegorical structure of human rights claims to this recognition. The paradox that such representations bring front and center, of course, is the figuration of the individual as an embodiment of group identity and group vulnerability—a sense of collective identity recognized by the genocide convention (the 1948 UN Universal Declaration of Human Rights; see also Slaughter 2007, 161). In contrast to instantiations of witnessing that deny that empathy and identification are political practices, *The Sky* (Mackenzie 1995) and *Homes and Gardens* (Friend 1996) stage the political aesthetics of recognition by foregrounding the problem of implication and identification through incorporation.

## Absent Presence: Proximity without Intimacy

Claps of thunder sound as dark, ominous clouds trudge across the opening frames of *The Sky: A Silent Witness*, a 1995 documentary video by the British independent filmmaker Midge Mackenzie, produced in association with Amnesty International. The expansive yet oppressive sky functions as a haunting reminder of human rights violations around the globe. Religious-sounding piano music accompanies shots of the sloping hills of Guatemala, commemorating 180 Quiché Indians who were massacred in 1982. We see dozens of women and men kneel as they empty human ashes and bones into small coffins. Women place fresh flowers on rough wooden boxes. Children look on, both curious and sad. A woman speaks: "My name is Juan de Paz González. I belong to the Quiché Indian tribe." González recounts how her father, a preacher, was killed by army soldiers in Guatemala, and how her family hid in ravines and mountains before coming to the city, where her husband was later kidnapped and she was left alone with her daughter, hungry and displaced. "It was a difficult situation for me as a woman with a child," González continues. "The situation is very difficult for all one and a half million displaced here in this city, this country of Guatemala."

González's testimony, set against the backdrop of excavations, funeral rituals, and protest marches, establishes the narrative pattern followed by the other women featured in the film: name, cultural affiliation, and date of the action that led to individual and mass trauma, followed by a rhetorical gesture that highlights the importance of community and collective grieving. The film features six women—from Bangladesh, China, Guatemala, Tibet, Bosnia, and the United States—all of whom describe experiences of victimization and state-sanctioned violence. Taslima Nasrin from Bangladesh spoke out against violence against women. She describes how as a result she was beaten and tortured by fundamentalists with, she argues, the government's complicity. Death threats forced her to flee her country. The other four women are Judy Richardson, an African American civil rights worker who was jailed in the 1960s for her participation in marches against racism; Tsultrim Dolma, a Tibetan Buddhist nun who was beaten by representatives of the Chinese government for her work on behalf of human rights and the fight for Tibetan independence; Lu Jing Hua from Beijing, who was arrested, taken to a detention center, and tortured by the Chinese government for her participation in demonstrations at Tiananmen Square; and an unnamed woman who was raped by soldiers in Bosnia. The camera focuses on one woman at a time, with the exception of the Bosnian woman—the only white woman—whose face we do not see. Each face is lit from the side, with one half embraced by dark shadows. The slow panning between frames of the sky and the women's faces creates the illusion of a seamless visual narrative. Similarly, each woman's testimony retains the rhetorical appeal of the particular, yet situates the particular within a communal "we." At work here, as is common to the protean genre of the *testimonio* is a "lateral identification through relationship, which acknowledges the possible differences among 'us' as components of the whole" (Sommer 1988, 108). As Beverley notes, "The word *testimonio* translates literally as 'testimony,' as in the act of testifying or bearing witness in a legal or religious sense" (1992, 94). Testimonio is a genre deeply connected to human rights advocacy, and yet testimonio troubles human rights' universalizing rhetoric through its claim to a differential universalism and its projection of solidarity onto witnessing publics. Midway through *The Sky*, an unnamed woman speaks explicitly, though briefly, about the trauma of rape warfare. We hear her voice but do not see her face. She speaks through a screen of dark thunderous clouds:

> In Bosnia on September 3, 1992, the soldiers came to take the young women. They said they would beat us and rape us and kill us. I was raped by two of them. They brought more soldiers to rape me. I cried and screamed. I wanted to kill myself. They said it was war. There is no law and order. In my dreams, it's happening to me again. I have these bad dreams all the time.

This woman recounts the horror, haunting memories, and lingering trauma of rape warfare, dreams that expose the wounds and that function as evidence—archives of memory that establish her authority and ethos. The visual absence of her body reminds viewers of the vulnerability of victims in speaking out, even as her testimony is also on behalf of the thousands of women who could not speak out: those who were killed or who kept silent out of fear for their lives and because of the social stigma that a rape victim carries in patriarchal cultures. Absence and presence are configured not only in terms of the belatedness of trauma, but also in terms of the witness, whose rhetorical function is to give trauma a presence.

But this scene from *The Sky* also unsettles the relationship between viewer and speaker, and it functions in ways that parallel formulations of empathetic unsettlement in trauma studies. This scene marks a point of tension in testimonials, which, as Leigh Gilmore notes in another context, often "invite and rebuff identification" (2001, 23).[12] Thus we might ask: Does the visual absence of the rape victim in *The Sky* provide an opportunity for our rhetorical presence and for the construction of a scene of self-recognition? Or does the suspension of the visual spectacle of victimization prompt a politics that moves beyond recognition? Does this particular representation exemplify testimony without intimacy? In what ways does the cinematic absence of the victim's body reconfigure the ethics of recognition? Patricia Yaeger suggests that to focus on the aesthetics of testimony—specifically, on how "the figures of testimony enact specific rhetorical or bodily effects that push us away even as they pull us toward intimacy" (2006, 402)—is not to admit that trauma is unrepresentable. Rather, Yaeger's emphasis on the formal and structural aspects of testimony turns our attention to how the secondary witness "gets stuck in the gap between what is said in testimony and the way a speaking body or written text says it" (402). Yaeger is concerned with the ethical dimensions of proximity and scale (405), and how aesthetic estrangement and the diversion from familiar frames of rhetorical engagement shed comforting illusions of empathy and identification (410), giving readers a "glimpse of desuetude, of one's own uselessness, of failed intimacy" and the possibility of an ethical stance based on "proximity without intimacy" (415).

As the unidentified woman speaks, the film captures a reflection of the sky on the surface of water. This reflection reverses, distorts, and contains the sky; it establishes boundaries where there are none and therefore draws attention to the crisis of witnessing. The sky functions as an image metaphor for trauma's unattainability: trauma is often conceptualized as out of reach, unknowable, shifting, yet always present. The sky as a metaphor encompasses both the potential inhumanity and humanity of shared visions. The primary motive for the testifier's anonymity may have been protection, but her refusal to become a visual text also places the viewer in a curious relation to this rhetorical refusal. This particular sequence and mapping of conceptual domains does not permit the viewer to appropriate trauma or the suffering of others through the spectacle of visual identification; however, the speaker's verbal testimony bears the cultural stigma of identification as a rape victim. The visual absence yet auditory presence of the material body also represents the psychological dislocation associated with traumatic experiences, the experience of "going elsewhere," and a dislocation of another sort—namely, the historic absence of rape as a human rights violation within international law. As I mentioned above, it was not until 1996 that the ICTY recognized rape as torture and a war crime. And international recognition and coverage of rape warfare in the former Yugoslavia stands in marked contrast to the relative invisibility of wartime rape in other contexts, such as Latin America, where it was a common practice throughout the 1980s, or Rwanda. Rhonda Copelon argues that the visibility of rape in Bosnia is a result of its association with genocide (64). She is critical, however, of the emphasis on genocidal rape as unparalleled and of the "notion that genocidal rape is uniquely a weapon of war." She argues that to "exaggerate the distinctiveness of genocidal rape obscures the atrocity of common rape" (69). Thus, this scene not only attests to the risks of testifying but also serves as a reminder of how voices speak through or are silenced by the image (Shohat and Stam 1994, 214).[13]

Aida Hozic observes the power of mass-mediated imagery of "distant violence" (2000, 229) in the production of global crises. She argues that the "attention and media space given to war-torn areas is proportional to the propensity of the international community to intervene in their troubles" (229), which explains the international focus on ethnic violence in Sarajevo instead of other regions in Bosnia, or Somalia, Rwanda, or Chechnya. We might call this phenomenon the realpolitik of recognition. Initially, victims of persecution by Serbian nationalists welcomed media attention, expecting publicity to persuade the international community to intervene. Soon, however, many began to realize that the voyeuristic nature of the news media exposed Bosnians to "an unwanted parody of genuine witnessing" (Weine 1999, 183) without adequate responses from international agencies and governments. The wars that have stricken the region since 1991 have "turned more than a million people into refugees, killed tens of thousands, and resulted in rape, torture, separation of families, and widespread physical and psychological traumas" (Benderly 1997, 59). Some of the strongest support for survivors has come from antiwar feminists. Feminists have been divided, however, over the objectives of their nation-states, and there are opposing views among feminists in the states that succeeded Yugoslavia about who was doing the raping and why. For instance, while evidence points to the "preponderance of genocidal rape by the Serbian paramilitary and army . . . atrocities were abundant on all sides of the conflict. Even United Nations peacekeeping forces appeared to be involved in the traffic in women" (66).[14]

Significantly, in *The Sky* the woman who testifies to being raped by soldiers in Bosnia does not identify the perpetrators' or her own ethnic or religious affiliations. This lack of identification requires viewers to contextualize this absence within the complex identity politics, cultural mythology, and history of the region.[15] As Lynda Boose notes: "In the Balkans—and especially Serbia—a type of racial ethnicity is largely assumed to be synonymous with religious difference, and ethnic identity synonymous with national boundaries" (2002, 75). Yet in the guise of critiquing essentialist notions of ethnicity, Boose reconstructs them when she claims that "all three of these peoples actually belong to the same racial and linguistic group, Southern Slavs"—a connection that, she argues, Serbian culture denies in its struggle to retain heroic uniqueness constructed around fantasies of racial purity and denial of interethnic marriages and cultural hybridity (76). According to the testimonies of many Bosniak[16] survivors, "the usually drunken, enraged soldiers raped and beat them, the rapists screamed either 'Turkish whore' or 'Ustaša' [a term that refers to a Croatian fascist separatist movement] whore' at their victims" (75). Boose links the figure of the enemy "Turk," the image of the Turkish practice of impalement, and its transference onto Bosnia's Muslims to Serbian culture and national mythology. Given the 500-year Ottoman domination of Serbia, she argues, it should come as no surprise that the figure of the Turk is entrenched in Serbian cultural memory.[17] The "Turk remains an ever-internalized figure of occupation," a figure who "threatens to conquer, victimize, feminize, and humiliate Serb national selfhood (always a masculine construct)" (78). The displacement of identification was also geographical. It was Bosnia, not Croatia, that suffered the force of Serbian aggression and violence. (Though the Serb military did invade Croatia in 1991, and leveled the city of Vukovar, the Serb army crossed back over the river.) "Crossing the Drina to create rape camps and subject Bosnia's Muslim women en masse to the authority of the Serb phallus," Boose continues, "not only enacts a repetition and a return to subjugate the omnipresent Turk but tries to reciprocate the humiliating violation of male impalement/rape" (93).[18] The rape of Bosniak women works as a form of resentment against the Turk because "in constructing women's bodies as property signifying the honor of the male community, patriarchal culture has produced the equation that makes this substitution possible" (ibid.). Accordingly, Boose views "ethnic violence" as a representation of actual ideology—a historical inheritance. Conversely, Andrew Herscher prompts us to consider the "performative dimension of 'ethnic violence'" and to question the inference of an ethnic identity that exists "prior to and separate from its material representations, violent or otherwise." "Sometimes ethnic violence is posed as the result of a top-down manipulation of ethnic communities by states or elites," Herscher argues, and "sometimes it is posed as the result of a bottom-up appropriation of ethnic ideologies in local conflicts; occasionally it is posed as a result of primordial antagonism between ethnic communities" (2010, 81).

The dynamics of substitution and displacement must also be seen, as some scholars have argued, in relationship to the internationalization of identity politics and its link to the globalization of capital—an analytic that posits rape as an epiphenomenon of economic conflict and contrasts with MacKinnon's claims that rape is an epiphenomenon of the pornographic imagination. For instance, Neil Davidson argues that two conditions were necessary in order for the "upsurge of 'ethnic' identifications to take place" (1999): the need to distinguish one group from another and rapid social change. "Where that change is destructive of established ways of life, and in some cases whole societies," Davidson continues, "then distinguishing oneself as part of a specific group in order to struggle over the resources, or . . . rubble left by the onward march of international capital, may appear to be the only available option even when group membership may previously have meant little or nothing to the people concerned."[19] Thus, according to Davidson, the internationalization of identity politics that figure prominently in the conflicts must not be seen in isolation from the economic conditions.[20] For instance, the ultranationalist Slobodan Milošević went to great lengths to polarize people by manipulating the economy. Hence, when considering the mobilization of identity categories, we need to take into account the economic motivations of the leaders of regions involved in the conflicts. Moreover, as Susan Woodward notes, nationalist politics emerged in areas that were more integrated with Western markets and was pushed by politicians who had support from Western sources for their reforms. When this Western drive overflowed into areas that were less able to cope with liberalization strategies, adverse political and economic consequences emerged (2000, 31). Davidson and Woodward challenge us to understand how identifications based on historical processes of domination can be mobilized as structural elements of national and foreign policy, and as tools of war as well as tools of peace.

Boose's theoretical premise of rape warfare as a rationally deployed instruction to "undermine ethnic mixing"—as an epiphenomenon of historical inheritance—and Davidson's theoretical positing of ethnic genocide as an epiphenomenon of economic conflict are, to varying degrees, at odds with an understanding of violence as a confluence of material and symbolic realms, which is my own position. Specifically, in this case, Žarkov argues: "It is this link of ethnicity and territory through raped female bodies that[,] in effect, makes both the victims and the perpetrators imaginable only through their ethnicity. It is the ultimate victory of the ethnic war and the media war that raped women and rapists were so consistently counted, included, and excluded, exclusively through their ethnicity, and because of it, that the analysis of rape repeated—instead of subverting—the ethnicization of both victim and the perpetrator" (2007, 154).

Ron Haviv's photograph of a defaced portrait of a Bosnian Muslim family visualizes the material and rhetorical violence of identification in the hands of an ultranationalist regime. The depicted Muslim family fled Sarajevo before the siege. When they returned to their home in 1996 after the Dayton Peace Agreement, they found all their material possessions had been looted and only one item was left behind: this defaced photograph, in which each body had been impaled with carefully placed slash marks (Boose 2002, 89–90). This image highlights the visual instrumentality attributed to the ultranationalist configuration of the other as a defaced spectacle: a spectacular scene of nonrecognition and violation.

Marija Gajicki's documentary *Vivisect*, which premiered at the New York Human Rights Watch film festival in 2003, captured the public reaction among Serbian visitors to an exhibition of photographs by Ron Haviv in Novi Sad, Serbia, in 2002 (fig. 5 among them). Gajicki is an activist, filmmaker, and journalist from Novi Sad. Due to the Haviv exhibit's controversial reception and perception as anti-Serbian propaganda, it was open for only ten days and seen by 5,000 people before being closed by the Serbian government. Visitors were asked to write their reactions to the exhibit on long white sheets of paper tacked alongside the displayed photographs. Some of the comments were: "This is terrible because it's a lie," "The exhibit

5. A defaced photograph found by a Bosnian family when they returned to their home in a suburb of Sarajevo on 17 March 1996. The Serbs who had occupied the house left as the city was reunified under the Muslim-led Bosnian government, taking the Bosnian family's furniture and the rest of their belongings. Only the photograph was left behind. Photograph by Ron Haviv / VII.

is a disaster," and "We are not Gypsies." One visitor captured on film implies that the sequence of photographs tells a particular story about whom to blame—namely, the Serbs. Another visitor says: "The exhibition should have included Serbian victims." In sum, *Vivisect* illustrates the violent materialist and representational force and imprint of identifications in the act of witnessing, and the fact that witnesses may not identify themselves; rather, they may deny or negate the identifications imposed on them, and their contextualization.

## Suspending the Spectacle

*The Sky* suspends the spectacular as a mode of recording violence by staging its absence, a political aesthetic of witnessing tied to various formal moves of subtraction, depletion, or abstraction. A similar aesthetic characterizes *Homes and Gardens/Documenting the Invisible: Images from Kosovo*, a

6. The person who lived in this house reports: "It was 4:30 in the afternoon. A police patrol of nine cars arrived. The policemen jumped over the wall and knocked at my door . . . they came in, tied up my hands and called all my family to come over . . . they started to torture me and search for arms and documents. All this lasted for about one hour and thirty minutes. Afterwards I was taken to the police station . . . there they beat me up so badly that I lost consciousness and didn't know where I was. They hit me on the head, kidneys, arms and legs with a rubber truncheon and metal piping" (Melanie Friend, 1996, xx). Photograph by Melanie Friend. By permission of Melanie Friend and Cleis Press.

photo-testimonial exhibition by the British photojournalist Melanie Friend (1996). *Homes and Gardens* depicts the homes of Albanian Kosovars raided by the police in the 1990s.[21]

In the quote shown in the caption to figure 6, it is interesting that the homeowner refers to his persecutors as "the police," rather than essentializing them as "Serbs." For over a decade, the ethnic Albanian population in Kosovo (or Kosova) followed a strategy of nonviolent noncompliance with the police-state regime that had taken away their autonomy in 1989.[22] Thus *Homes and Gardens* works against essentialist ethnic identity categories. Friend, who worked in the Balkans from 1989 to 1995 and returned in 1999–2000, offers an alternative visual rhetoric that contrasts with the mass media's spectacular use of graphic images to represent mass trauma and violence. Her photographs are accompanied by oral testimonies, with an audiotape of them played in the exhibition. Excerpts from the sound transcripts appear on pages opposite to the photographs in the 1996 exhibition catalog. The juxtaposition of testimonials and photographic images of domestic spaces encourages viewers to consider the relationship between testimony and visual evidence, and the distance between what one sees and what one hears or reads (see fig. 7).

With the exception of one image that provides evidence of a burned house, Friend's images reference but do not visually depict the eruption of violence or the violation of private domestic space. The oral testimonies that anchor *Homes and Gardens* carry the burden of historical context, of memory, and—as with the rape victim's testimony in *The Sky*—of imagining what occurs beyond the boundaries of visual representation. *Homes and Gardens* does not make the visual into the custodian of violence but grants this role to delivery, or oral testimony. In a number of cases, for instance, the testimonial narratives create a violent mental picture. In this sense, *Homes and Gardens* engages the paradox of representing trauma in its challenge and also support of theories about the links between representations of violence and the construction of empathy.

In contrast to dominant news media representations of the trauma of ethnic violence in Kosovo/Kosova, *Homes and Gardens* uses its imaging of absence to prompt viewers to contemplate how they are positioned by the media to see themselves, and to consider the problem of implication—that is, how they as observers may be implicated in the object of observation (LaCapra 2001, 5). The domestic spaces captured by *Homes and Gardens* project a rhetorical gaze of gender and class identification, particularly with middle-class Western viewers. But, as Wendy Kozol notes, in not providing graphic images of embodied trauma, the exhibit refuses "conventional icons of victimization" and counters dominant Western images that mobilize

7. The person who lived here remembers: "Every day we hear of terrible new happenings . . . every minute we are afraid that they may come back, and every time the bell rings, the kids get frightened and ask me to open the door. Any time this happens they jump and say 'Mum it's the police, come to take Daddy away'" (Melanie Friend, 1996). Photograph by Melanie Friend. By permission of Melanie Friend and Cleis Press.

ideals of domesticity to construe American viewers as rescuers (2004, 17). Witnessing may not require identification with the audience in the traditional rhetorical sense of shared experiences, but rhetorical modes of identification and recognition are readily employed by these works. *The Sky*, for example, projects rhetorical identification—that is, group identification—through the discursive register of human rights law and, in the case of the former Yugoslavia, the genocide convention (the 1948 UN Convention on the Prevention and Punishment of the Crime of Genocide). These identifications, however, are also suspended by scenes like that of the rape testimony, which in its absence of markers of visual suffering forges a differential proximity between the testifier and secondary witnesses (viewers). And while the images of middle-class homes in *Homes and Gardens*, with which many Euro-American viewers may identify, counter the mass media depictions of the Balkan other as undesirable, the testimonials dislodge easy identifications and transferences. In both *Homes and Gardens* and the scene under consideration from *The Sky*, absence creates the consubstantial space for rhetorical witnessing and listening. Significantly, this space is not predicated on identification alone, but on evidentiary unsettlement coded here as a rupture in, if not a crisis of, witnessing. In not providing a spectacular image to accompany the trauma narrative, *Homes and Gardens* suspends the spectacle. In contrast to MacKinnon's "Turning Rape into Pornography" (1993), which reproduces distant suffering for Western audiences by framing rape warfare as a spectacle within the pornographic imaginary, *Homes and Gardens* restages the spectacle of violence through the visual framework of the ordinary and normative, making the audible testimonies of violation all the more shocking and intimate. In the next section, I focus on *Calling the Ghosts*, a documentary that exposes the tensions between the legal dependency on the nationalist and ethnic identities imposed on material bodies during the Balkan wars and the politics of nonrecognition that they support. *Vivisect* reveals the same tensions, but *Calling the Ghosts* also exposes the desire for independence from those identities.

## Testimonies and the Politics of Recognition

*Calling the Ghosts: A Story about Rape, War, and Women*, a documentary film directed by the South African filmmaker Mandy Jacobson in collaboration with Karmen Jelincic, of Croatia, addresses the political limits and risks of identification and the violent consequences of an essentialist nationalist politics of recognition.[23] One of the ways the film engages the ethical traps of representation and of the politics of recognition is by interrogating "the disjuncture between images and witnessing" (Zimmerman 2000, 65). The film employs the testimonies of Croatian and Muslim women interned at the Serbian concentration camp of Omarska.[24] Reportedly, the filmmakers did not turn their cameras on for the first seven months but instead focused their energy on building trust with the women they met. Jacobson and Jelincic state that they were interested not in what happened to the women but in how they were making sense of their experiences and channeling their pain into a struggle for justice, which involves tracing the women's process of recognizing themselves as human rights subjects before the international community. The filmmakers sought to counter dominant representations of the war that focus solely on its ethnic dimensions. Their intention was to use media to influence public policy and to do so in a way that did not recreate a victim narrative but that depicted how the women responded to victimization (Jacobson 2003). This process of self-recognition aims to counterbalance the dehumanizing nationalist and hierarchical politics of recognition that underlies ethnic violence. *Calling the Ghosts* focuses on two middle-class women: an attorney, Jadranka Cigelj; and a civil judge, Nusreta Sivac. The two are childhood friends who were captured, tormented, and tortured by former neighbors and who, as Jacobson puts it, "defy all those stereotypes about peasants and mad savages" (2003). By focusing on the experiences of middle-class legal professionals, the film works against Western expectations about what a sexually abused Muslim woman might look like.[25] In the first scene, Cigelj washes her face before swimming in the ocean. Water, as a sign of purification, functions ironically in the horrific story of "ethnic cleansing" that follows.[26] As Cigelj speaks, it is clear that washing cannot wipe away her memories: "There was a period of self-questioning before me. To stay silent or to speak.... If I stay silent, how moral would that be? When I remember the night when I was taken out my own broken bones start to hurt. If I speak how good is that for me? I would actually have to expose myself." This statement articulates the intersection between embodied memory and speech acts: the individual's trauma is implicated in the social, regardless of whether she chooses to speak. Yet, as Cigelj notes: "Without the live witness, one can only speculate about the crime. The crime has not been filmed with a camera. It is only recorded in the memory of the witness." Still, Cigelj and the filmmakers know all too well what price survivors pay for their testimonies. As the camera slowly narrows in on the face of an old woman in a headscarf, visualizing how violations and abuses cross generational lines, Cigelj states: "In order to expose the crime, you violate the witness. You don't force her, of course—you beg her to speak. But you do make her live through it again." In reliving the trauma so as to give evidence, the witness and the viewer are implicated—albeit inadvertently—in recreating the spectacle of victimization as a scene of forced recognition.

Recognizing the problem of voyeurism embedded in many representations of rape warfare, *Calling the Ghosts* addresses the question of spectacle and foregrounds the crisis of witnessing in its highly ambivalent critique of the media. On the one hand, the film condemns the news media's insatiable voyeurism. A long, slow shot pans across a still photograph of a group of women of different ages as Cigelj speaks: "Journalists and TV crews would come, always with the same question: 'Are there any women here who were raped?' I mean, as if one could possibly divide women between those who were raped and those who weren't. As if they were in some sort of display." This critique of voyeurism interacts with the camera's pan across the picture, implicating the viewer in the desire to know if these unidentified women were raped. On the other hand, the film credits news reporters for bringing the ethnic genocide in Bosnia to international attention and, indeed, for saving the lives of many women at Omarska. A scene in a refugee camp explicitly presents the ethical choices of filmmakers and reporters. A group of women and children crowd around the camera as a woman yells: "I am telling you: If you are going to help, then shoot! If not—then don't film us." As the film cuts to a train pulling away from a station, the viewer is left with only the ambivalent and unresolved issues surrounding the need to publicize this violence, and the costs of such publicity. For instance, there is a powerful scene in which Nusreta Sivac directly challenges cultural fantasies and the voyeuristic gaze that links violence to the other: "It bothers me when someone says raped women. . . . Abused women, women victims of war, find some other appropriate term. But raped women—that hurts a person, to be marked as a raped woman, as if you had no other characteristic, as if that were your sole identity." Here Sivac not only alludes to the reductive label that casts women who have been raped as passive and powerless spectacles, but she also points to the use of the category of raped women as a form of social stigma, itself attached to that spectacularization. This scene thus shows how rape scripts the perception of women, and how its representation may further traumatize women.[27]

Although the film shows us victimized bodies, we also see bodies surviving their wounds. For example, *Calling the Ghosts* features individual and group interviews, montages of many women's faces, and close-ups of stacks of 3″ × 5″ photographs of tortured body parts. Cigelj's dilemma—whether to speak or stay silent—articulates the relationship between the spectacle of trauma and oral testimonies as empowering and voyeuristic, collective and individual. The material presence of women's bodies and their excruciating experiences of torture produce important tensions between witnessing and spectacle. To find human rights testimonies and images of suffering simultaneously empowering and voyeuristic is not to remain undecided about their role but rather to recognize their complex rhetorical dynamics.

Despite an explicit critique of voyeurism, however, the film clearly recognizes the crucial role that news reporters played in saving lives and publicizing this violence. As a result of the publicity surrounding a visit by a group of reporters to the camp, the majority of women still held there, including Cigelj and Sivac, were released. The film also shows Cigelj working with the reporter Roy Gutman, who first publicized the existence of the death camps and later the rape and torture of women. But in another scene, Cigelj watches a television news report that features both her testimony and a refutation by the commander of Omarska, Zeljko Mejakic, who tortured her. The irony is chilling, for on television, they appear similarly calm and authoritative, Mejakic as credible as Cigelj. It is only within the wider context of the film that Mejakic's credibility—his delivery—is undermined. But *Calling the Ghosts* does more than position these women as victims or injured subjects; it also grapples with the notion of testifying as a collective act. Against the visual backdrop of their home city of Prijedor and the Omarska camp, Cigelj and Sivac identify their torturers by name and provide specific details about their incarceration, release from Omarska, and subsequent resettlement in Zagreb, Croatia. There they join with other women to create support communities for providing legal aid and the gathering of testimonies. Turning from victims to activists, the women dramatize the "epistemological travel" in testimonial work, a mobility signaled initially by Cigelj's choosing to speak out. Through individual testimonies the atomistic self is reconfigured as plural (where the "I" becomes interchangeable with the "we") and construe a "collective 'I' witness" (Sánchez-Casal 2001, 87). One might argue that the testimonies in *Calling the Ghosts* contest the formulation of the sovereign subject of liberalism and its established universalism through the articulation of collective, yet particularized, experiences. But we also have to remember that the transformation from the singular to the plural subject in the context of human rights law—namely, the notion of collective identity at the core of the genocide convention—is, in some cases, also a product of resurgent and violent nationalisms.

Little critical work exists on the modes of witnessing evoked by human rights testimonies embedded in documentary film. This neglect stems, in part, from assumptions about the authenticity of firsthand accounts and the referential nature of testimony as legal evidence. Patricia Zimmerman's study *States of Emergency* is one of few exceptions that considers the rhetorical relationship between the atrocity spectacle and human rights testimonies in independent documentary films. In her incisive analysis of *Calling the Ghosts*, she observes that the film "visually excises Serb atrocities, diminishing their importance as registers of the real by supplementing them and then obliterating them with the testimonies of the women. Words of women destroy male nationalist imagery and imaginaries. In the end, *Calling the Ghosts* disarms the Serbs by burying their images through testimony" (2000, 76). But, as she also importantly notes: "Sounds and image traces do not retreat, but repeat in dreams and nightmares. They burrow deep, tunneling into the psyche, history, and archives" (77). Although oral and written human rights testimonies may shift attention from the visualization of suffering, individual testimonies are shaped by culturally available scripts and an international moral economy attached to an identity-based politics of recognition.

*Calling the Ghosts* highlights how the trauma of rape warfare intrudes into the domestic and the seemingly private space of the unconscious. Sitting at a kitchen table, Cigelj's mother explains that among the effects of the camp on her daughter is her profound anxiety when people walk behind her while she is eating. During this conversation, Cigelj's son gets up from the dinner table and walks behind her, to no apparent effect. The ordinariness of the visual scene speaks to the belatedness and often invisibility of trauma in the spaces of daily life. Rape and other acts of violence in the Balkans were deliberate attempts by Serbian paramilitary forces and the army to destabilize communities by violating bodies and the domestic spaces that contain them. If the domestic signals a private space, rape warfare violently destroys that illusion. *Calling the Ghosts* invokes domestic imagery but complicates expectations about the maternal. Throughout the film, Cigelj's concerns revolve around her son. Yet domestic ideals are destabilized here because this young man continually speaks about the need to care for and protect his mother. Even when small children appear in this film, their vulnerability and suffering is contextualized through images of community. A series of scenes shows Cigelj, now working with a UN agency collecting testimonials, talking with young women surrounded by or holding one or more children. Instead of the vulnerability frequently emphasized in photojournalism, these scenes promote an ideal of empowerment and agency through the presence of Cigelj, the witness, and through the multiple scenes of testimonials that work against individualizing trauma. This culminates in a scene in which over a dozen children gather with Cigelj to have their picture taken. After numerous scenes of survivors speaking and crying, often with children, it is evident that these children themselves are survivors. And yet they move around, joke, and pose as people often do when they gather for a photograph.

Similarly one of the earliest scenes in *Calling the Ghosts* uses Cigelj's and Sivac's home movies and childhood memories of Prijedor to depict past moments of multiethnic middle-class community. Grainy, black-and-white film shows children on swing sets, people swimming in a river on a sunny day, and a backyard family picnic. These images, which evoke a peaceful childhood in which different ethnic groups swam and raised their children together, have a sentimental value in their association of women with the domestic. Yet these are not merely utopian or traditional images. At work here is not a melancholic rhetoric of loss, nor a narcissistic response that subsumes the lost other into oneself, reproducing the dialectical self-other struggle for recognition. Rather, these scenes point to the formation of communities not premised on identity alone. Rape warfare was one of many strategies whose goal was to "undermine the ethnic mixing that had been openly encouraged in Tito's Yugoslavia, where intermarriage had become increasingly common and people had really begun to see themselves as 'Yugoslavs' rather than Serbs, Croatians, Macedonians, and so forth"

(Boose 2002, 73–74). Rhetorical sentimentality also functions as an acknowledgment of the shifting identities of the two major characters, and how their look back is a return with a difference. The fact that former ties and multiple loyalties have become fractured by a resurgent nationalism is itself an expression of the crisis of identity of the nation-state. As *Calling the Ghosts* makes clear, ethnic genocide inscribes nationalist identities on individual bodies, upon which such acts of violence are literally dependent for their validity. At the same time, nationalist and internationalist forms of identity politics have been relied upon, and to a certain degree have been "complicit in the constitution of realities they merely claim to describe" (D. Campbell 1998, 56). Additionally, the alignment between territory and identity has limited political discussions and responses, and, as David Campbell puts it, has "helped legitimate and sustain geopolitical positions of extreme nationalists" (80).

Stevan Weine identifies two common explanatory frames invoked to describe the conflicts in Bosnia-Herzegovina. The first frames these conflicts as the "perpetuation of ancient ethnic hatred" and describes the region as held "captive to historical memories of ethnic atrocities" (1999, 1). The second frames Bosnia as "a utopian multi-ethnic society that suffered from sequential betrayals. . . . The problem lies not in Bosnia . . . but . . . in the Serbian and Croatian nationalists who raped an innocent Bosnia; and in the international community . . . which stood by and did less than nothing to stop the killing" (1–2). According to Weine, neither explanation is satisfactory, because neither accounts for the complex social functions of memories of collective trauma (2).[28] Cigelj alludes to this very point at the end of *Calling the Ghosts*, when she says: "The world watches coldly while everything passes through women's bodies. . . . When they were killing and raping older women, they were killing and raping living history; when they were raping younger women they were destroying future generations." The claim that they are "killing and raping living history" suggests that it is not only material bodies that are violated, but that these violations "leave the trace of an incision right on the skin; more than one skin, at more than one age" (Derrida 1996, 20). This claim also points to the use of rape as a form of ethnic genocide. One of the specific characteristics attributed to the ultra-nationalist Serbian policy of genocidal rape was the use of rape as a means of enforcing pregnancy and eventual childbirth. But, as Beverly Allen notes, "in the case of enforced pregnancy, its illogical reasoning is founded on the negation of all cultural identities of its victims, reducing those victims to mere sexual containers" (1996, 100). Within the context of such theories, we must ask what victims of rape warfare would gain if they were to give up the identity of trauma. As Katherine Stiles aptly notes: "One of the etiologies of trauma is that the subject cannot help being attached to her experience, since that trauma is simultaneously part of and often lost to memory. That is, attachment to the trauma is part of the trauma."[29]

In *Forgetting Children Born of War*, R. Charli Carpenter argues that the inattention by the international community and governmental and non-governmental organizations to the human rights of children born of wartime rape in Bosnia-Herzegovina was based on a construal of these children as symptoms of sexual trauma and "symbols of human wrongs" rather than as subjects of human rights law (2010, 52). Carpenter's case study reveals the myriad political, cultural, and legal forces that condition these representational silences and a profound paradox at the heart of the battle for the recognition of gendered violence and rape as a war crime in international law. Transnational advocacy networks, she points out, were conditioned in the 1990s to view children born of wartime rape as a "side effect of war rape rather than a population of concern for children's advocates in their own right" (2). For instance, the emphasis on forced pregnancy—a legal construct first articulated on the basis of these mass rapes—inadvertently pitted children's rights against women's rights and kept rape survivors as the advocacy focal point (42). *Forgotten Children* therefore draws attention to how advocacy issues emerge from and are attached to existing institutional discourses on trauma and violence (43).

## The Postcard as a Scene of Address

One of the final scenes of *Calling the Ghosts* features Cigelj and Sivac's trip to The Hague for the opening of the ICTY's prosecution of crimes of ethnic violence. The convening of the tribunal featured Judge Elizabeth Odio Bento addressing the panel of jurists. In the film, she states that this is the first time in human rights law that rape has been listed as a human rights violation, and she says emphatically: "There can be no justice if there is no justice for women." At this moment, when rape becomes recognized as a human rights violation, women who are rape victims become distinct subjects of international human rights law. They become postnational citizen-subjects in the sense that their identities are not defined exclusively by the nation-state. Their citizenship and identities, however, are not defined solely in terms of suffering and injury either. *Calling the Ghosts* works against a dichotomous conception of women's agency between those who act and those who are acted on. The film exemplifies how women's agency, as Inderpal Grewal puts it in another context, is "differentially constructed within formations that come not only from state and nation, but also from geopolitics, economics, religion, sexuality," and so on (1998, 516). Human rights testimonies can, and often do, serve to claim a legal identity, especially when the context for the testimony is juridical. But human rights testimonies also function in extrajuridical contexts, as acts of memorialization and as sites of healing and cultural resistance. If one of the rhetorical appeals of a documentary like *Calling the Ghosts* is the hope of social justice and the promise of human rights, the film also foregrounds the fact that the juridical does not heal the wounds of atrocity or loosen attachments to identity, and in the process undermines the instrumentality of human rights discourse. *Calling the Ghosts* reveals how human rights claims and social desires for retributive justice are dependent on configurations of identity as "wounded attachments" (to use W. Brown's term [1995b, 199]), a configuration that supports a dialectical politics of recognition—even as the documentary seeks to counter that dependency.[30] Similarly, Julie Mertus prompts us to question the unequivocal endorsements of legal responses to rape by "the champions of 'universal justice'" in her analysis of instances of public testifying at the ICTY that reproduced women's victimization (2004, 112). What becomes clear here are the links between a dialectical politics of recognition and the political aesthetics of traumatic realism.

Walking through an amusement park in The Hague, Cigelj and Sivac select a postcard from several large racks. They send the card to former friends of Sivac with whom she had worked before the war, with a message that reads: "We hope that you will join us shortly in this lovely city." Cigelj and Sivac use The Hague as a symbol of human rights to remind the postcard recipients, and the viewer, of the (promised) ability of international law to hold accountable those responsible for ethnic genocide. This message thus both remarks and reclaims shared identity categories between Cigelj and Sivac and their former friends, Bosnian Serbs. The postcard signifies women victimized by rape warfare as juridical subjects, a rhetorical move that reclaims a collective identity in opposition to the degrading and dehumanizing denial of subjectivity produced by acts of violence and torture (see Scarry 1985). This collective identity is asserted, in part, through the articulation of injury and justice within the literal and figurative space of international human rights law. Interestingly, the articulation of the juridical subject here is packaged within the rhetoric of tourist and consumer culture. The postcard as an image metaphor signifies a chosen, rather than a coerced, mobility—yet in this scene, it also signifies experiences of displacement and enforced movements.[31] The postcard reveals tensions between a return home and continued displacement. It is sent from a place other than one's home, indicating movement away from the domestic sphere, a self-consciously ironic move for refugees forced to flee their homes. In this way, the postcard signifies both movement and the preservation of borders. The limited writing space coupled with the mobility of the mail resonates with the imposition of geopolitical borders as well as their transgression.

The postcard scene in *Calling the Ghosts* also reproduces the process of making the private text public. The postcard is a rhetorical situation—an open letter—that has a destiny, an addressee, and an audience. But the rhetorical situation is ungovernable; the postcard can be intercepted, interrupted, read by unintended audiences. For Jacques Derrida, the "tragedy" is that "everything becomes a postcard" that never reaches its destination (1987, 23), which speaks to the inadequacy of representation, the limits of narratability, and the risks of speaking out. The public reproduction and exposure of the private represented by the postcard point to yet another risk of testimonial travel: the anxiety and material consequences that surround its interception and reception. Will the postcard reach its destination? Who might intercept it and its message along the way? Hence, we need to consider, in both the literal and theoretical sense, the "irreducible twists in any sending system" (Bass 1987, xii). What role do we play as interceptors of the postcard, as international witnesses of the testimonies of victims of rape warfare?

The postcard scene prompts us to think about how the global economy and international politics, including the interests of the United States, have intervened in supposedly local conflicts, and how such conflicts are configured rhetorically. For instance, the scene might be used as an occasion to formulate an intercontextual rhetorical approach to transnational reading and viewing practices that does not simply intercept or colonize the other. Human rights testimonies, like human rights images, risk voyeurism and commodification, and I do not want to minimize these risks. However, the "you" to whom the human rights testimonies are addressed also open up the possibility for alternative forms of listening, witnessing, and "unforeseen memory" (Simon 2000, 19). Human rights testimonies ask us to consider, as Roger Simon puts it in another context, "how and why it would matter if accounts of systematic violence and its legacies were part of [our] memorial landscapes?" (17). We might view this embodiment an instantiation of the intersubjectivity of memory and witnessing.

If we take our cue from scholars who address the methodological and ethical challenges posed by human rights testimonies, we might begin to fashion a rhetorical witnessing attuned to the national, cultural, and discursive frameworks and limitations of our disciplinary orientations and methodologies. For example, Renata Jambresic Kirin, a Croatian feminist scholar, frames her study of the testimonies of displaced persons of Croatian and Serbian nationality not as a search for something "'sensationally tragic,' silenced and kept hidden from the public eye, and finally scholarly revealed" (1996, 67). Instead, Kirin suggests that our goal, as feminist scholars and human rights advocates, should be not "just to turn silence into speech that compels listeners, but to change the nature and direction of exile discourse . . . to turn the 'passive' voice . . . into an active powerful one, which can, with force of argument, participate in political discourses from the local to the parliamentary level" (67–68).

If we look at rhetorical identification and the politics of recognition as fundamentally social processes that presume both discontinuity and continuity with the past, we come to realize the need for representations that do not simply turn passive or silent voices into compelling speech, or reproduce the traumatic real, but that reconfigures witnessing in rhetorical and ethical terms. *Calling the Ghosts* suggests that the international community, including international human rights communities, needs to better negotiate the enormous risks of identification and the consumption of the spectacle of female victimization. This entails an awareness of the ongoing need for a call to action predicted upon the incompleteness of the present and the ungovernability of the past. The differentiated politics of recognition and reflexive witnessing that *Calling the Ghosts* puts forth may provide a model for the emergence of new transnational publics to offset the nationalist politics of recognition and the spectacular gaze of the international community in the face of wars and other violent conflicts.

# CHAPTER FOUR

# Global Sex Work, Victim Identities, and Cybersexualities

Spectacular representations of women as passive and naive victims lured or tricked into sex work are prominent in international human rights campaigns, including feminist antitrafficking campaigns, and in international news media representations of the global sex trade.[1] Western audiences are familiar with this narrative of sex trafficking as one of the most prominent human rights violations; it is a pervasive narrative that situates human rights violations elsewhere.[2] In 2004, Nicholas D. Kristof wrote a series of op-ed pieces for the *New York Times* about his visits to brothels in Poipet, Cambodia, where he posed as a customer to interview two young prostitutes—whose freedom he later purchased by paying off their debt to the brothel owners. Kristof's stated intentions were to "address the brutality that is the lot of so many women in the developing world," an issue that he claims "gets little attention and that most American women's groups have done shamefully little to address."[3] Kristof overlooked feminist organizations that work to counter sex trafficking, and his interaction with these two young women set in motion a paternalistic rescue narrative defined through the very parameters of the global sex trade—the purchase of human beings. Kristof's actions therefore risk constructing advocacy on the same grounds as exploitation. What cultural, political, and economic forces contribute to making particular audiences readily accept such identifications and narratives? For whom, and in what contexts, are such narratives persuasive? To what degree do feminist antitrafficking campaigns promote justice as a politics-of-recognition paradigm through their construction of non-Western women and girls as sympathetic victims in need of rescue? An exploration of these questions reveals the intersection of a Western-inflected human rights internationalism with feminist, securitization, and antimigration agendas.

Feminist antitrafficking campaigns have been framed largely by moral distinctions between those who are considered to be the victims of trafficking and those who choose sex work as a form of survival. This tension in feminist activism between the rights of trafficked victims and of voluntary sex workers highlights the need for a differentiated politics of recognition and an understanding of identification practices as material and rhetorical acts. Feminist antitrafficking campaigns fall on a continuum running from neo-abolitionist campaigns—which use women's testimonies to influence antitrafficking legislation and to resist the movement to legalize prostitution—to campaigns that stress sex workers' agency and implicate discriminatory law enforcement as the major cause of their exploitation (Simmons 1999, 132).[4] Despite ideological differences, all the antitrafficking campaigns, including those that address trafficking as a complex problem involving context-specific issues of migration and labor, rely on women's victimization narratives to structure their rhetorical appeal. To the extent that these campaigns uncritically turn to women's narratives of victimization in making the invisible visible, they ignore the complications of transnational movements and privilege certain rights over others. The right to be protected from violence and exploitation (admittedly a crucial right) is privileged over the right not to live in poverty and the right to control one's sexuality, for instance. The focus on sexual victimization reveals the hegemony in women's human rights discourse of liberal individualism based on one kind of notion of morality and sexuality.

The spectacle of female sexual victimization is a central component of the international women's human rights movement and its focus on violence against women, especially the trafficking of women and girls for sex work. Violence against women became an important topic for transnational social movements in the early 1980s and gained prominence in human rights concerns in 1985, when it became an object of UN activity. In 1983, Charlotte Bunch and Kathleen Barry organized a global feminist workshop in Rotterdam against traffic in women, which situated sexual slavery in a broader debate about women's human rights. Violence against women was also a central part of the platform at the UN Conference on Women in Beijing in 1995. But the danger of restricting such varied practices as battering, incest, rape, and female genital mutilation to a single category—violence against women—or collapsing trafficking and prostitution is that such representations fail to account for the different ways in which women and activists interpret and resist these practices in different regions of the world (Basu 2000, 78).[5] Despite the achievements of transnational feminist activists in engaging a wide range of concerns that affect the lives of women and children, including poverty and the lack of education and health care, spectacular representations of sexual violations of women and girls continue to attract international media attention in part because such stories subscribe to Western myths of deserving victims and to the shaming tactics of human rights organizations. Similarly, transnational feminist activism tends to be publicly recognized when the issue is sexual victimization (82). Ratna Kapur uses methodological terms to frame the challenge of understanding the contrary functions of victimization rhetoric in human rights campaigns: "What is missing from the VAW [violence against women] position, and the writings of scholars . . . who endorse it, is an analysis of how the mechanisms of discursive engagement produce the victim subject and the accounts of violence to which she may be subjected" (2005, 108).

In analyzing the deployment of victimization rhetoric in antitrafficking campaigns, I am not calling for the silencing or repression of narratives of violation; the stories of trafficked and enslaved persons need to be told and heard in a range of contexts. The Freedom Network, a national coalition of antitrafficking organizations and advocates in the United States, notes that to empower trafficked and enslaved persons to gain full access to justice and victim-centered services, organizations must ensure that these persons are perceived, in part, as victims. U.S. legislation on human trafficking requires individuals to prove they were victims of a severe form of human trafficking in order to receive legal benefits and social services.[6] But human rights activists and feminist scholars need to become more attuned to the ways in which strategic and at times uncritical mobilizations of victimization narratives, both verbal and visual, may revictimize the subjects represented and support repressive cultural and political agendas. My goal therefore is to draw attention to women's accounts of violation within the context of feminist antitrafficking video campaigns, paying particular attention to contrasting mobilizations of identity claims and to representations of sex work and the global sex trade that challenge the pathology of recognition—namely, the idea that the oppressed desire recognition by the oppressor—by highlighting multiple, shifting identities. Additionally, we must account for the geopolitical structures and technological developments that affect the mobility and marketability of certain identifications and recognition practices associated with female bodies and sexuality. Rhetorical analysis will not resolve the seemingly incommensurate theoretical and ideological positions taken by advocates and scholars, but it can help us to better understand the politics of recognition that structure the discourse about the global sex trade and antitrafficking campaigns and policies.

## Identifications, Recognitions, and Misrecognitions

At the very same time that identification sets into motion the complicated dynamic of recognition and misrecognition that brings a sense of identity into being, it also immediately calls that identity into question.
—Diana Fuss, *Identification Papers*

The concept of identification occupies a central position in psychoanalytic theory, feminist film theory, and rhetorical theory.[7] Diana Fuss argues: "Identification is a process that keeps identity at a distance, that prevents identity from ever approximating the status of an ontological given, even as it makes possible the formation of an illusion of identity as immediate, secure, and totalizable. . . . Identification inhabits, organizes, and instantiates identity" (1995, 2). Fuss's psychoanalytic view of identification as "the detour through the other that defines a self" (ibid.) echoes Hegel's dialectical formation of self-recognition, which links subjectivity to the incorporation of the other. Feminist film theory is invested in the politics of recognition in its focus on how cinema manipulates spectatorial identifications. In *Desire to Desire*, Mary Ann Doane claims: "The female spectator overidentifies with her image on the screen, binding identification to desire to the point where identification operates for women as 'the desire to desire'—the desire to take on and to inhabit the desire of the other" (quoted in ibid., 7). Kaja Silverman insists that critics account for the "libidinal politics" of identification, the interaction of subjectivity and ideology, and the potential of cinematic identifications to counter oppressive ideologies (1996, 7). In her seminal work, *The Threshold of the Visible World*, she calls for viewing practices that resist incorporative identifications that result in self-affirmation and praises representations that "invest the other with the ability to return the look" (1996, 95). Despite the differences among these theorists, one area of contention that cuts across their work concerns the "ethical-political significance of identification" (Fuss 1995, 8).

Critical of the neo-Aristotelian emphasis on identification as a form of persuasion, Krista Ratcliffe argues that seminal scholars such as Kenneth Burke do not sufficiently account for how cultural differences and disidentifications might function as a place for positive rhetorical exchanges and collective political action (2005, 58). Kenneth Burke argues that difference is foundational to identification: "In being identified with B, A is 'substantially one' with a person other than himself. Yet at the same time he remains unique, an individual locus of motives. ... [T]o begin with 'identification' is ... to confront the implications of division" (1950, 21–22). Ratcliffe insists that in order to generate productive cross-cultural exchanges, we need to recognize the partiality of our visions and become conscious of our mistaken identifications (2005, 73). Burke may not have accounted for productive exchanges based on differences, but he was sensitive to the coercive functions of identifications based on the creation of a common enemy or scapegoat. He was well aware of the politics of recognition and nonrecognition; he knew that the range of possible identifications was limited by context, and by the subject's position in the identity hierarchy. Burke describes how in Nazi Germany faulty identifications (stereotypes) were a means of dehumanizing the other and incorporating the dominant public into the state (1950). The problem with Burke's theory of rhetorical identification is not that it ignores differences, but that it operates in an economy of recognition that repeats the subject-object hierarchy. In the context of this chapter, I foreground the political role of identification in the development of anti-trafficking policies and campaigns and examine how the identifications and the politics of recognition that those policies and campaigns set in motion challenge or reinforce social and political hierarchies. I argue that the problem of human trafficking might be better addressed if activists, policymakers, and scholars were to turn away from identity categories of victim and agent and to consider instead the mobilization of identity claims in action-defined contexts. Such a shift would open up important new ground for thinking through the coalitions and clashes among advocates.

## Feminist Antitrafficking Campaigns

Recent feminist antitrafficking campaigns' emphasis on victimization narratives can be understood, in part, as a consequence of the primacy of violence against women as an organizing device in the international women's human rights movement. When that violence became a prominent focus of the movement in the early 1980s, it helped to counteract historical divisions between Western feminists, who emphasized discrimination against women, and feminists in the developing world, who focused on development and social justice and their effects on both men and women. The rhetorical appeal of the transnational identity of women as victims of oppression is persuasive. Margaret Keck and Kathryn Sikkink suggest that the issue of "bodily harm resonate[s] with the ideological traditions of Western liberal countries like the U.S. and Western Europe [and] with basic ideas of human dignity common to most cultures. . . . Issues of bodily harm also lend themselves to dramatic portrayal and personal testimony that are such an important part of network tactics" (1998, 205).

In the course of creating sympathetic visibility[8] for women and girls coerced and trafficked into the sex trade, antitrafficking campaigns often isolate women and children as objects to be seen and then rescued. Women and girls in the sex industry not only become instruments of pathos but also evidence—proof—of the need for antitrafficking agencies and policies. Neoabolitionist antitrafficking campaigns, such as that of the Coalition against Trafficking in Women (CATW), mobilize women's testimonies of victimization as a means of influencing antitrafficking legislation to resist the movement to legalize prostitution as a form of work, and of making the harm of prostitution visible. In CATW's campaign materials, experiential narratives appeal to a moral understanding of human rights premised on the coherence of "women" as a universal category. Despite recognition of women's consent to sex work, CATW claims that prostitution "reduces all women to sex" and therefore that all prostitution is exploitative (http://www.catw international.org). CATW employs a broad definition of prostitution, which includes casual sex, work in a brothel or escort agency, military prostitution, sex tourism, the selling of mail-order brides, and trafficking in women.[9]

In its representation of sex workers as victims, CATW's campaign video *So Deep a Violence: Prostitution, Trafficking, and the Global Sex Industry* (2000) highlights the global and local contexts and forces (such as poverty and sexism) that drive women into sex work and the material forces that constrain women's choices. But the video does not expand upon the contextual forces in its portrayal and identification of women as victims. In other words, an ethos of individual victimization takes precedence over a contextual understanding. Close-ups of sad and angry faces, along with the testimonies of women and children who were beaten and confined, frame the video's portrayal of "prostitution as a form of violence against women and . . . a human rights violation." According to the testimonies, these women have "little or no sexual autonomy." Women are seen as radically naive. The video claims, for instance, that they "don't understand that the mail-order bride marketers are promoting women of their country as subordinate domestic and sexual servants." The testimonies of women provide evidence that they were duped and trapped into prostitution. As one woman, a former sex worker, puts it: "I felt trapped, like I had no other choice." She continues: "We have no resources or money to create our own business . . . [prostitution] is a survival strategy. . . . I just wanted to live a normal life." This woman's narrative alludes to contextual constraints, including the lack of economic opportunity, but the larger abolitionist argument places little or no responsibility on those contextual constraints.

*So Deep a Violence* also highlights the role of men in the proliferation of prostitution and as victims of its ideology. An unnamed "expert" and CATW activist notes that prostitution "teaches men and boys that women are simply things, commodities to be used for sex." Another unnamed CATW activist says: "Economic analysis is not enough because it does not address the men, the so-called customers, or the male-dominated values that assume that prostitution is inevitable, a male's rights or a male's needs." Patriarchy is the contextual frame applied here. The commonplace that sex workers or consumers of commercial sex are passive victims of patriarchy assumes a static notion of gender identity attached to victimization—an injury or wound—and ignores the myriad forces and range of identity markers (race, ethnicity, sexual orientation, and so on) that shape human agency and subjectivity.[10] This configuration also produces a static notion of context that does not account for how the economy structures sexual desire and the demand for commercial sex work (A. Wilson 2004).

According to Jo Doezema, an activist and researcher with the Network of Sex Work Projects and a former sex worker, images of "trafficking victims" as naive, innocent young women lured by traffickers bear little resemblance to the realities of the majority of women who migrate for work in the sex industry. Yet, as she notes, "it is easier to gain support for victims of evil traffickers than for challenging structures that violate sex workers' human rights. . . . The picture of the 'duped innocent' is a pervasive and tenacious cultural myth" (1998, 42–43).[11] Moreover, a segment of the antitrafficking lobby depicts "victims of trafficking" as unemancipated, poor, third world women "kidnapped or lured from [their] village[s] with promises of a lucrative, respectable job overseas" (1999, 165). Choice is an option, Doezema claims, that in some antitrafficking campaigns is given only to Western prostitutes (166).[12] At work here is an international, hierarchal politics of status recognition. Many migrant sex workers, she notes, are aware that they will work as prostitutes; what they are lied to about are the slavery-like conditions under which they must work (2000, 24).

Stereotypes of prostitutes as social deviants or as helpless victims maintain their rhetorical appeal because they keep the audience's focus on the other and thereby deflect attention from the national and international policies, economic and sociopolitical forces, and cultural traditions that contribute to the material conditions that drive many women to work in the sex industry. The identification of women solely as victims also serves a crime-control agenda. The persuasiveness of neo-abolitionist campaigns in the current climate, for instance, is achieved through their *kairotic*—that is, timely and opportunistic—association with U.S. national narratives of crisis, vulnerability, and security. The anxiety and panic over the violation of moral and geographic boundaries that characterize neo-abolitionist antitrafficking campaigns might be considered, as Doezema suggests, a modern version of old cultural myths about "white slavery."

Campaigns against white slavery in Europe and the United States in the late nineteenth century attempted to regulate female sexuality under the pretext of protecting women. Then, as now, such claims reflect uncertainties over national identity and fears of women's increased desire for autonomy (Doezema 2000, 23–24).[13] Dominated by repressive moralists, these campaigns forged alliances with religious and social-purity organizations and feminist organizations that sought to abolish prostitution (28). Opportunistic alliances continue to exist today between neo-abolitionist feminists and right-wing groups. Although a range of forces paved the way for the passage of the U.S. Victims of Trafficking and Violence Protection Act of 2000 (TVPA), including the efforts of Senator Paul Wellstone, right-wing and feminist groups coalesced around the passage to advance their own political agendas. As Anna-Louise Crago notes: "A successful joint campaign was mounted to ensure that the TVPA would not only condemn forced labor and forced prostitution but condemn sex work as a whole—forced or not" (2003).[14] For instance, on 15 January 2003, the United States Agency for International Development (USAID) notified organizations around the world that no funds would go to antitrafficking projects that advocate "prostitution as an employment choice or advocate or support the legalization of prostitution" (quoted in ibid.).[15] The U.S. government is not alone in its antiprostitution abolitionist agenda but is joined by feminist groups and right-wing Christian groups. As Laura Lederer, the former senior advisor on Trafficking in Persons for the Office for Democracy and Global Affairs of the U.S. Department of State, puts it, faith-based groups have brought "a fresh perspective and a biblical mandate to the women's movement. Women's groups don't understand that the partnership on this issue has strengthened them, because they would not be getting attention internationally otherwise" (quoted in ibid.). Likewise, Donna Hughes, the education and research coordinator at CATW (1994–1996), in her response to the new USAID policy, states: "The challenge now is to implement these landmark [antiprostitution] policies in order to free women and children from enslavement" (quoted in ibid.).

Such couplings, however, can have serious consequences. For example, Josephine Ho from ZiTeng, a sex workers' rights group in Hong Kong, notes how domestic policies designed for their national appeal can be imposed on other nations:

First-world feminists and women's NGOs . . . have now joined with UN workers and other international organizations in characterizing Asian sex work as nothing but the trafficking in women and thus is to be out-lawed and banned completely . . . the immense power of Western aid, coupled with the third-world states' desire for modernization . . . [has led to interpretations of] all forms of women's migration toward economic betterment and sex work as mere trafficking. (quoted in ibid.)

One possible outcome of the new USAID policy—beyond the reproduc-tion of paternalistic rescue and rehabilitation narratives, as Crago rightly notes—is the prospect that USAID will give financial support only to orga-nizations with antimigration agendas (Crago 2003). To collapse the terms *trafficking* and *prostitution* is also to downplay the role of migration in un-derstanding the increase in human trafficking, as well as to eclipse the men, women, and children trafficked for other labor than sex work. In addition to the trafficking of women and young girls for sex work, men, women, and children are trafficked for sweatshop labor, domestic labor, marriage, and, in the case of children, for illegal adoptions.

Many antitrafficking campaigns that advocate the decriminalization of prostitution find the voluntary-forced distinction problematic because it as-sumes that voluntary prostitutes don't have rights: only forced prostitutes (trafficked women) have rights that have been violated. In their 1997 re-port *Trafficking in Women, Forced Labour and Slavery-Like Practices in Mar-riage, Domestic Labour, and Prostitution*, Marjan Wijers and Lin Lap-chew (1997) argue that the forced-free distinction and its mobilization negates sex workers' rights to self-determination and oversimplifies the complex-ity of women's agency as both victims and agents.[16] Similarly, the Global Alliance against Traffic in Women (GAATW) campaign importantly argues for the application of human rights principles in order to address traffick-ing as a complex problem that involves context-specific issues of migration and labor. GAATW aims to combat the restrictive trends of crime-control campaigns and neo-abolitionist agendas, which the organization argues in-fringe on the rights and protection of trafficked persons. GAATW's position is that trafficking as a concept is insufficient because it does not account for the link between trafficking and migration.[17] *Bought and Sold: An In-*

*vestigative Documentary about the International Trade in Women* is directed by Gillian Caldwell (a lawyer and filmmaker born and based in the United States, and a former executive director of Witness)[18] and Steven Galster (a U.S.-born animal-rights activist and director of WildAid's operations in Thailand). The video represents a more mediated view and integrated approach to the politics of recognition than *So Deep a Violence* in its focus on the experiences of migrant women, its attention to economic and social circumstances that enable and support the global sex trade, and its embrace of GAATW's definition of trafficking (Caldwell and Galster 1997). Caldwell and Galster made *Bought and Sold* while they worked with the Global Survival Network (a group whose investigative work focuses on exposing environmental and human rights abuses). The video is based on a two-year secret investigation of the trafficking of women from the newly independent states of the former Soviet Union. The video argues that the transition from communism to capitalism throughout Russia and Eastern Europe and decline of the economic status of women have both contributed to the increase in human trafficking. Sex workers go into sex work not because they are just naive but also because the transition to capitalism in the Eastern bloc has led to women's economic decline: "Poverty like this leads women throughout the world to migrate for work. But they face limited opportunities and substantial risks." *Bought and Sold* focuses specifically on the representational strategies of recruiters who position women in competition with each other: "White women from the former Eastern bloc are regarded as the hottest new commodity in the sex trade and are being marketed as alternatives to Asian and Latin American women"—they are "from a modern, yet meager society."

*Bought and Sold* also has a strong thread of victimization narratives, which amplifies its call for both the recognition and the protection of trafficked women: these women are all "lured" with promises of a better life and recruited by friends, and some women are portrayed as seduced by the profession of sex work. However, the video negotiates the agent-victim and economic-cultural binaries carefully, deploying victim narratives in ways that portray the complexities of trafficking and the issue of transnationality. In other words, the video presents the kairos of identification in relation to the geopolitical conditions and contexts that shape women's actions. These conditions include growing unemployment and declining economies in their home countries, which drive many women to seek work abroad; the recruitment of women through front companies that present a legal façade as travel, modeling, and marriage agencies; and debt-bondage, or contracts between trafficking networks and women. Travel debts can range from $1,000 to over $10,000, and women also incur debts for food and housing, as well as financial penalties for misbehavior. Finally, *Bought and Sold* illustrates the roles of international networks of organized crime and government complicity—often related to traffickers' bribes of national security units and local law enforcement. *Bought and Sold* exposes how the systems meant to protect individuals facilitate their exploitation. The Global Survival Network emphasizes training law enforcement officials not to treat trafficked persons as criminals, but as victims of human rights abuses.

*Bought and Sold* does not fall into the trap of representing women as only duped victims, even though some of the women's stories fit that mold. For instance, the video's opening scene depicts the agency of a woman (Lowena) in dealing with a man who is trying to lure her into sex work and who is consciously choosing a life in sex work abroad. The voice-over says: "Lowena is ready to go. She is twenty-two. She is willing to work as an escort abroad. She hopes it is her ticket to a life of adventure and glamour. This film is made for people like her." Moreover, in its call to action at the end (a section titled "What Can Be Done?"), the video calls for a variety of strategies by activists, governments, and media groups. Besides insisting that trafficking be recognized as a human rights violation, *Bought and Sold* demands: "Governments must stop treating sex workers as illegal migrants." Instead, governments should provide stays of deportation as well as services for sex workers, including health care, education and training, and witness protection. In other words, the video represents advocacy as a necessary transnational collaboration among many sectors.

*Bought and Sold* has been distributed to more than five hundred NGOs in countries around the world and to U.S. embassies. The Global Survival Network identifies multiple audiences for the video, including at-risk women—namely, those from countries undergoing socioeconomic transition; NGOs; governmental and intergovernmental organizations; university students; the general public; and the media.[19] One of the major pedagogical goals of the film is to foster an understanding of trafficking as a human rights abuse, in order to promote the development of policies that offer protections and compensation to victims and governmental and nongovernmental programs that address the socioeconomic causes of the problem and to counter media coverage that sensationalizes or dehumanizes women whose human rights are being abused). As my analysis of the videos of feminist antitrafficking campaigns suggests, the timeliness of certain identifications and the recognitions and misrecognitions they activate might be understood as adaptive, strategic, or motivated by and meaningful only in certain circumstances.[20]

## A Differentiated Politics of Recognition?

The manifesto of the Mahila Samanwaya Committee (1998) exemplifies the strategic mobilization of identification practices. The manifesto also illustrates some of the social and political processes by which certain identities are recognized or resisted, and by which certain individuals or groups are classified as human and therefore deserving of human rights. The stated aim of the committee, comprised of sex workers from Calcutta and Howrah, is to attain "social dignity, justice and security for the sex workers and their children" (Pal et al. 1998, 202):

> We are recognized for the business we profess—a trade that has continued since time immemorial. . . . Many tricks are manipulated to conceal the wicked propensities of men. These hapless women are marked as fallen. . . . When we are not even accepted as humans, can we expect to be honored as citizens of this country? . . . Whether we like it or not, we have been identified and continue to be identified by the same name . . . our profession is our life and death as also our caste and creed. We cannot aspire to differentiate. (200–201)

Here the committee highlights how sex workers are configured as the "fallen ones" (200), drawing attention to status recognitions and the difficulty for sex workers in shedding this label due to social stigma. The committee both critiques the essentialist politics of recognition imposed on its members by dominant groups and imagines the possibility of a more differentiated politics of identity. However, the material conditions of isolation—

with sex workers in cubbyholes in the red-light district—fractures the rhetorical collectivity and potential solidarity among them: "As the sun sets everyday, we are out on the streets, standing in close proximity to each other, soliciting clients. We are close, but why are we not attempting to remove the barrier amongst ourselves?" (202). The manifesto employs a dual rhetorical address: the committee speaks directly to fellow sex workers and at the same time to readers positioned as listeners or eavesdroppers. It continues: "For long we have lived in terror, it is time we overcame this fear and fought for our rights. . . . We do not ask for much, except to be accepted as human beings" (ibid.). The rhetorical appeal to women as a unified group—rhetorical identification—has been a fundamental strategy of women's human rights campaigns, which anchor their call to action in the experiences of individual victims. The phrase "we cannot aspire to differentiate" foregrounds the necessity of a universal appeal to a common humanity—in this case, the necessity of claiming a normative gender identification—and, at the same time, highlights identity as embodied rhetorical action, a configuration that frames identification practices and the recognitions and misrecognitions they set in motion as both symbolic and material struggles.

Joshua Price urges us to consider the situational nature of sex workers' range of identifications and the "logics that govern identification" (2001, 20). He also points out the hypocrisy of the private-public split—another dimension of an essentialist politics of recognition—as it applies to sex workers and their rights. He argues: "The public sphere is not amenable to the context of living sex workers, hence, voicing in that sphere promotes self-betrayal" (16). And he notes: "Publicly their voice has no authority, their testimony is disbelieved, while on the street they are silenced. In private spaces, they serve as johns' confidantes or as police informers" (8). Price calls for a different kind of listening, which urges the "cultivat[ion] of an ear for the highly contextualized subject positioning of different actors, including discursive positionings that ought to be critiqued" (30) and the recognition of alternative rhetorical spaces that counter the logics of an imagined bourgeois public sphere. The shift here is to listen to the invocations of identity as action rather than as characteristics of the rhetor (32). Cultivating this ear requires us to become more attuned to the strategic mobilization or transformation of normative identity narratives, cultural myths, and rhetorical commonplaces by advocates on all sides of the debate. The concept of identity as action also suggests that we revisit the identity-based politics of recognition and the cosmopolitan rhetoric that have come to characterize Western feminist scholarship and human rights activism.

## Cybersexualities and Cosmopolitan Attachments

Ursula Biemann's experimental videos *Remote Sensing* (2001b) and *Writing Desire* (2001c) trace the routes and displacements of female bodies in the global sex and mail-order industries and provide an opportunity to explore further how transnational movements and migrations trouble the cultural politics of recognition that inform liberal feminist antitrafficking campaigns and Western-centric cosmopolitanisms. Biemann is a white Western experimental videographer, activist, and scholar, born and based in Zurich. Her videos are distributed by Women Make Movies, in New York City—which targets an educational market, selling chiefly to universities. But her videos have also been shown at documentary festivals and in art exhibitions, and NGOs have used them in lobbying and to promote debates. *Writing Desire* was made for an art exhibition in New York City on the body image in bio- and cybertechnology, but it has been frequently shown in art exhibitions on globalization processes. Biemann says that she is interested in revealing the constructedness of different positions articulated by NGOs rather than in reducing issues to messages that can be used to bring about change on a legislative level.[21]

Throughout *Remote Sensing*, the screen is divided into parts that show multiple images and offer different viewing positions, including a close-up video shot of a space shuttle taking off, a distant view of a weather satellite, and what seems to be an aerial view from a fighter jet. The latter situates the viewer in the pilot's seat, gazing through a targeting device. The divided screen, like the title *Remote Sensing*, refers to the abstraction of geography and gender by satellite technology as well as the contradictions produced by and within transnational publics generated through the production, circulation, and reception of representations of global sex work (see fig. 8).

*Remote Sensing* points out how global capital and technologies sexualize and facilitate women's movement into the sex industry and at the same time police geographical boundaries (see fig. 9).[22] The film insists that stricter

HONG KONG
SUNRISE : 6:08 AM
SUNSET : 6:42 PM
MOONRISE : 8:54 PM
MOONRISE : 7:42 AM
CIVIL TWILIGHT : 5:47 AM 7:04 PM
TIDAL: 10:43 AM(2.1M)I@1:47 PM(.8M)

香港天文台

8. Commuting between a Manila slum and the Hong Kong Bunny Club. Still from
*Remote Sensing*. By permission of Ursula Biemann.

migration policies and control of borders will not necessarily reduce the
trafficking of women. Rather, the result might be an increase in prostitution
and trafficking worldwide, because states' policies forbid women to migrate
for work in other professions.

*Remote Sensing* reports: "Five hundred thousand women migrate into
the European sex industry every year. Two-thirds come from postsocialist
countries." As the narrator notes, migration laws reveal "the place of sex
in . . . national space. These laws protect the flourishing sexual life of male
citizens as privileged, and a source of power."[23] Focusing on the border between the former East Germany and the Czech Republic, "where two nations come together, one united, one dissolved," the camera moves down
a long road—the famous highway between the two countries—sparsely
populated by cars. It is winter, and snow covers everything (see fig. 10).
The voice-over says: "Women standing on the roadside come from as far

9. Travel schedule from Moscow to Tel Aviv, through the Bosphorus. Still from *Remote Sensing*. By permission of Ursula Biemann.

away as Bulgaria, Ukraine, and elsewhere. Glass house brothels, where girls dance naked under disco lights, or simply stand out in the cold, dark forest" to await their German tourist consumers. The video also challenges the victim-agent binary through its portrayal of the identity of sex workers at the border between the two countries: "Here, everything is transitory, no sentimentality, no clinging to the past. The prostitutes are from distant places, many smuggled in, captured, and illegal. They all know that where they are, and what they are, is only temporary. The consumers, the German tourists just passing through—they too are aware that their time here is only temporary. Everything resonates with impending change." Hence, this segment suggests that both feminine and masculine identity is constructed, and that male desire is also a result of social conditioning.

Neither of Biemann's videos resolves the victim-agent binary, but both do expose the oppositional logics, cultural values, and public policies that

10. In a brothel on the highway from the Czech Republic to Germany. Still from *Remote Sensing*. By permission of Ursula Biemann.

create and sustain such categories. Bandana Pattanaik, one of the sex workers in *Remote Sensing*, says:

> Seeing them as victims creates a lot of sympathy and therefore people find it easier to accept. If I'll say that I have been forced into prostitution, people say, oh poor thing, like let's help her, she is in a really bad situation. But if somebody says I chose to become a prostitute that's very difficult to accept or to understand. Why would you choose to be a prostitute? So many times it's framed in this either-or debate. Either you are a victim or you are an agent. Either you have chosen to be a sex worker or you have been forced into prostitution. And I think there are such large gray areas in between.

Both *Remote Sensing* and *Writing Desire* struggle against the logic of oppositions and reveal just how large the obstacles are to systematic change and processes of resignification, even within transnational feminist advocacy. Despite Biemann's claim that she is not primarily interested in the evidentiary function of representation, or in reinforcing the victim-agent binary, both films include narratives of women lured and tricked into sex work. For instance, *Remote Sensing* focuses on a case involving eight Filipinas who were recruited by a German man and his Filipina wife in Manila. One of the women says: "One morning the recruiter approached me personally and promised me $350 a month if I agreed to work in a restaurant in Germany. We didn't have to pay any placement fees . . . all the fees would be gradually deducted from our salary. At the moment of departure, we noticed that on the ticket it said Nigeria instead of Germany as we believed."

Yet this "lured and tricked" narrative is complicated by several factors, including the narrative of Naomi, whose story ends in Cyprus, where prostitution is legal, and who used the money she earned through prostitution to return home. Like several of the other women presented in the video, Naomi was recruited in Manila and sold into Nigeria. She was then sold into Lome, Toga, before she fled to Cyprus. When Biemann asks Naomi if she has ever had a boyfriend, Naomi responds that she has never had sex without getting paid for it. "No boyfriend . . . someone you loved?" Biemann asks again. Naomi clarifies: "I never say to a customer . . . I love you." But she is perplexed by the question: "No boyfriend. But customer, yes. But free, no. Why?" Naomi inhabits a radically different framework than that inherent in Biemann's question. The politics of this exchange resides in the videographer's insertion of the cultural and rhetorical commonplace of the romance narrative.

The audio representation in *Remote Sensing* provides yet another framing device for the women's experiences. In the case of Filipinas in Nigeria, Biemann includes a strong mediating device, an English voice-over—which she seldom uses in her work. She has said that she typically aims to let her subjects, who include former sex workers and women employed by NGOs, speak and analyze the international situation, rather than theorizing about their experiences in a voice-over.[24] This voice-over might be read as an ethical breech by the Western white videographer in representing sex workers in the global south (a breech that reproduces the social dominance of the global north). But we might also view this editorial decision as evidence of the representational challenges of transnational feminist advocacy and of the lure of a feminist cosmopolitan analytic.

As its deployment in postcolonial theory, feminist theory, and cultural anthropology suggests, the term *cosmopolitan* reveals contradictory uses and meanings (R. Wilson 1998, 352). On the one hand, the term has been used negatively to signify liberal self-invention, tourism, and global travel, and to refer to carnivalesque cosmopolitanism (Buell 1994). Cosmopolitans are associated with the movement of capital, with "knowing no boundaries" (Robbins 1998b, 249; also see C. Kaplan 2001). On the other hand, the term has been used positively to categorize a new class of transnational cosmopolitans (Hannerz 1990), and to refer to migration, diasporic movements, and refugees, as in James Clifford's notion of the "discrepant cosmopolitan" (1992, 108). The philosophical concept of cosmopolitanism can be traced to ancient Greek and Roman thought. The Cynic philosopher Diogenes (404–323 BC) coined the term "citizen of the world." Martha Nussbaum observes: "Diogenes refused to be defined by local origins and group memberships" (1998, 6). The Stoic philosophers over the next few centuries followed his lead in arguing that we each dwell in both local communities and the community of human aspiration (7). Broadly speaking, cosmopolitanism upholds "the view that we are citizens of the world, members of a common humanity, and that we should pay no more regard to the claims of our co-nationals than to those of any other human beings regardless of where they happen to reside" (D. Miller 1995, 3).

Invocations of cosmopolitanism in human rights education and politics tend to invoke modernist philosophical conceptions of the cosmopolitan, especially Kant's project for perpetual peace, in which he called for international commerce as a form of sociability and a way to activate, as Pheng Cheah puts it, the "humanizing processes of self-cultivation" (2006, 81). Such invocations emphasize a universal humanism that transcends particularism (19). For instance, Nussbaum calls for a cosmopolitan approach to civic education based on the view that we are all citizens of the world and members of a common humanity. For her, literature and the arts play a "vital role [in] cultivating powers of imagination that are essential to citizenship" (1998, 85). But cosmopolitanism, as I have argued elsewhere (Hesford 2010), can function as an alibi for neoliberalism and national interests in a global guise.[25] To address the risks of cosmopolitanism for human rights politics, feminist scholars and advocates need to engage its all-consuming vision and acknowledge the differential conditions of mobility and the shifting dominance relations among men, women, and children in diverse locations. Moreover, we need to acknowledge that human rights law and culture work together to sustain normative frameworks of inclusion and exclusion, and that cultural predilections and entrenched conceptions of identity and difference shape an individual's imaginative capacity to identify with others (see chapter 1).

Biemann generates a critical ambivalence through her critique of the victim-agent binary and her simultaneous inclusion of the testimonies of women victimized by the sex industry, which is indicative of her navigation of cosmopolitan and transnational feminist analytics. This ambivalence illuminates the representational challenges posed by the rhetorical conventions of a human rights internationalism based on UN discourses and treaties for transnational feminist scholars and advocates, especially the challenge of how to document victimization. For instance, *Remote Sensing* exposes the risks of documentary techniques in revealing multiple layers of surveillance: "Locked up in tiny rooms, confined in semi-darkness, guarded closely, she lives in the ghettos and the bars of the underworld, the semi-world, living a half-life. Guarded step by step, number by number, trick by trick." The camera travels down long, dark corridors of brothels at night, dimly lit by streetlights and the lights from clubs. The corridors echo the "semi-darkness" and the "underworld" quality of the narrator's description of sex workers' lives. The halls are dirty and crowded, choked with prostitutes and potential customers. Because of the danger of filming in this milieu and the fact that the women didn't want to be filmed,[26] the camera does not focus on any individuals. Instead it lingers on women's eroticized body parts—breasts, lips—fragmenting the bodies it seeks to represent. Here the video plays on the cultural expectations that women will be objectified. But we might ask: Are such identifications necessary as forms of persuasion in transnational feminist advocacy? This choice, according to Biemann, is a result of difficult recording circumstances, but it also indicates the embrace and limitations of certain representational strategies and journalistic conventions. These images of captivity progressively dissolve, as later parts of the film speak to more self-motivated decisions to enter the sex trade.

*Writing Desire* suggests that critical agency resides in the strategic mobilization and juxtaposition of dominant discourses and counterdiscourses, and in this way the video draws attention to the fundamental intercontextuality of rhetorical agency. The first scene shows a beach with palm trees, and we hear upbeat music. Over this touristic image, the following lines appear in succession: "Geography is imbued with the notion of passivity." "Feminized national spaces awaiting rescue." "With the penetration of foreign capital." The opening sequence foregrounds the increasing disembodiment of sexuality, the links between sexual desire and electronic communication technologies, and the production of subjectivities through the compressed space of virtual exchanges. This sequence constructs the viewers as consumers: we hear Internet dial-up sounds, then categories and links appear on the screen, representing a search by the categories of country, age, height, weight, and education. The cursor scrolls down a list of third world countries. The link for the Philippines is then opened, and digital representations (photographs and online videos) of young women appear. Women are ranked and described according to their country of origin; in this way the video highlights locational identifications and cultural stereotypes and myths: Women from the Philippines are described as the "most friendly." Women from Brazil are listed as the "best lovers." Women from Thailand are listed as the "most beautiful," and those from Costa Rica as the "most eager to please."

*Writing Desire* focuses on commercialized gender relations on the Internet —namely, the market for mail-order brides and virgins in the former Soviet Union and the Philippines (one of the poorest countries in Southeast Asia). The video argues that women's bodies, as symbols of global products, are racialized as objects of desire waiting to be either conquered or rescued (see fig. 11). At one point in the film, the screen represents an Internet page with the following links: Distant Communication, World Sex, International Women, Travel, and Browse. Distant Communication is opened, and the following text appears. "Every year thousands of happy relationships between Western men and Eastern women begin by electronic communication."

The video implies that new media and technology create mobile subjectivities, make context irrelevant, and in so doing enable alliances that other-

11. Still from *Writing Desire*. By permission of Ursula Biemann.

wise might never occur. Yet it also portrays the fantasy that individuals can bridge distance through technology without confronting the consequences of those fantasies: "a stream of desire troubled by nothing." A woman lying across a bed says: "What's interesting about it [e-mail desire] is that you create these love stories in which you are the protagonist.... What is important is the act of writing. While the real bodies are absent, it's all in the writing. That's why the sexual discourse becomes important. It would be wrong to infer that it replaces the body." Instead, the body is "present in the writing." This sequence highlights the challenge of technology in configuring a locational feminism, in which identity is embodied as technology. Here the body and identity become first and foremost rhetorical, highlighting Biemann's feminist agenda of representation—which, as she puts it, is "to bring the representation of women in poverty in connection with high technology and other concepts [such as mobility] that have a progressive high status in our eyes."[27] Although both films attribute some level of agency to the women represented, we might ask whether the act of bringing "women in poverty" before "our" eyes reiterates a cosmopolitanism that once again positions poor women as objects of sight for the privileged gaze.

In the case of *Remote Sensing*, "women become agents of transport and transformation for countries who struggle to make themselves a place on the global chart."[28] The video proposes a link between the proliferation of global sex work and sex tourism and the technology of the Internet, which "capitalizes on this vulnerable set of motivations" (Biemann 2001a, 3). *Writing Desire* fractures presumptions about the stability of identity and geographical contexts, yet it also reminds us that these new technologies foster inequitable material relations and oppressive conditions for much of the world's population.

At one point in the film, the rhetorical strategies that women in the global sex industry employ become strikingly clear. On the screen overlaying videos advertising brides from the former Soviet Union, the following text appears: "she is beautiful and feminine / she is loving and traditional / she is humble and devoted / she likes to listen to mellow music / the smile is her rhetorical gesture / she believes in a lasting marriage / and a happy home / she is a copy of the First World's past." The phrase her "smile is her rhetorical gesture" acknowledges the rhetorical dimensions of identification and agency in the context of transnationality. Biemann notes in her commentary on the film: "To present herself as humble and unambitious, [the woman] denies the desirability of the financial and social rewards of marrying a Western man. Morality remains an economic issue but if women want to be seen as moral at all, they better mask their awareness of their relationship to property, mobility, and privilege" (2001a, 3).

In this sense, *Writing Desire* exposes the foundational Western idea, as Caren Kaplan notes in another context, that "travel produces the self, makes the subject through spectatorship and comparison with otherness" (1996, 36). A critical ambivalence characterizes *Writing Desire*, just as it does *Remote Sensing*. However, the critical ambivalence in *Writing Desire* does not emerge so much from the deployment and critique of victimization narratives as from the portrayal of cosmopolitan conceptions of identity. These conceptions are acquired through travel, virtual or otherwise, as represented in the figure of Maris Bustamante. Bustamante is an artist based in Mexico City who finds an American husband through an Internet dating service. She is a middle-aged, self-identified feminist, widow, mother, university professor, and, as she puts it, "radical of my own will." After an "examination of [the] Mexican environment . . . the 'Cradle of Machismo,'" and after working through "intellectual guilt," she posts her profile on an Internet dating service. She corresponds for six months with a man named John, a lieutenant in the U.S. Marine Corps, whom she later marries and with whom she establishes a new family. Bustamante indicates that the Internet enabled her to suspend judgment and reformulate her expectations: she would not ordinarily have been attracted to a military man. Her narrative is emblematic of the historical trajectory of future promise (construed in familial, heterosexual terms), a narrative that recasts the white, middle-class feminist subject at the center and as normative. She and the lieutenant are pictured in a classic family portrait. The centerpiece of the black-and-white photograph is the father, seated front and center, surrounded by his wife and three teenage children. His wife's hands rest on his shoulder. The whole family is smiling.

Bustamante is depicted as a virtual feminist cosmopolitan, whose worldliness is acquired largely via technology. The position of her story, defined by a conventional narrative arc, affords her character a certain status in *Writing Desire*. We might read this narrative as an example of the idiomatic particularity of contemporary geopolitical feminisms, or of the temporal rhetoric of awakening and rebirth common to second-wave feminism. Either way, Bustamante's narrative highlights the venerable power of rhetorical stasis to usurp the transnational feminist project by reclaiming rhetorical commonplaces and hegemonic notions of freedom, movement, and liberation, and securing normative identifications through structures of opportunity, technology, and privilege. The rhetorical weight of Bustamante's narrative in *Writing Desire* offers a cautionary tale to feminist scholars and human rights advocates about the risks of transference (rhetorical, methodological, and cultural) and the prominence of a cultural cosmopolitanism that construes the global citizen subject as a consumer of difference.

Claudia Colimoro, an advocate for prostitutes' rights, attests to such risks in an interview with Amalia Lucia Cabezas, when she notes the lack of financial support for sex worker advocates in the third world and points out that sex workers do not seem to benefit from academic interest: "There are sociologists, anthropologists and others interested in the different research and education projects. But the sex workers do not benefit. The academics are the ones on the board of directors, not the sexual workers. We need to have a group of academics around. But this does not permit us to advance. They are the ones who go to the congresses, the ones who take the organizations forward. It is a good business for the academics but not for the prostitutes" (1998, 199). I return to the issue of academic appropriation in the following chapter, in my discussion of children as subaltern subjects. Here I want to simply reassert the importance of understanding identity as a field of action because such a view allows us to question the victim-agent binary and to consider the strategic deployment of such contrasts in particular contexts. But if this conceptualization loses all traces of the materiality of identification practices, it risks becoming the methodological equivalent of cultural tourism. Just as we need to look beyond the academic transmission of new conceptions to consider how "social movements appropriate and transform global meanings, and materialize them in local practices" (Thayer 2000, 207–8), we need to understand how identity claims, recognition practices, and localities are produced through the visual and affective economies of the global morality market to which human rights is tethered. The performative contradictions that characterize women's experiences within the global sex trade, as several of the works discussed in this chapter suggest, compel us to read the geopolitics of recognition rhetorically, in terms of the timeliness of certain identifications and their deployment, and to account for the colonial and imperial histories of global sex work and the technologies that continue to position sexual subalterns as objects of sight and surveillance.

# CHAPTER FIVE

# Spectacular Childhoods:
# Sentimentality and the Politics of (In)visibility

The potentially subversive element of childhood agency is kept at bay by
the sentimental and idealized vision that dominates our thinking, at least
as far as human rights instruments and interventions are concerned.
—Jacqueline Bhabha, "The Child"

he development of transnational human rights networks and
international human rights treaties and conventions, including the UN's 1990 Convention on the Rights of the Child (CRC),
has made children's human rights more visible. But what is the
nature of this visibility? To whom are the myriad images of children under
duress addressed? What moral obligations do they solicit? How can we look
at images of children whose basic human rights are not being met and then
look away? What are the ethical and political stakes in circulating images
of endangered children in our media-saturated global morality market? To
what degree has the spectacle of the sexualized girl-child created a new neoliberal subject in the transnational human rights imaginary, extending the
long-standing sentimental tradition in the feminization of childhood?

The media scholar Susan Moeller argues that within the last few decades, children have replaced women "as the public emblems of goodness
and purity"; children have become "the moral referent" and "motives for
action" (2002, 38). In her study of the rhetorical functions of children in
international news, Moeller demonstrates how international media deploy
images of endangered children to dramatize the righteousness of a cause, to
symbolize a nation's identity and future (39), and to "invoke an audience's
sympathy on a plane that appears apolitical or suprapolitical—'purely'
moral" (48). Similarly, Karen Sánchez-Eppler illustrates how children have

been historically depicted as passive recipients of culture rather than as cultural actors, as "vulnerable, innocent, ignorant beings [who] require adult protection and training" (2005, xvii). We also need to consider the hierarchy of children's suffering because domestic U.S. media tend to represent non-white children outside of its borders in more sympathetic terms than those within. This is particularly true for black male youth and the children of illegal immigrants, who are often construed as deviant and unlawful (Wanzo 2009, 190–91).

One of the challenges of establishing political status for children is that under modern law, the possession of rights is premised on the concept of the autonomous individual subject and that subject's capacity to exercise rights; children have not been perceived as autonomous agents but rather as dependent beings (Bryst 2004, 31). The child rights advocate Kate Federle has argued that "if having a right is contingent upon some characteristic, like capacity, then holding the right becomes exclusive and exclusionary" (1994, 343). It was not until the CRC that children were construed as "bearer[s], not merely . . . object[s], of human rights" (Bhabha 2006, 1529). The CRC may recognize the child as a rights holder, but, as Vanessa Pupavac has noted, the convention does not unequivocally position the child as a moral agent capable of exercising those rights (2001, 99). The recognition of the child as an agent with rights, for example, is not necessarily compatible with the other cardinal principle of the CRC—the "best interests" principle (Bhabha 2006, 1528–29).[1]

Despite the child-centered research in anthropology and sociology in the second half of the 1980s—which rejected the notion of childhood as a "state in development psychology or a time of universal dependence and powerlessness" and recognized childhood instead as a "culturally constructed, social phenomenon" (Montgomery 2001, 17), the CRC institutionalizes a Western model of child development preoccupied with individual character and individual causations (Pupavac 2001, 103).[2] Wedded to Western idealized notions of childhood as a universal state of innocence and dependence, the developmental-psychological model tends to isolate children from the socioeconomic conditions in which they live and to fuel the moral crusades of international child organizations that "highlight the suffering of children as a moral failing of their society" (102).

The social investment in children's innocence and moral salvation is nowhere more vivid than it is in U.S. and international news media representations of the problems of child prostitution and child labor.[3] Western media typically project human rights problems outward to expose the ineptitude of other nations, deflecting attention from the United States and issues, such as poverty, that severely impact children's rights.[4] The ideology of innocence that surrounds childhood, the shocking nature of child prostitution, and the fact that children are increasingly subjected to local and global economic forces that exploit their sexuality make children's human rights politically salient yet also voyeuristic. The U.S. news media have not approached child prostitution as a human rights issue, which would necessitate an explicit focus on the role of the state and state actors, but have individualized the problem by focusing on child predators lurking on the Internet and sex tourism.[5] Although images of the sexual exploitation of children appear to capture more media attention than images of other kinds of violence against children, as Henry Giroux points out, "it is not a form of abuse that can only be assessed, as much as the Western media might suggest, through the horrible behavior of sexual predators" (1998, 34). Rather, "such abuse needs to be situated within a broader set of political, economic, and social considerations." The central threat to children worldwide, Giroux suggests, and I concur, "lies not in the figure of the pedophile or sexual predator but in the diminishing public spheres available to children to experience themselves as critical agents" (ibid.).

Lauren Berlant argues that the spectacle of a child suffering—"the wounded image"—"speaks a truth that subordinates narrative: [since the child] has not 'freely' chosen his exploitation; the optimism and play that are putatively the 'right' of childhood have been stolen from him" (1999, 52). However, I argue that it is not narrative that is subordinated by the spectacle of children suffering, but children's agency, including children's *rhetorical agency*, a term I use in this context to refer specifically to children's ability to represent themselves. The spectacle of children suffering relies on certain international and national scripts—such as the rescue narrative and deterministic models of child development—that displace children's negotiations of enveloping discourses and material circumstances and thereby reinforce their disenfranchisement as moral agents and historical actors in the public sphere. Indeed, we need to look at children's agency as "differen-tially constructed" (to use Inderpal Grewal's term) within the transnational human rights imaginary, that is, we need to consider the repertoire of im-ages, narratives, and normative frameworks that mediate children's human rights and children's self-representation of these rights (1998, 516).

When children's human rights are examined, age-old questions about agency arise as methodological issues and ethical challenges. Like tradi-tional notions of the public sphere in Western philosophy and thought, which correlate the democracy and the persuasiveness of public opinion with a sovereign power as the addressee,[6] human rights discourse has not sufficiently accounted for the disaggregation of agency at distinct levels or for interlocutors that do not constitute a national citizenry. Moreover, agency has been considerably romanticized in human rights discourse through its intellectual origins in liberal humanist philosophy. As Carl Herndl and Adela Licona note: "The language of the humanist individual . . . haunts [our] discussion[s] of agency" (2007, 137). In rhetorical studies, agency has traditionally been construed through the concept of intentionality— a concept that depends on an autonomous subject and an identifiable (often understood as a temporally and geographically static) audience and rhetori-cal context. Postmodern critiques of the autonomous subject have usefully troubled the usually static notions of authorship, rhetorical agency, and in-tentionality.[7] Interest in agency is growing in feminist rhetorical studies, as contemporary rhetoricians begin to focus more on who has access to rhe-torical agency (N. Johnson 2002, 1–18) and "how rhetors without taken-for-granted access do, nevertheless, manage to exercise agency" (Geisler 2004, 3). Implicit in such rhetorical work is the important recognition of multiple agencies and heterogeneity in all locations, as well as the consideration of forms of agency that cultural and legal representations make available to or imagine for the subjects represented and their audiences. Thus, to under-stand agency as "a property of the rhetorical event or performance itself" (147) requires us to acknowledge that, as Carolyn Miller points out, "at-tributions of agency may rely on prefabricated conventions, ideologically imposed or culturally given" (2007, 151).

At the same time that the spectacle of the endangered foreign child, spe-cifically the sexualized girl-child, continues to dominate Western media and to function as the glue that binds human rights and humanitarian appeals together, we see the transformation of the spectacle of endangerment into a narrative about children's empowerment, a narrative that is strategically deployed to support a range of political and cultural agendas. In the discourse of human rights education, for example, this empowerment narrative is increasingly linked to a notion of visual literacy, a coming-of-age story about children's capacity to represent themselves in visual forms and media. In many instances, self-representation is framed as a rite of passage that draws children into an imagined cosmopolitan public through the transgression of local boundaries. In my analysis of the documentary *Born into Brothels*, I trace the transformation of the human rights spectacle of childhood victimization into the spectacle of children's empowerment, framed as a form of self-expression, as *Bildung*—"the inner-directed formation of an individual in the image (*Bild*) of a personality prescribed by moral norms" (Cheah 2006, 96). As I argue in the book's introduction, the term *human rights spectacle* refers not to individual images but to the social and rhetorical processes of incorporation and recognition mediated by visual representations and the ocular epistemology that underwrites human rights discourse. Self-representation is an important form of rhetorical agency. But children's self-representations can also serve as a means of self-recognition for the powerful—a representational pattern that shows how children's agency is caught up in the global politics of recognition and economic distribution.

In contrast to Western humanitarian, missionary, and human rights rescue narratives, Heather Montgomery's ethnographic study of child prostitutes in Thailand (2001) and Tareque and Catherine Masud's documentary about the struggles of child workers in Bangladesh (2007) emphasize children's complex identity negotiations as cultural and moral agents. Together, these cases and the truth-telling forms of cultural authority they take (documentary film, photography, and ethnography) reveal an international ambiguity about the meaning of childhood, the political relevance of children as rights holders, and the participation of children as moral agents in imagined and socially recognized publics. The cases in this chapter demonstrate the pressing need for human rights advocates and scholars to recognize children as complex moral and political subjects who must negotiate the economic and social inequities of globalization at the local level. Specifically, one of this chapter's goals is to question moral universalism and its elevation of the depoliticized victim in children's human rights law, and to demonstrate the potentially subversive elements of children's agency when the substance of morality is not innocence but children's sense of familial and social responsibility. I suggest replacing a view of agency as an individual possession and the freedom from constraint with a relational understanding of children's agency. Agency is not an individual enterprise; rather, an individual's agency is enabled and constrained by cultural discourses and material forces. By rethinking our approach to children's agency and sentimentality, in particular, we can begin to address the internal contradictions of the CRC, and to counter the symbolic repertoires and hierarchical scenes of suffering that dominate representations of children in transnational human rights discourse.

## On Sentimentality and Children's Rights

Lauren Berlant characterizes sentimentality as a rhetorical "means by which mass subaltern pain is advanced" (1999, 53) and the public recognition of suffering is equated with its amelioration (84). Sentimentality ignites a relationship of rhetorical identification that presumes that the recognition of one's own vulnerability will lead one to eradicate the other's pain. Critical of sentimental politics and its misrecognitions, I agree with Berlant that sentimental politics often "over-organize[s] social antagonism" into utopian feelings and traumatized affects (57). The direct connection between sympathy and visual display can be traced to the eighteenth century, when scientific investigative work and emotional appeals coincided in their "strategy of placing the object before the eyes of the observer" (Van Sant 1993, 42). The combination of objectivity and engaging rhetorical modes of presentation, like the tension between curiosity and pity, continues to shape cultural representations of endangered children. In early usages, *sensibility*, associated with bodily sensations, referred to an "immediate, almost involuntary sympathy," whereas *sentiment*, associated with the mind, referred to thought and reflection (48). By the eighteenth century, *sentiment* came to be associated with refined feeling; the meaning of sensibility and sentiment converged as part of the "eighteenth-century realignment of categories for mental and emotional experience" (8). Eighteenth-century usages of *sentiment* linked sympathy to virtue and to the development of a modern moral identity, a connection exemplified by Adam Smith's *The Theory of Moral Sentiments*, which proposed that morality derived from the human capacity to sympathize with others (Howard 2001, 223–24). In the eighteenth century, reading and the visual arts were viewed as a way to cultivate identification and sympathy across social and economic boundaries. Indeed, historians and philosophers (Hunt 2007; Nussbaum 1998; and Rorty 1993) have linked the development of human rights' moral imaginary to this cultivation of sympathy. The spread of sentimental education—fostered by the cultural work of epistolary novels, portraiture, and public exhibitions in the eighteenth century—did not dismantle the hierarchy of the subject and the other or object, or the social and political inequities on which these empathetic identifications were based. These projected identifications and scenes of self-recognition, through which eighteenth-century bourgeois readers distanced themselves from European hegemony, reinforced their status before the law as rights-bearing subjects distributing rights and recognitions to others unable to claim them.

Even in the context of critiquing sentimental appeals, however, we need to acknowledge the historical and cultural work that sentimentality performed and continues to perform in the social imaginary. In the nineteenth century, for example, sentimental ideas about children's separateness helped to justify the passage of important child-labor laws in the United States (Sánchez-Eppler 2005, xix).[8] The expansion of government agencies that accompanied the passage of these laws led to more governmental interventions, but they were not always perceived as benevolent acts. Popular uses of the term *sentimentality* tend to stigmatize the sentimental as an emotion that is "either affected and shallow or . . . excessive" (Howard 2001, 218). June Howard prompts readers to question critics who merely condemn or celebrate sentimentality (215). She argues that emotions are social phenomena, not isolated, individual, and internal experiences (220). Specifically, I interrogate the cultural and rhetorical power of sentimentality, which links sympathy and visual display to virtue, in advancing the human rights of children growing up or working in the sex industry in South Asia, a region that Western depictions have infantilized through a rights-based humanitarianism that denies the moral and political capacities of children and adults alike. This chapter also critiques liberal internationalism and revivals of cultural cosmopolitanism, as well as their failure to address the geopolitical and economic dimensions of children's agency.

## Spectacular Identifications and Horrified Gazes

The *New York Times* columnist Nicholas D. Kristof's advocacy on behalf of foreign children in the sex industry exemplifies a form of transnational sentimentality and moral righteousness that confers upon U.S. viewers the power to judge, interpret, and frame the issues—thus demonstrating the entanglement of human rights internationalisms and American nationalisms. As I discussed in chapter 4, Kristof disclosed that he had purchased two young women from brothels in Poipet, Cambodia.[9] His act set into motion a rescue narrative enabled by the terms of the global sex trade itself—the purchase of human beings—and created, as Leti Volpp put it, "a new market in abduction and redemption" (2006, 1631). Kristof later acknowledged that "buying enslaved girls" is not the solution to global poverty and sex trafficking.[10] Featured in this article is the work of a literacy project in an elementary school in rural Cambodia, developed with the aid of American Assistance for Cambodia. At the school, a teacher and volunteer students from the United States teach English-language skills to Cambodian children. Kristof acknowledges that education will not solve the problem of young girls' enslavement in brothels, but he also notes that traffickers "prey on illiterate girls from the villages."

Many of the world's children live in poverty, are enslaved as child laborers, and are displaced in war-torn states. But Kristof's rhetorical appeal to transnational intimacy and the acquisition of the English language once again ignores the local and global economic realities that sustain child prostitution and limit children's political and moral agency. As Alexander Cockburn points out in his article "Nick Kristof's Brothel Problem," published in *The Nation* on 8 February 2006: "If Kristof wants to confront the prime promoter of prostitution in India and many other countries besides he doesn't have to leave the East Coast of the United States. He can take his video camera into the World Bank and confront its current president, Paul Wolfowitz." Cockburn rightly suggests that we need to consider the material conditions and policies, such as structural adjustment policies, that weaken economies and propel women and girls into sex work. In other words, we need a multidimensional understanding of sex work and the sexual exploitation of children that accounts for the material and discursive forces—both local and global—that enable or constrain, in this case, young women's and children's capacity to act as human rights subjects.

In "Hitting Brothel Owners Where It Hurts" (January 22, 2006), Kristof prompts readers to identify with Hasina Bibi, a sixteen-year-old girl who worked in a garment factory where an older employee pretended to mother her. "Imagine what you would have done if you'd been in Hasina Bibi's sandals," he writes. Hasina was drugged by the older employee and sold to a brothel in Gujarat, India, where she was beaten and threatened with violence if she tried to escape. In this regard, Hasina is the paradigmatic victim, whose image is racialized, in part, through Kristof's reference to her sandals instead of shoes. Unlike many of the girls featured in Kristof's pieces and elsewhere in the popular media, however, Hasina is seen as an agent. "Hasina . . . had a fourth grade education and was literate. So, although she earned no money," Kristof continues, "Hasina asked customers for tips and was able to amass a secret stash of rupees. She learned a bit of Hindi. Finally, one day she jumped into a rickshaw and ran away. . . . Ashamed to return home, Hasina is now an independent streetwalker here in Calcutta." Kristof highlights the role of education in deterring girls from entering sex work: "Educating girls is the best way to give them the tools to resist trafficking or escape brothels. In the long run, one effective way to knock down brothels is to build schools."

In addition to the education-as-rescue narrative (in which education becomes the agent for change), Kristof's reference to Hasina's current occupation and identification as an "independent streetwalker" imply that certain occupations are forced on children while others are chosen. A streetwalker may be perceived as an independent agent, but she is still prone to all the risks of sex work: disease, abuse, even death. Moreover, *streetwalker* does not conjure up the image of an innocent child, victimized and betrayed (as child prostitutes are typically portrayed). Rather, the label presents a more ambiguous and suspicious image of a child onto whom a certain level of agency, if not blame, is projected. Kristof's acknowledgment of local activists who provide education and health services to women and children in brothels is a productive development in his columns. But his focus on rescuing girls and young women allows him to emerge as the virtuous reporter and advocate, whose value and agency are affirmed by the "lacking" other—a humanitarian narrative of self-actualization with an imperialist history (Spurr 1993, 20).

Humanitarian and human rights campaigns have long construed women and children as symbolically appealing victims through a paternalist framework, which has both national and international dimensions. The spectacular figure of the exploited child is most often depicted as foreign (racially or ethnically different) and nonautonomous, an innocent being betrayed by familial and cultural traditions.[11] Kristof acknowledges that these young women's agency is reduced by their limited choices and opportunities—a significant recognition—but in the end he sees himself as both the consumer and the agent of change. Finally, his purchase of these young women's freedom turns them into valuable commodities. Kristof capitalizes on humanitarianism's investment in consumerist culture and its privatization of gendered violence and rescue.

## Through Children's Eyes?

The Academy Award–winning documentary *Born into Brothels* (Kauffman and Briski 2004) marks a key rhetorical shift toward configurations of children as agents of their own stories. But what kind of agents are they depicted as? *Born into Brothels* has been marketed by ThinkFilm Productions as "touching and heartfelt, yet devoid of sentimentality" and as defying "the tear-stained tourist snapshot of the global underbelly. . . . [The children's] photographs are prisms into their souls, rather than anthropological curiosities."[12] Despite the film's portrayal of children's voices and visions, their rhetorical agency is nonetheless framed by an unequal relationship between the filmmakers and the children and their families, and by the economic and cultural logics of global capitalism.

*Born into Brothels*, directed by Ross Kauffman and Zana Briski, depicts the brothels in Sonagachi, the oldest and largest red-light district in Calcutta, as a site where children's rights (or lack thereof) are linked to their designated identities as children of prostitutes. Briski—a British-born, white photojournalist turned advocate, who was educated in theology and religious

12. "Group Shot," photograph by Zana Briski. By permission of Kids with Cameras.

studies—attempts to get the children into boarding schools and out of the brothels. But she quickly learns that virtually none of the schools will take the children because their parents are criminals, drug dealers, and prostitutes. *Born into Brothels* attempts to individualize the children; to identify them as agents and legal subjects, so they can claim their right to education; and to represent their differing familial situations and personalities. Despite their differences, however, the children share a common bond: they were all born into families working in brothels, and the film implies that without Western intervention, they will likely continue in this line of work (see fig. 12).

Briski went to India in 1995 and began photographing the "harsh reality of women's lives—female infanticide, child marriage, dowry deaths and widowhood" (Briski 2004). During trips to Calcutta from 1998 to 2000, she grew close to sex workers and their children. Ultimately, she convinced one brothel owner to rent her a room. Briski reports that the children would surround her, fascinated by her camera: "As soon as I entered the brothel . . . [the] children were all over me; they wanted to learn how to use the camera. That's when I thought it would be great to teach them and to see this world through their eyes." She taught them how to take pictures, gave them each point-and-shoot cameras, and set up weekly photography classes for them, in which she emphasized visual composition and encouraged individual creativity and choice.

Several of the children become key characters in a larger transformation narrative, which moves from pain and trauma (signified as growing up in a brothel, neglect, fragmented or nonexistent family structure, illegal family businesses) to personal expression (photography as a means of empowerment) to an imagined global citizenship (a globally funded right to education and development). But in the end, the narrative arc of the film is less about the right to education and economic remedies as it is about humanitarian or even missionary intervention. Nevertheless, this narrative of the transformative and redemptive power of art resembles the trajectory of children's development within human rights law itself. The language and narrative progression of the CRC, as Joseph Slaughter notes, configures "human rights incorporation as [a] coming-of-age story . . . by guaranteeing the child rights 'to a name' (Article 7), then to an 'identity' (Article 8), then to 'freedom of expression' (Article 13) . . . and finally a responsibility to 'respect . . . the human rights and fundamental freedoms of others' (Article 40)" (2007, 333 n. 64).

The narrative trajectory of the film positions Briski as a savior, and the children as having been transformed by the power of art. But throughout the film, and in public discussions of the film, including a presentation that I attended at the International Center for Photography, Briski struggles with her own cinematic positioning. In one film scene, she says of one girl: "She's never said no in her life, so you can imagine what's going to happen to her very soon. The children ask me for help. They ask for it all the time, and it's heartbreaking, I mean there's so little I can do. All I can do is try." In another scene, she struggles with her lack of qualifications as well as agency: "I'm not a social worker; I'm not a teacher even. That's my fear, you know, that I can't do anything and that even helping them to get an education is not going to do anything. But without help they're doomed." Briski acknowledges the "literacy myth" (Graff 1979), namely the universalizing idea that irrespective of the particularities of any given context, literacy correlates with social standing and economic advancement. Yet she proceeds to work under its pretense.

*Born into Brothels* bears witness to Briski's journey through the creation of a rhetorical space of transnational intimacy between the children and her along with imagined Western audiences. Although the subtitle to one of the scenes is "To See Through Children's Eyes," what we see is the film-maker's perception of the children. In many ways, we might consider *Born into Brothels* a cosmopolitan bildungsroman, in which Briski incorporates herself and the children into a human rights plot about the rights and responsibilities of citizenship, including the right to education. Indeed it is through the children's artwork that they are poised in the film to join the sociopolitical public and to aspire to become global citizens. Here visual literacy is valorized just as reading and writing often are—"as tools for acquiring the knowledge necessary for socioeconomic advancement and as the primary media of modern transcendental personal fulfillment through the imaginative extension of the individual into the world" (Slaughter 2007, 272). The film's attention to visual literacy reasserts the liberal public that is central to the implementation of human rights, reaffirming a set of social institutions and assumptions about education as empowerment.[13]

Briski and Kauffman, a New York–based filmmaker, shot 170 hours of video of the children, much of it under cover given the danger of shooting in brothels. The film opens with a series of closely cropped images of the children's faces, with emphasis on their eyes, intermingled with images of women lined up and waiting for customers, men counting their money, and young babies in small, crowded rooms in Calcutta's red-light district. The camera pans in close on the bodies and faces of the people in the district, replicating the tight quarters in which many of the children live. A close-up of two rats eating reinforces the dreariness and filth of the scene. The brothel shots are cast in warm red and orange overtones. Interspersed black-and-white photographic stills reinforce the documentary feel of the film. Authorial identity, however, is elusive in these opening shots. It is unclear whose point of view the stills represent. On a second viewing, however, it becomes clear that some were taken by Briski. Several of the children's photographs also appear in this opening sequence, though they too are identifiable as such only on a second viewing. The juxtaposition of Briski's and the children's photographs creates a paratactic structure that positions all the photographs on a single, rhetorical plane, prompting the critical question: Who is representing whom?

### The Mothers of *Born into Brothels*

Kochi is one of the film's success stories, and her success is attributed to Briski's intervention. In the commentary on the DVD, Briski indicates that Kochi was "really treated like a slave. . . . She really knew what was in store for her; she totally got it; but yeah, she had a real inner strength." Kauffman adds that through Briski's photography class, Kochi "learned that her opinion actually meant something." Similarly, on NPR's *All Things Considered*, Briski characterizes Kochi as "completely transformed in the photography class."[14] In an early scene in the documentary, Kochi talks about her mother: "I live here with my grandmother because my mother can't take care of me. My father tried to sell me. . . . I worry that I might become like them." At a meeting at the boarding school where Briski hopes Kochi can go—a meeting that Briski worked hard to set up—the camera closes in on Kochi's face as a school representative talks to her grandmother about why she wants to put the girl in school. When the representative warns the grandmother that she will have to be committed to Kochi's education and do without her work at home, the grandmother begins to talk about how hard Kochi works; she barely has time to rest, her grandmother says. But she suggests that she'll "manage somehow" without the income that Kochi brings in by cleaning houses. What's alluded to here is the need for compensation to replace the child's labor and to enable families to send children to school. The school representative looks skeptical and asks why Kochi's mother isn't here. The grandmother says "she's sitting right over there," and begins to explain: "There's no problem with her mother, just that she's temperamental. She's lost six sons, her husband died too." The camera focuses on Kochi's mother for the first time. Kochi's grandmother continues: "She tried to kill herself by jumping off the Howrah Bridge. Since then, she doesn't behave normally." Kochi looks on hopefully as the school representative tells her grandmother that she can't promise anything, but that she can take Kochi's application. This scene presents Kochi's mother as a silent and mentally unstable figure who cannot participate in her daughter's boarding school interview. The camera shows her sitting there but not speaking, and she does not tell her own story. In this scene, in addition to being shown as irresponsible and incompetent, Kochi's mother is helpless and silent.

Throughout the film, the prostitute mothers are contrasted with Briski (whom the children call "Zana Auntie"), who spends hours working with the Calcutta bureaucracy to get the paperwork that the children need to enroll in a school away from their families and the brothels. In contrast to Briski's wise and compassionate words, the mothers' talk, like their work, is depicted as immoral, not nurturing, and ultimately not motherly. For instance, in one scene, Tapasi's mother screams at her: "Does her mother have to tell her to work? I'll throw you out, you little bitch." Later, Tapasi tells the camera: "I like her, but sometimes she says such mean things. But I don't care. After all, she's my mother. . . . I know what she does for work, and I feel bad talking about these things." Tapasi's mother, like many of the other mothers in Calcutta's red-light district, is always yelling and cursing at her children, saying "mean things." But the children love their mothers no matter what.

In another scene, Manik is dragged by his legs, beaten, and cursed by a woman (it's not clear if she is his mother) and the group of women who surround her. He struggles and screams. "Beat that son of a bitch," one woman yells, "beat the son of a cunt-fucking bitch." Another woman, whose face is never shown, apparently reprimands the women who are yelling and beating Manik, and they turn on her: "You aren't the only one who's brought up kids!" "Naked fucking whore . . . giving out all the time in your room!" "Acting the part of a fucking saintly wife!" "If we are sluts, what are you?" As the women yell at each other and the scene descends into further chaos and confusion, the children look on—or look away, hiding their faces. This scene of chaos illustrates once again the unmotherly character of these mothers. As the women switch from screaming at Manik to screaming at each other, they are revealed to be competitive but also irrational (calling each other "whores" and "sluts"). Interestingly, what seems to bother them most is the woman who defends Manik and criticizes them, appearing to think herself better than they are. Once again, the violence and chaos of this scene contrasts with Briski's reasonable and nurturing relationship with the children. The brothel mothers are shown as irresponsible and self-centered. The film implies that they do not put their children first. Nor does it ever offer an alternative view of the mothers to complicate this one-dimensional representation of them. As Svati Shah suggests, the film depicts Indian women as helpless and exotic in relation to the normative white woman (2005).[15] The film's portrayal of the mothers is indicative of the problem with spectacular human rights rhetoric and its emphasis on victimization, which doesn't account for the multiplicity of ways in which people function. The children's fathers are generally absent or unknown, and when they are depicted, their immoral behavior as drug users or black-market sellers of alcohol is highlighted. These scenes reinforce the perception of the need for external intervention on behalf of the children. The relative lack of attention to the agency of any of the adults in the community and their roles, or potential roles, as child advocates evinces paternalism toward the children's families and pathologizes the entire community.

In the context of postcolonial India, the perception of prostitution and the regulation of women's sexuality need to be understood against the historical backdrop of colonial encounters and legal regimes (Kapur 2005, 28). For example, the efforts of late-nineteenth-century social reformers to prohibit oppressive cultural practices, such as child marriage and subjugation of widows, were opposed by political nationalists and cultural revivalists, who perceived such reforms as interventions by the colonial powers into the private sphere of the Indian family. Political nationalists have countered colonial assumptions that "Indian women were victims of a backward culture and in need of rescue and rehabilitation" (29) by construing women's sexuality and the home as symbols of cultural autonomy and resistance to the colonial encounter (53). Ratna Kapur writes: "Indian womanhood became the embodiment of nationalism, as the nation came to be constructed as a divine mother, and women in general became the mothers of the nation" (31). Despite the increased visibility of sexuality and sexual subalterns in the public domain—via satellite broadcasting, commercial cinema, activist movements, and the AIDS crisis—sexuality continues to be the target of legal regulation in present-day India. The Hindu Right,[16] for instance, has advanced its exclusive understanding of culture and its neonationalist agenda through legal reforms that restrict affirmative expressions of sexuality, treat women as vulnerable and incapable of making decisions, and sustain the private-public distinctions in the law itself (42–43).[17] Sexual subalterns who challenge normative sexuality (including gays, lesbians, and commercial sex workers) are viewed as a threat to the purity of the Indian nation—as cultural contaminants (56). In India, sex work is regulated by the Immoral Traffic (Prevention) Act 1956, whose primary purpose has been to criminalize prostitution, including soliciting, trafficking, and the keeping of brothels. Although the act does not criminalize the prostitute per se, sex work is penalized through the provision against solicitation; the bill also contains measures to promote the rehabilitation of commercial sex workers. Legal reforms that recognize sex work as a legitimate exercise of the right to work have been drafted and submitted to the government by organizations such as the National Law School of India University. But the government has shown little interest in addressing the human rights of sex workers and has countered the activism of feminists and sex workers with even more repressive legal measures, such as those recommended by the 1998 "Report of the Committee on Prostitution, Child Prostitutes and Children of Prostitutes and Plan of Act to Combat Trafficking and Commercial Sexual Exploitation of Women and Children," including the removal from their mothers to institutional care of children above the age of six (74). Briski's efforts to get children out of the brothels and into boarding schools therefore colludes with what sex workers rights advocates consider repressive legal policies. Of course, there is also a long colonial history of forced removals of children from their mothers, including the removal of part-aboriginal children in Australia, Native American children in certain regions of the United States, and Adivasi children, believed to be the aboriginal peoples of India (Swami 2005).

Not surprisingly, the reception of *Born into Brothels* by some Western critics plays on images of the mothers as immoral agents (see Schickel 2005, 77). One reviewer characterized the mothers as "catty, vulgar women . . . who fully expect their daughters to join (or replace) them 'on the line' in their early teens. . . . A good number of the children manage to find places at schools, but the biggest barrier proves to be the kids' mothers or guardians" (McCarthy 2004, 41). The irrational maternal figure is depicted again at the end of the film. At this point, after Briski has spent much time and energy trying to get the children into good boarding schools, away from the brothels and their families, Puja's family doesn't want her to go. "I'm not worried about sending her off," says Puja's grandmother. The camera looks down on her from above as she squats on the floor and continues: "In fact, I feel happy, I feel good. If only it wasn't today. My mother died on a Thursday at five in the afternoon. Since then, I don't do anything special on Thursdays." The camera closes in on Puja's face; she is looking down at the ground. "Ma, can I go?" she asks. "You can go tomorrow but not today," says her mother. Briski warns: "Everyone's going today and it's the last chance, so this is the only opportunity." Briski apparently talks the mother and grandmother into letting Puja go, since in the next scene they are sending her off and Briski is saying to them: "This will be good for her."

The women's superstitious reluctance contrasts with Briski's intelligent persistence. Briski wins, but this scene foreshadows a gloomy future for Puja, who is taken out of school at some later point, according to the film's closing summary. Moreover, the scene illustrates that even though Puja's family is better off than the other families (because they work in an upper-class Brahmin neighborhood), their higher-class status does not translate into valuing education or escaping sex work. Puja is just as trapped by the matrilineal cycle of prostitution as the poorer children are. These scenes construct working as a prostitute and being a good mother as mutually exclusive and incompatible (Shah 2005). The film offers no discussion of sex work as a means to make a living—a means of supporting the children. Sex work is portrayed as an abusive familial cycle passed down through the matrilineal line. (Suchitra's aunt, for example, already wants to send her to work "in the line.") It is a trap for these children, especially for the girls.[18]

The film's recognition of the matrilineal cycle of prostitution and poverty is important. India's National Human Rights Commission reports that "hundreds of thousands of Indian women work as prostitutes. . . . Almost half of them began working as children" (Curry 2005, 63). A report by Human Rights Watch estimates that "probably more than a million women and children are employed in Indian brothels," and that many of the women and children have been trafficked from Nepal to brothels in Bombay (1995). The film's unilaterally critical view of the red-light district, as well as its construal of "prostitute mothers as unsafe for children," however, ignores the history of women's activism in the area of sex work and the successes of Calcutta's first cooperative of sex workers—the Indian Commercial Sex Workers—in decreasing the rate of HIV infection (Shah 2005).[19] The group, which was organized in Calcutta in 1997, works to promote the recognition of prostitution as an occupation, workers' rights, safer sex practices, and the control of sexually transmitted diseases including HIV and AIDS.

In 1999, *Newsweek* reported that Sonagachi's 5,000 women had "begun reclaiming their lives and their dignity, both individually and collectively" (Mazumdar 1999, 40). The Sonagachi cooperative of sex workers attempts to protect its members' rights by helping to ensure that sex workers keep 50 percent of their earnings; before the madams organized, pimps took a share of their earnings (40). The article reported that some members of the cooperative made and sold handicrafts at local fairs. More recently, the Sonagachi model and the DMSC union have been criticized by advocates for current and former prostitutes (such as Uma Basu who runs the New Light shelter for trafficked women in Kolkata) for operating as a front for brothel owners and as a cover for traffickers (Kristof and WuDunn 2009, 28). Moreover, as Shah points out, the organization Sanlaap, which provides shelters for the female children of prostitutes in Calcutta, and which appears in the film, is never properly identified. Shah notes that they were "portrayed as interpreters, school administrators . . . part of the background against the 'real' story of the filmmakers mounting their rescue" (2005).

In contrast to prostitutes' rights organizations, such as the Commercial Sex Workers, which argue that prostitution should be seen as work, the Calcutta-based Indian feminist NGO Sanlaap—established in 1987 and featured in the film—emphasizes the rehabilitation of sex workers and the prevention of second-generation prostitution.[20] Like Sanlaap, the film advocates the criminalization of prostitution. However, criminalization does not address the structural context of the sex industry. Many of the sex workers in Sonagachi, for instance, left their villages because they could not survive there as landless agricultural workers. The lack of information about women's economic challenges and local activism—even if the women featured in *Born into Brothels* were not involved with such efforts—reinforces the horrified Western gaze overlaid with an Orientalist script. It also suppresses women's agency and implicitly pits women's rights against children's rights, rather than representing them as interdependent. The film never acknowledges the emergent transnational publics, including activists and their audiences, and the discourses that define sex work and activism in India. The omission of any reference to the sex workers' rights movement ignores the potential radicalism of the human rights project and recasts the filmmakers' intervention as a type of missionary enterprise.

In addition to Kochi, whose success consolidates Briski's rescue narrative, Avajit is the film's other success story: he and Kochi are the only children still in school when the film ends.[21] Avajit receives special recognition for his photography, which, according to the filmmakers, shows a strong sense of composition and artistic vision. World Press Photo selected him to participate in its annual exhibition in Amsterdam. As depicted in the film, Avajit is the potential artist whose environment and circumstances stifle him and whose family doesn't understand the significance of this talent. A representative from World Press tells Avajit's grandmother: "This is a very special thing. As a grandmother you should feel very happy and very proud." However, the gruesome violence of his mother's murder (she was burned by her pimp, although her death was reported as a kitchen fire) does not bode well for Avajit, who begins to lose hope in his art. He says to the camera: "I used to want to be a doctor. Then I wanted to become an artist. There is nothing called 'hope' in my future." Briski becomes the rescuing substitute mother, who must intervene to save Avajit from an equally gruesome future. The film suggests that she succeeds: although she has trouble getting him a passport, she eventually manages to get him to Amsterdam to show his work, after which he returns to school in India. We learn in material produced after the film that he later traveled to the United States to study photography and film.

## Selling the Spectacle of Empowerment

In contrast to one reviewer, who claims that *Born into Brothels* "bears witness to . . . the pervasiveness of unfeeling capitalism (even deep within a Calcutta slum, there are advertising signs for Pepsi-Cola)" (Howell 2005), I argue that the film illustrates the pervasiveness of *feeling* capitalism in humanitarian terms. In the film, Briski describes organizing auctions and exhibits of the children's work as a means of fundraising, "using their own photography, selling their photographs to raise money for them. . . . The whole point of this is to get the kids out of the brothels." At an auction at

Sotheby's, fine art collectors and other upscale Westerners gaze admiringly at the children's photographs and, if they are moved enough, purchase a print. The camera cuts to the children in India, watching their photographs being looked at on television. The scene links transnational sentimentality and capitalist consumption by framing both with a rights-based humanitarian politic and aesthetic.

Through Kids with Cameras, an organization that Briski founded to "empower children through the art of photography," prints of the children's photographs are for sale, along with the soundtrack for the film and a book titled *Kids with Cameras: The Book*. Proceeds from the sales of the prints go directly to the children's education; the proceeds from the soundtrack and the book support the mission of Kids with Cameras. Visitors to the organization's website can click a link to e-mail the children directly. As of February 2005, after the film had been nominated for an Academy Award, Kids with Cameras "had raised $100,000 for the children's education . . . [and had] begun negotiations to open a boarding school in Calcutta for children from the brothels" (Collins 2005, 4). Controversy has surrounded the claim that Briski's efforts and the film have helped the children. Among the most strident critiques has been launched by Partha Banerjee, who worked on the film during the production stage as an interpreter. In a letter to the Academy of Motion Picture Arts and Sciences, Banerjee disputes the claim made by the filmmakers and the Academy that the children's lives have been improved as a result of Briski's efforts:

> I visited these children a number of times during the last couple of years and found out that almost all the children are now living even a worse life than they were in before Ms. Briski began working with them. The children's despair has exacerbated because they'd hoped that with active involvement in Ms. Briski's camera project, there would be an opportunity for them to live a better life. At the same time, their sex worker parents believed that with so much unrestricted access to their secretive lives they had provided to the filmmakers, and that too, so generously (were their written consent [*sic*] ever requested and received by the filmmakers?), there would be a way their children would also be sharing some of the glories the filmmakers are now shining in. Alas, very

likely, they don't even know that their misery, helplessness and traumas are now being widely exposed and exploited to find fame and prosperity. (Banerjee 2005)

One week after *Born into Brothels* won an Academy Award for best documentary feature, Jeff Sackman of ThinkFilm, the film's distributor, reported that the film would generate at least $2 million for the company and another $1 million for the filmmakers (Westhead 2005).[22] Most of the photographs that have been formally exhibited, including the photograph that appeared as the cover of Amnesty International's 2003 calendar, are landscapes and portraits of the children set against a backdrop of slabs of radiant color, swaying trees, and blue skies. Many of the exhibited photographs, especially the closely cropped portraits of the children, abstract the architecture of the brothel as a series of geometric lines and blocks of color.

Beyond the narrow spaces of the brothels, these images reflect calm, bright, and expansive natural landscapes (see figs. 13 and 14). These are essentially photographs that reproduce an exotic, touristic aesthetic for Western audiences and advance—especially within the global morality market—a cosmopolitan argument based on the projected identifications with the "foreign" other. More broadly, the popularity of these images exemplifies Western humanitarianism's investment in transnational sentimentality and capitalist consumption.

In a film review for *Maclean's*, Brian Johnson argues that "by showing us an underworld through the eyes of children, *Born into Brothels* inverts a documentary gaze that's usually stranded between pathos and voyeurism. This is an inspiring story of kids learning to see." He continues: "We sense that if they can capture the world through a lens, maybe they can avoid being captured by it. If photographs do indeed steal souls, these children are stealing theirs back."[23] The assumption here is that the children were "blind" prior to being seen by Western eyes. The witnessing public that *Born into Brothels* imagines echoes the cosmopolitan discourses of travel and visibility created by colonial histories. The legacy of colonial discourses, however, need not annul the possibility that human rights discourses and the witnessing publics they imagine might have effects that counter such histories. For example, the funds generated through the sales

13. "Girl on a Roof," photograph by Suchitra. By permission of Kids with Cameras.

14. "Bucket," photograph by Avajit. By permission of Kids with Cameras.

of the children's photographs are reportedly routed to a fund that Kids with Cameras established to build a school that will house 150 children from Calcutta's red-light districts. Yet the intervention of removing children from their families, as I've mentioned, has ties to colonial histories. This is not to proclaim a blanket critique of this particular intervention, which has yet to be realized in this case. Rather, the challenge is not to reproduce the colonial legacy of pathologizing societies as uncivil and repressing the agency of both children and adults, then recreating the spectacle of salvation through such interventions. Thus we might also ask, as Roberta Smith did in her review of *Born into Brothels*, "if a 10-year-old living in a brothel in Calcutta could ever not take pictures that would prove interesting to Western eyes" (2005).

Like the UDHR, the implicit narrative of the CRC is one of human personality development. The notion of that development in international human rights law is a "process of socialization, a process of enfranchisement into the . . . 'social practices and rules . . . which bring individuals together to form a functioning political community'" (Slaughter 2007, 20). The development narrative is one that "plots a story of sociocivil incorporation by which the human rights personality becomes legible to the self and others" (23). Visual forms of expression and visual literacy narratives, as I suggested earlier, are becoming major components of children's social incorporation as rights-bearing subjects and part of a larger movement of youth participatory photography.[24]

The objectivist documentary aesthetic of *Born into Brothels* presumes that sight equals agency and that seeing is power. But what if one sees, all too well, but can't change anything? What kind of power does seeing enable? The film defines children's agency within the parameters of individual choice and the consumer logics of global capital and compassionate cosmopolitanism. As the film progresses, Avajit's identification and demeanor shifts, possibly influenced by the continual praise of his work. On the plane on the way to Amsterdam for the World Press Photo exhibit, he assumes the attitude of a world-class business traveler and artist, snapping pictures the entire time. At the exhibit itself, he adopts the language of the art critic and educator, teaching others how to read his work: "This is a good photograph," he suggests, even though it is hard to look at, "because it shows the truth." Avajit resurrects the image of the Indian male, asso-ciated in the film with degenerative excesses (of drug users, drug dealers, and pimps), as a cosmopolitan subject. Avajit's identity and agency become caught up in this mobility and the mobilization of individuality defined by a particular aesthetic sensibility. The emphasis in the Amsterdam scene, when Avajit shares his artistic expertise, and the prominence of Avajit as one of the film's success stories, presents individual choice as the ethical framework for understanding agency. Earlier in the film, Avajit's agency is framed as freedom of movement and choice (Briski struggles to get him a passport). At the film's close, his agency is aligned with geographic mo-bility and consumption—an alignment that suggests the imbrications of children's rights and global consumer culture. *Born into Brothels* animates the spectacle of endangered children growing up in a brothel in Calcutta as a human rights narrative about children's personal development and their lack of access to fundamental social services, including schools. The chil-dren and the products of their development as portrayed by the film—their photographs—become conduits for a cosmopolitan aesthetic that cham-pions their redemption as subjects of a heroic narrative in which they and the imagined Western viewer triumph over the deficient moral-aesthetic boundaries of the brothel. This transformation narrative distracts atten-tion from the severe poverty and exploitation to which the children are sub-jected in favor of the expert gaze of the cosmopolitan art critic, which the children are encouraged to emulate, and new forms of neoliberalism and its regulation of social difference, subjectivity, and public morality.[25]

A multitude of factors—employers, parents, the state, and international actors—assist the global sex industry and sustain the need for child labor. Transnational corporations and international financial agencies, such as the International Monetary Fund and World Bank, often "create socio-economic conditions which are not conducive to the protection of child rights or elimination of child labor" (Arat 2002, 185). UNICEF notes: "The real cost of adjustment is being paid disproportionately by the poor and by their children" (quoted in Arat 2002, 190).[26] Therefore, a multidimensional analysis of children's agency is needed that considers the interdependency of human rights, including how poor labor conditions for adults (inad-equate wages, lack of health or disability benefits, and unsafe working conditions) contribute to the family's dependency on child labor (183). Human rights advocates and scholars need to be skeptical of the dualisms (forced versus chosen, moral versus immoral) that dominate representations of women and children in the sex industry, and we must account for the transnational, national, and cultural forces and narratives that define our alignments with children and those that limit children's agency as moral and political subjects.

A scene midway through *Born into Brothels* powerfully captures the relationality of children's agency and breaks down the film's otherwise structuring opposition between childhood innocence and knowledge and between adulthood and childhood in its depiction of embodied cultural discourses. The children are on a bus, returning from the beach excursion that produced many of the exhibited landscapes and many cartwheels on the sand. The girls dance in the aisles as Bollywood music blares on the radio. The scene exudes sexuality and childhood states of joy. In the background, we hear horns beeping, the bustle of the city approaching. The constant motion of the camera on the children's faces and swirling dresses washes them in exterior light and blurs their movements, lending an impressionistic feel to the scene. The girls' gestures mimic the gendered scripts and sexualized roles available to them. The music itself is highly sexualized and is a type of music that many young women love to dance to, not just girls heading to the red-light district. These rituals unfold as playful rhetorical acts, but as viewers we also know (we are told this numerous times in the film) that these girls are likely to end up as sex workers, and thus we project their future onto the young girls' playful movements. Briski comments that this transitional scene from the beach to the brothels is one of her favorites. There is "something very sexual about it," she says; "There's this lure of the red-light district, and then it's the Bollywood music that I love." She continues: "One of the most brutal parts of the film, for me, is the transition from the beach—the freedom, what it represents, being outdoors, the sea—to this claustrophobic, clawing red-light district. And the kids having to go back and walk through this, knowing this is their future."

Briski suggests that this scene highlights the transition from freedom and innocence to entrapment and exploitation. But it does much more than that. It also illustrates the indeterminacy and relational nature of the children's agency, and how they perform transnational and cultural scripts with their bodies. The children in this scene are "anomalies in the discourses of children and childhood" (Montgomery 2001, 133). These children exist in a gray zone—an ambiguous category—that threatens Western constructions of childhood innocence by blurring "the categories of adult and child, knowledge and innocence, force and choice" (134). Once the children return to the red-light district, the camera follows them as they walk through the brothels' narrow, dark corridors lined with women and men. The camera pursues Avajit as he walks past a prostitute, who tugs on his short-sleeved shirt. He shrugs, shakes his arm back to his side, and rejects, at least for now, the lure of this transnational gendered script (the third world mother-prostitute as a figure of excess and failure) in order to pursue an alternative script (the sought-after subjectivity of the capitalist and cosmopolitan man of fortune). Finally, one could argue that this scene highlights agency as a negotiation among social location, subjectivity, and the politics of social recognition.

In the next section, I consider *Modern Babylon?* (Montgomery 2001), a feminist ethnographic study of children in the sex industry in Thailand, which powerfully highlights the local particularities of sex work and children's rhetorical agency, the impact of Thai nationalist discourses, and the transnational movement toward middle-class values as it affects the children and their families. *Modern Babylon?* provides a promising opening for future studies of children in the sex trade because it directly engages the ethical challenges in counteracting the spectacle of children's victimization and illustrates the potential of a rhetorical analytic for understanding the complexity of children's agency. My intent is not to endorse ethnography as an alternative to documentary film; both genres share a troubled history of objectifying representations of the other.[27] The question is not whether ethnography should supersede documentary as a genre for human rights advocacy, but rather how particular instantiations of these genres or combinations of the two can increase our ability to attend to the local and global politics of recognition and the affective and material economies that shape children's agency, or lack thereof, as human rights subjects.

## Children as Rhetorical Agents

As part of the growing interest among social anthropologists in studying childhood—especially children in the global sex industry—Montgomery aims to shift the rhetoric of protection and self-idealization of children in public discourse in order to emphasize children's relative autonomy, self-determination, and agency. This shift reflects the view that the protection of children as property is not the same thing as recognizing children's political status as persons. The absence of children's points of view has fed stereotypical images of children as passive, helpless subjects. Montgomery claims that "child prostitutes . . . fulfill a special need in Western iconography" (2001, 21) and that "the only image of the child prostitute in the public arena is that of a tragic martyred child" (49). As the cases analyzed earlier illustrate, Western representations of women and children in the sex industry follow a similar narrative trajectory: the narrative is one of betrayal (the child is abandoned by parents or trafficked, sold, or debt bonded into brothel life), abuse, and then rescue by good outsiders. Ultimately, however, rescue is not lasting, as many of the children die, often of AIDS. This betrayal-abuse-rescue-death narrative seems to provide endless opportunities for sentimental moralizing (146).

Montgomery recognizes the exploitation of children in the sex industry and the physical, mental, and emotional consequences of sexual exploitation for children. But she is concerned that the voices of boys and girls have not been well represented by U.S. or international news media, or by NGOs campaigning to end child prostitution (1998, 140). Many children are kidnapped into prostitution, or sold or debt bonded by their parents, but the children that Montgomery observed did not fall into these categories. Conducted in the mid-1990s, Montgomery's case study focuses on children's experiences in a small community, a slum on the edge of a tourist resort in Thailand, which earned most of its income through child prostitution. These children worked in the prostitution industry and lived with their parents. She describes the children as "technically 'free.' . . . These children worked because they felt a strong obligation towards their families and believed that it was their duty to support their parents financially" (143).

Contrary to popular Western depictions of sex workers, such as those in

Kristof's columns and *Born into Brothels*, which assume a "straightforward link between identity and sexuality," of the forty children she studied who were under the age of fifteen and who had worked as prostitutes, Montgomery found that neither prostitution nor sexuality defined their sense of themselves (1998, 146–47).[28] These children developed a private morality in relation to prostitution and exhibited qualities such as a sense of familial loyalty and duty (140). The children also "could delineate clear boundaries between what happened to their bodies and what affected their personal sense of identity and morality" (143). Labels and identity categories were very important to the children, who did not refer to themselves as prostitutes. Children, as their parents would commonly say, "*pay thiaw kap farang* (go out for fun with foreigners), *jap farang* (catch foreigners) or even *mii kheek* (have guests)" (144). Montgomery highlights children's images of themselves and the coping strategies they employ, including their rejection of the label and status of victims, to counter popular characterizations of children in the sex industry as "suffer[ing] from a form of false consciousness" (146). At the macro level, Montgomery argues, it is hard to see the children as having any choice: "Poverty and poor social status consigned them to the margins of society from where they had no structural power. With no welfare state or social safety net, there were few options which enabled them to exist even at a subsistence level" (148–49). At the local level, however, the children "did not passively accept their low status and lack of choice, and their own sense of worth and identity were bound up in being in control of their lives. . . . Even though they were socially and economically very marginal, by most definitions they were dutiful children whose respect and [deference] toward their parents was honorable and admirable" (149).

Montgomery's study primarily addresses the material conditions and discourses that structure children's sense of identity and agency through an analysis of how the children rationalize their behavior. For example, the children's separation of experiences and systems of values and ethics into public and private domains allows them to adhere to moral codes concerning family and loved ones while continuing to sell sex for profit (143). Moreover, the children are likely to romanticize clients by considering them friends and potential lovers rather than customers (1998, 145). Children's rationalizations reveal how local or micro practices are contingent upon, and therefore not separate from, global or macro forces. This micro-macro analysis is just one of the features missing in the *Born into Brothels* portrayal of children growing up in the sex trade. Montgomery recognizes that the children tell the stories "that are expected of them" (2001, 22), but she only hints at how the children's identifications and rationalizations reflect competing logics and the gender and class-based discourses that circulate within and between nations when she describes the children's awareness of how outsiders view them.

The children are particularly upset by the label of prostitute, which they use only when they are trying to deeply offend each other. One boy, Nong, refuses to speak to Montgomery for two days after she asks him "if he ever *jap farang* (caught foreigners)" (1998, 144). "In his own terms he was not a prostitute and hated to think that others saw him in this role" (144), a role that comes with a whole set of negative associations concerning morality and identity. Montgomery's attention to the children's rationalizations, language, and sense of identity construes children as subjects with rhetorical agency—however limited. Notably, she acknowledges that resistance and agency are possible in even the harshest of circumstances: "For people who are poor and powerless, prostitution does not seem a unique and ultimate horror (as many outsiders view it) or something they have to be forced into but one difficult choice among many" (149). What many code as "passivity," she notes, "may in fact be a form of protest" or an "unwilling compliance" (148). Her study focuses on collective consent (familial, cultural, national, and transnational). Specifically, she highlights how communal factors of identity formation—namely, the children's understanding of sex work—developed dialogically among themselves, their parents, their peers, and their customers. Indeed, Montgomery's representation of child sex workers' agency as exemplary of familial loyalty and duty importantly shows how vexing the issue of children's rights and sexual agency can be.[29]

In order for morality "not to degenerate into self-righteousness," Montgomery argues, it must be placed in a context (2001, 3). Montgomery notes that "commercial sexual abuse is not a new phenomenon imported by foreigners, but it is, rather, a contemporary distortion of many cultural norms in Thailand" (160), which include control of female sexuality through social and legal codes (many of which do not apply to men).[30] Motherhood is viewed as a state that brings a woman's sexuality under control. The state has not tried to counter traditional ideas about men's uncontrollable sexual needs, including the view that "without prostitutes, many women and girls would have been raped" (115). Yet Montgomery also notes nationalist Thai imperatives to control childhood prostitution. Several NGOs in northern Thailand, along with government officials, advocate the removal from their homes of children who are at risk of becoming prostitutes. Poor children from non-Thai ethnic groups are taken from their families and moved to Thai-speaking communities to be taught the virtues of Thai citizenship, and families who do not comply with the move risk losing their parental rights completely (66). In other words, the removal of children at risk is linked to the need to sustain the nation-state of Thailand. As Montgomery notes, social and political battles are waged with the image of the violated child as a symbol of social distress: "The child's body has taken on the symbolic role of Thailand itself" (153).

In focusing on political and economic imperatives, Montgomery distinguishes herself from the intrinsic moral biases that researchers have long brought to prostitution (2001, 141). She notes, for instance: "It is extremely difficult to study the children's lives objectively and to say that the children do know something of 'hope or joy or uplift' without accusations of condoning child abuse which is automatically equated with child prostitution" (141). Overwhelmingly, the global media feed—and, some argue, create—the cultural desire for sensational stories: Montgomery notes that child prostitution is an issue that "both repels and allures" (142). Child prostitution became an international concern in the 1990s. In 1996, the World Congress against the Commercial Sexual Exploitation of Children was held in Stockholm. Many countries passed severe laws against their citizens' committing sexual offenses against children abroad. But even when they are framed by calls to action, the prominent placement of child victimization narratives "confer[s] a special commodity status on the subject of 'child sex'" (142). Similarly, the emphasis in *Dateline*'s series "Children for Sale" on foreign predators shifts attention from "situations where the sexual abuse of children is endemic and has become normalized and, indeed, institutionalized" (32). That is, "those who concentrate on the extreme, ignore the mundane" (28). Ultimately, Montgomery's study provides a model for human rights advocates and scholars of how to take into account the relational nature of children's identifications and agency, and to counteract the spectacle of children's victimization and cultural voyeurism by attending to mitigating texts and contexts. However, we also need to consider the potential appropriations of representations of children's agency in service of neoliberal tolerance, cultural relativism, and the regulation of feminist critiques (Bray 2009, 185).

## A Kind of Childhood:
## Moral Ambiguity and the Political Aesthetic

I conclude with a brief discussion of Tareque and Catherine Masud's *A Kind of Childhood* (2007), a documentary about the struggles of working children in Dhaka, Bangladesh, which challenges the privileged discourses of childhood as a state of innocence and dependence.[31] *A Kind of Childhood* does not address the problem of child prostitution or children growing up in brothels but—through its chronicle of the lives and struggles of working children as young as six—foregrounds representational and ethical questions at the heart of this chapter. Unlike *Born into Brothels*, where recognition of the children's agency is perceived as being conferred by Western intervention, *A Kind of Childhood* begins with the premise that children are cultural actors. The documentary reformulates what it means to see children as complex subjects, whose subjectivity is not grounded in a struggle for recognition but in their ability to respond to impoverished social and economic circumstances. In *Born into Brothels*, vision operates as a means to bridge the gap between Zana Briski's world and that of the children she filmed. *Born into Brothels* invokes a humanitarian politics of recognition, whereas *A Kind of Childhood* invokes a nonhierarchical politics and aesthetic of recognition that creates "proximity without intimacy," to use Yaeger's term (2006). *A Kind of Childhood* undercuts familiar frames of rhetorical engagement and the spectacle of the endangered child by chipping away at comforting illusions of empathy and identification (Yaeger 2006, 410) associated with Western representations of children in non-Western contexts. By focusing on the children's daily struggles and resilience, the film counters the spectacle of children as passive victims that is common to human rights and humanitarian campaigns, specifically those that target Western audiences. Although the film shows the difficult life of a child worker, its emphasis is the children's resourcefulness and the paradoxes of international efforts to halt child labor.

The film's central story is that of Idris, one of thousands of child laborers who earn a living working on the streets of Dhaka. Idris is a young boy who has to work to support himself and his invalid father. Child labor is not new to Bangladesh; it has long been part of the normal socialization process in rural areas and is viewed as an essential contribution to household economies. Despite the government's initiatives to reduce child labor during the 1990s, the proportion of children aged ten to fourteen who participate in the labor force in Bangladesh increased from 21 percent in 1981 to 39 percent in 2000 (Rahman, Khanam, and Absar 1999).[32] The UN Human Development Report of 2004 indicates that at least 5 million children work in Bangladesh (out of about 35 million children in the country's total population of 143 million). Moreover, nearly half the population of Bangladesh lives below the national poverty level.

In the film, after an international campaign against underage sweatshops exposes the labor practices in Dhaka, Idris loses his job as a garment worker and goes to work in the street fish market.[33] To compensate him and the other child garment workers for the loss of their incomes, a school is established for them. A program negotiated by UNICEF gives each child six dollars a month to stay in school, but this proves to be not enough for Idris to survive. When there is a change in the school hours, he can no longer keep his job at the street fish market, so he decides to work as a "tempo boy," standing on the back of a rickety taxi-bus, collecting fares as it buzzes through the crowded city streets. Idris wants to stay in school, but the long working hours take their toll, and he finally drops out to work full time as a tempo driver. After he is injured in a crash, he decides to go back to his village to pursue farming. In the film's final image, Idris is walking along the edge of a farmer's field, but a postscript tells us that after a few months he was back in Dhaka driving a tempo. However, after a government crackdown on urban pollution, the postscript continues, he was forced to abandon that job and ended up pulling a rickshaw. In short, the film is not structured as a transformation or rescue narrative; there are no heroes or villains. The film documents the children's struggles, their lack of choices and resources, and the generational cycle of poverty, and it exposes the contradictions of advocacy work.

Like Montgomery, the Masuds maintain a noninterventionist, observational gaze in the film by withholding information about whether they interceded on the children's behalf at any point. The filmmakers' suspension of moral judgment is exemplified in their portrayal of Idris's relationship to his mother. At the outset of the film, Idris tells us that his mother was taken back by her parents after her marriage because of his father's disability. When the filmmakers search for Idris three years after their initial filming, they are told that he now sublets a room in a veranda for ten dollars a month, which he shares with his half-brother Sohel. At the boys' home, the woman who rents the space to them addresses the camera directly: "It's my fate that I should have to put up with you two. I curse myself for subletting you my veranda. There's no one to care for them but me. They need a guardian— a mother. They still owe me for last month's rent. I am poor myself. How can I take care of this burden? But I still try." The film provides no moral judgment about Idris's mother's absence, saying simply that she and Idris have a strained relationship.

When the Masuds catch up to Idris after his tempo is involved in an accident, his sister tells them that he is very sick; he has been coughing for the last three months and can't support his father. His sister speaks to the camera: "Why should Idris be involved with you? It doesn't benefit him at all." An elderly woman then speaks: "He should be taken to a doctor." When we see Idris at a doctor's office in the next scene, we assume that the Masuds took him there after hearing the pleas of Idris's family. The film never states this directly, though, and the filmmakers remain off camera—a classic technique of observational documentary filmmaking (Nichols 1992).

Yet several scenes in the film disrupt the observational documentary gaze: when the filmmakers question their roles in a voice-over, when the children question the value of their participation in the project, and when footage from the film is shown at the school for former child garment workers. These moments give viewers an opportunity to think about their role as witnesses—a small fissure in the otherwise continuous observational gaze—and the potential pedagogical role of the film in the context of its making. In a final scene, Idris is shown the footage that was also shown to young children at the school. However, Idris does not acknowledge that his story could help younger children facing similar dilemmas and material conditions. Rather, he contemplates how his participation has benefited himself: "Now I'm older, I wonder what good it's done me. . . . Now you've seen what I've become. What have I become?" The filmmakers' brief contemplation of the ethics of their observational gaze and unacknowledged intervention exposes the fissures in the objectivist paradigm and ocular epistemology (seeing is believing) that underlies both documentary and human rights advocacy. The facts that Idris does not take on the pedagogical role that the occasion seems to offer him and that child labor laws put him and many other children from the garment factory on the street highlight the moral and political ambiguities of advocacy outcomes and of human rights internationalism more broadly, and raise complex ethical questions about the documentation of children's struggles and of violations of children's human rights. Although the filmmakers show little self-reflection, their construal of the local as a multilayered locality is a perceptive look at childhood in the context of identity producing materialities—in contrast to the humanitarian gaze of *Born into Brothels.* In documenting these ambiguities at the material and—to a lesser degree—the methodological levels, *A Kind of Childhood* presents an occasion to contemplate the political aesthetic of documentary as human rights advocacy. This is so even though the film is not marketed as a human rights documentary per se.

Jacques Rancière argues: "Political art cannot work in the simple form of a meaningful spectacle that would lead to an 'awareness' of the state of the world" (2007a, 63). For Rancière, political art negotiates between a political signification and a perceptual shock (68). He maintains that "aesthetic politics always defines itself by a certain recasting of the distribution of the sensible, a reconfiguration of the given perceptual forms. . . . [T]he dream of a suitable political work of art is in fact the dream of disrupting the relationship between the visible, the sayable, and the thinkable" (63). *A Kind of Childhood* recasts the distribution of the sensible in its refusal to construe the children as mere victims or to infantilize their families or the society in which they live. In its portrayal of a family of children who sing on the streets of Dhaka to survive, the film blurs the boundaries between play and work—boundaries that *Born into Brothels* upholds when it portrays children's photographs as apolitical, neutral forms of personal expression. Scenes at the beginning and end of *A Kind of Childhood* feature the children singing about their hard-working lives and their dreams:

> I am a dropout, yes I am,
> Caught in life's traffic jam.
> I keep riding on my dreams.
> Please spare me your pity, if I have a little love
> Someday I'll turn this traffic nightmare into dream.
> I keep riding on my dreams,
> Riding, riding on my dreams.

My intent is not to position *A Kind of Childhood* as the exemplary model of ethical representation or to suggest that the film is beyond criticism. But there are several defining features of the film that make its depiction of children's struggles distinct and powerful. Among these features is its nonsentimental appeal. The film does not persuade by soliciting viewers' imaginative identifications with the children or fostering a sense of transnational intimacy, but by enabling a relationship built on the recognition of children as cultural actors and moral agents and by not translating the children's experiences in the terms of idealized Western models of development. The lesson of *A Kind of Childhood* is that scholars, documentary filmmakers, and human rights advocates need not succumb to sentimental or colonial narratives of moral salvation and mastery, which rob children of their agency and erase the ambiguity of moral responsibility and political action. If we are to recognize children as political and moral subjects, we need to reimagine the discourse of childhood dependence. Dependency, as Jessica Kulynych notes, is a "normal human condition [that] can no longer be a justification for the exclusion of some humans from the common political culture" (2001, 249). Children's human rights advocates have argued that "making capacity a prerequisite for rights has excluded marginalized and weak groups in society, notably children" (Pupavac 2001, 98). But as the cases in this chapter have shown, and as the bus scene in *Born into Brothels* powerfully visualizes, the tensions between individual capacity and vulnerability, and between protection and empowerment, are not easily resolved. Only when we begin to see children's agency as a matter of social and economic rights and not solely civil and political rights, as a matter of both political recognition and the redistribution of resources, will our engagement with the issue of children's human rights become ethically grounded.

# Conclusion: Posthumanism,
# Human Rights, and the Humanities

homas Keenan claims that "the image remains, without guarantees, always available for reinterpretation and reuse, of necessity the focus of an endless vigil and a struggle for reinscription" (2002, 114). "The image or specter of the camera," Keenan submits, "haunt[s] our consciousness [and] form[s] the most privileged figure of our ethical consciousness, our conscience, our responsibility itself" (105). His characterization of the image captures the rhetorical force of the spectacle in human rights politics and the "spectral turn"—to use Weinstock's phrase (2004, 3)—in contemporary cultural theory, philosophy, and rhetorical criticism. Though human rights advocates are aware of the ethical dilemmas involved in representing violence—acts of representation risk complicity in the violence they depict, endangering both those representing and those represented (Dawes 2007, 178)—they nevertheless continue to call on publics to witness distant suffering, to join the "endless vigil" (Keenan 2002, 114).

Human rights organizations collaborate with the humanities, summoning the power of culture and the arts to cultivate the "imaginative capacity to enter into the lives of people of other nations" and cosmopolitan sensibilities, which, as this study shows, retain nationalist leanings (Nussbaum 1998, 51). The presumption that cultivating affective cross-cultural and transnational identifications through the arts and humanities will lead to social justice can be traced back at least to the ancient Greeks. The humanities are tied to the human rights movement through the implied universality of the idea of humanity and the cultivation of an expansive "circle of identification and belonging" (Cheah 2006, 1) instilled through *the universal feeling of sympathy*" (Kant quoted in Cheah 2006, 1). Contemporary cultural critics have exposed the risks of constructing a sentiment-based ethics and compassionate ethos that sutures human rights to the suffering body. As Lauren Berlant argues, "the important transpersonal intimacies created by calls to empathy all too frequently serve as proleptic shields, as ethically uncontestable legitimating devices for sustaining the hegemonic field" (1999, 46). The misprision in humanist orientations of human rights and the universal imaginative capacities that scholars cite as the animus for a cosmopolitan world citizenry ignores the cultural and material differences that shape the politics of identification, recognition, and belonging and, in so doing, removes suffering as a universal. To account for these differences as well as potential solidarities, human rights scholars and advocates alike need both to restage the universal (Butler 2000, 11) and to locate the vicissitudes of human rights recognitions and identifications in a wider, intertextual sociality. *Spectacular Rhetorics* therefore calls for an ethical rhetorical vision that critically engages the norms and theoretical narratives that characterize the transnational human rights imaginary, particularly as these norms and narratives shape processes of cultural and legal recognition—an ethos based not on philosophical universalism but on an awareness of the historical contingencies and rhetorical exigencies of ethical responsibility in its entanglement with institutional structures and individual lives.

The discordance between human rights advocates and the humanities scholars is often framed as a modernist-postmodernist divide, especially with regard to the distinct ways in which the two fields understand pivotal concepts like subjectivity, agency, and identity (McClennen 2008, 8). Broadly speaking, human rights advocates are said to uphold modernist notions of the self and its other and to be "fixated on the nation-state as the source of both violations and protections" (Stanton 2006, 1520). In contrast, contemporary humanities scholars, particularly those on the cultural left—in their distrust of totalizing concepts, such as civilization and universal humanity—are said to embrace postmodern concepts of fragmentation, deconstruction, and the particular and to question the hegemony of master narratives and the status of the nation-state under globalization (McClennen 2008, 6).

An entire body of cultural theory and criticism is devoted to the critique of humanism begun by Martin Heidegger, in his repudiation of the philosopher's narrow focus on individual subjectivity and in his formulation of "being-in-the-world" ([1947] 1993), and furthered by Baudrillard (2002), Derrida (1994), Gordon (1997), Haraway (1991), Hayles (1999), and Žižek (2002) through the idiom of haunting. In their critique of humanism, these theorists reject the existentialist philosophy of freedom through choice and the humanist subject of modernity—namely, the modernist construal of the autonomous, self-transparent subject. They embrace the death of the subject of certainty. Joshua Gunn explains: "The result of this willed embrace of indeterminacy is that it reframes the self/other relation so central to our fantasy of communication as an ethical relation between a decentered or uncertain self and some*thing* that confounds our sense of place in time, our sense of control: this *thing* is the specter, or as Derrida [1994] prefers, the revenant, a spirit that always comes back" (2006, 81). What would it mean to bring a posthumanist stance to human rights advocacy and scholarship? Are the two discourses compatible? If we approach human rights scenes of recognition as scenes of rhetorical address (see chapter 1), we begin to reconcile the perceived incompatibilities between practitioners and scholars. More broadly, a rhetorical perspective that emphasizes the intercontextuality of human rights discourse and its truth-telling conventions can help us bridge the ostensibly impassable gulf between the humanist subject of modernity and the postmodern death of the subject of certainty.

Sophia McClennen argues that the critical engagement between human rights and the humanities depends "on displacing the construction of the subject [and] developing an ethically just comparative method" (2008, 8). I share her comparative vision, but I do not believe we can displace the subject, particularly the human rights subject of the image. Rather, as I have argued throughout this book, human rights activists and scholars need to better understand how culturally and legally based human rights representations legitimate certain identities, subjectivities, and social relationships. The field of human rights may not have sufficiently engaged the visual rhetorics of recognition, identification, witnessing, and agency that inform its practice, but—as the case studies in this book demonstrate—human rights representations reveal what Ernesto Laclau calls the "parasitic attachment" (quoted in Butler 2000, 33) that human rights universalism maintains to its particular cultural articulation.

To theorize human rights through its cultural representations is to imagine points of convergence between human rights advocates and humanities scholars. Thus, part of the argument of this book has been methodological: in exploring the value that human rights advocates and humanities scholars attribute to visuality and the way each field critiques the political role that recognition, identification, and witnessing play in the formation of ethically engaged publics, I have called for greater critical engagement between the two fields. The gap between the humanities and human rights could be narrowed if scholars and activists were to focus on shared goals, which might include developing—in our audiences and ourselves—the capacity for ethical engagements and representations that expose the contending universalities that underlie culturally induced suffering. We also need to question, as media coverage of the 2010 earthquake in Haiti prompts us to, the promises of transnational media to create a common humanity by conferring a suffering body on "our globalizing world" (Cheah 2006, 178). Moreover, we need to be wary of the dilution of human rights appeals through humanitarian frameworks, which draw attention away from crises and social injustices tied to everyday situations of poverty, economic exploitation, and corruption. Human rights advocates and humanities scholars understand the power of cultural representations in shaping public opinion and their success in raising funds, but what has not been sufficiently addressed—and what *Spectacular Rhetorics* has attempted to illuminate—is the rhetorical force that visual media exert in mediating the public's engagement with human rights principles and inscribing human rights internationalism into the texts of global capitalism and its nationalist and militarist correlates.

Humanist critiques of the spectacle of suffering tend to highlight the moral atrophy, mechanisms of denial (Cohen and Seu 2002), and compassion fatigue among the publics that human rights media target (Kleinman and Kleinman 1996; Moeller 1998). Rhetoricians and philosophers have long linked compassion (and, more broadly, the passions) to the development of modern moral identity (see chapter 1). But, as Daniel Gross rightly notes, whether in the case of Aristotle's apathetic slave, Adam Smith's notion of universal beneficence, or even more recently in Martha Nussbaum's conception of the compassionate cosmopolitan, "the constitutive power of emotions depends upon their uneven distribution" (2006, 5). The elitism of Aristotle's theory of emotion, for example, is revealed when you consider that, for Aristotle, "pity is directed toward those of equal status who have suffered a wrong unjustly. An equal, and not an inferior, represents the possibility that one might similarly suffer without cause" (Gross 2006, 42). In *The Theory of Moral Sentiments* ([1759] 2000), Smith attributes these passions, as Gross characterizes this work, "to the good graces of a benevolent Being" (Gross 2006, 170). Yet, as Gross also notes, "far from a symmetrical phenomenon felt equally by everyone for everyone else, for Smith . . . sympathy is precisely about negotiating social difference *from a particular perspective* . . . and *in a particular circumstance* where some commonsense notion of propriety prevails" (172). Whether in the context of ancient Greek rhetoric and philosophy, eighteenth-century sentimentality, or the history of modern human rights, "emotions . . . must be read as markers of social distinction rather than just as expressions of a human nature essentially shared by all (178). "Instead of wondering perennially why it has taken so long to extend the range of human compassion to women, to slaves, to non-Europeans, to the poor, to the disabled, and so on," Gross suggests, "we would do better to track the history of terms such as pride, humility, pity, and compassion and see how they have been mobilized for strategic purposes; how, for instance, particular communities are composed by the notion that they have a monopoly on that compassion that would be extended to others" (179).

Similarly, as Megan McLagen reminds us, "the process of summoning witnessing publics" is complex and not reducible to the persuasive tactics of rhetorical identification or rhetorical assent (2007, 312). Rather, this process is both enabled and constrained by a range of cultural, social, and political forces; rhetorical conventions; ideological frameworks; and technologies of interaction. Therefore, to understand how the suffering body becomes sutured to the universal body of human rights, we need to attend to the "structures of feeling," to use the term of Raymond Williams (1997, 114), and the structures of visibility and invisibility that regulate the relations and actions of individuals, communities, and nations. Understanding how the visual economy of human rights renders certain identities and scenes of recognition more legitimate than others is important to the development of a posthumanist ethical vision—a theoretical orientation to human rights that builds on a body of cultural theory and rhetorical criticism devoted to the critique of humanist notions of rhetorical intentionality, transparency, and autonomy. However, a posthumanist approach need not disavow notions of political agency, social justice, equality, and democracy.

Though many scholarly critiques of humanism promote an idiom of haunting, a posthumanist approach to human rights need not avert the corporeal body in favor of the spectral (ghostly) dimension, nor need it be construed as antihumanitarian (Gunn 2006, 81). But a posthumanist vision should be distinguished, as Pheng Cheah observes, "from humanistic critiques of rapid development as creating an empty shell or a mechanically efficient economic machine without a human soul or heart" (2006, 230). A posthumanist orientation to human rights interrogates the discourses of humanity, loosens humanism's hold on feeling (emotion and the passions), and departs from the purportedly benign universalism and moral, civilizing claims of philosophical modernity, which the history of colonialism exposed as malignant (81). Cheah puts it well: "what is at issue here is precisely the crafting of the human, how humanity and all its capacities are not primary, original, and self-originating but product-effects generated by forces that preceded and exceed the *anthropos*" (10). It remains an open question whether a posthumanist approach is politically viable or even imaginable at this historical moment in the development of the relationship between human rights and the humanities, especially given the assault on both human rights and the humanities in U.S. domestic and international politics.

Discovering the political limits and instrumentality of human rights law and culture and the ideological complicity of this law and culture in moral imperialism is an important task. But recognizing the "contaminated normativity of human rights" (Cheah 2006, 172) and how the human rights spectacle both haunts and consolidates hegemonic power is only part of the critical project that this book seeks to advance. *Spectacular Rhetorics* also aims to spotlight cultural and rhetorical interventions that contest abuses of power and the collusion of the discourses of human rights internationalism with the conquests of global capitalism. When human rights abuses are framed by predominantly humanitarian discourses, for example, certain political and ideological agendas are privileged over others, and the longevity of the commitment to help is tied to the staying power of charitable fortitude rather than to the principles of social and economic justice. In other words, the humanitarian response follows the logic of cultural recognition and its limitations in addressing social injustices.

Numerous scholars have critiqued the "messianic ethos" and "missionary zeal" of human rights advocacy that is geared to help those who presumably cannot help themselves (Mutua 2001, 231) and have exposed the limitations of an identity-based paradigm of justice (e.g., W. Brown 1995b; Fraser 2003). But what such perspectives often obscure, as the case-study chapters in this book show, is how human rights victims and advocates (nonexclusive categories) strategically mobilize the discourses of human rights internationalism in ways that simultaneously contest violent inscriptions of identity and invoke these same identity categories in claiming their rights as legal subjects. As scenes of rhetorical address, human rights claims reiterate a set of social and legal norms. But these reiterations never align perfectly; therefore, we need to account for the variability in repetitions that not only respond to particular contexts but that generate contexts. Hence my focus on the paradoxes of recognition and the potential, as well as the limitations of identity-based paradigms for addressing social injustices. Contrary to the position of many scholars, I argue that as those of us in the humanities and on the cultural left contemplate the possibilities of posthumanist principles for human rights advocacy and scholarship, we should not yield the study of the potential efficacy of identification and recognition (or lack thereof) to humanists.

The genealogy of struggles for recognition and reinscription can be tracked in the historiography of human rights (see chapter 1) and, as I demonstrate throughout the case-study chapters, in the paradoxes of the human rights spectacle as it develops in and travels through transnational advocacy and media networks, cultural productions, and academic scholarship. These struggles might be understood as interrogations of the discourses of humanity, and therefore as part of a posthumanist human rights project. This is not to exaggerate the political efficacy of cultural productions or rhetorical criticism in the movement toward social justice, but to account for the rhetorical intercontextuality of culturally and legally based human rights representations and how they effectively derive from provisional and strategic articulations.

In chapter 1, I argued that the history of human rights is itself a struggle for recognition and reinscription—a story troubled by the contradictions of visibility and by hierarchical scenes of suffering. Chapter 2 explored how the 11 September 2001 terror spectacle simultaneously activated an endless vigil for those whose lives were lost and scripted American empire through the trope of the traumatized nation and the creation of the racial other— the Muslim Middle Eastern terrorist. Even as it acknowledged the need to represent, to partake in the endless vigil that is cultural memory, chapter 3 explored how women's testimonies about rape in the context of war can be caught in the objectifying processes that they seek to expose and in this way entrench the pain of subjugated identities in human rights politics. Struggles for recognition and reinscription occur at both the individual and communal level, as illustrated by U.S. nationalist identifications of detainees as unlawful combatants in the War on Terror (chapter 2); women's collective activism and testimonies by rape-warfare victims at the International Criminal Tribunal for the Former Yugoslavia (chapter 3); the identity negotiations of sex workers' rights collectives in response to the neo-abolitionist, antiprostitution agendas of many antitrafficking campaigns and policies (chapter 4); and child workers' navigations of intricate familial, cultural, and national expectations (chapter 5).

Human rights advocates and critics are attuned to the ideological capacity and seductive power of images of suffering, but we need not remain caught in a critical paralysis over the spectacle of victimization or beset by humanitarianism's grip on human rights appeals, a hold abetted by the self-other dyad and normative properties of cultural and legal recognition (chapter 1). Even though the visual economy of contemporary human rights politics is tainted by the legacies of colonial pasts and present imperialisms and beset by the paradoxes of humanitarianism, several of the cultural works featured in the case studies show how human rights advocates, artists, and scholars can strategically mobilize normative frames—including restaging the human rights spectacle and its humanitarian gaze—to generate new discursive formations and cultural contexts through which human rights becomes a site of possibility and contestation.

I conclude, then, with a call for an ethical rhetorical vision that draws together the insights of the featured cases by imagining the humanities, and, more broadly, culture as a site of human rights advocacy and human rights law as a cultural site. This is a call for ethical visions that focus on how human rights law and culture are mutually implicated in, and set the parameters for, social and political recognition and identification practices. Visions attuned to how human rights discourses and practices are complicit in the rationalities that substantiate the hegemony of global capitalism and nationalist militarisms. Visions that extend the ethical parameters of our engagement with distant others by infusing human rights advocacy with a social imaginary predicated on an engagement with the contingencies that compel the pursuit of justice. Visions that contextualize human rights as rhetorical practices of institutional and cultural actors. Visions attuned to the cultural readiness (kairos) for certain representations and the social and political relations they enable.

Others have called for ethical visions predicated on constructs of critical distance, self-estrangement, and heteropathic identification (Silverman 1996); empathetic unsettlement (LaCapra 2001); ethical spectatorship (Kozol n.d.); moral spectatorship (Cartwright 1995); witnessing beyond recognition (Oliver 2001); an ethics of the other (Lévinas 1981); and the "impossibility of full ethical engagement" (Spivak 1995, xxv). While none of these theorists write explicitly about the role of the spectacle in contemporary human rights politics and the ocular epistemology that underwrites it and while their primary orientations include feminist film theory, trauma studies, philosophy, and history, aspects of their arguments are congruous with my own. Building on Kyo Maclear's notion of ethical vision as a "fraught process of understanding our complicity and responsibility to witness, to interpret, to act, towards the cessation of violence and oppression" (1999, 5), Wendy Kozol offers the concept of ethical spectatorship, which requires attention to the histories of imperialism, militarization, and inequalities that structure witnessing (n.d., 5). For her, witnessing is a historical process constituted by power relations. Similarly, *Spectacular Rhetorics* has emphasized the gendered, racial, and sexual scenarios of power that constitute the rhetorical politics of staging the human rights spectacle, which permeates legal and cultural representations. I have been particularly interested in how spectacular texts and contexts project identifications onto audiences; in the recognitions and misrecognitions these identifications set in motion (Fuss 1995, 2); and in how human rights subjects are represented both as possessing certain identities and as being emotionally compelling objects of identification.

*Projective identification* typically refers to misidentifications and mis-recognitions—the defensive projection of parts of the self onto another. However, Lisa Cartwright suggests that projective identification may be an important aspect of empathetic identification. Instead of characteriz-ing identification as a form of ventriloquism, as a process of becoming the other, she defends empathetic identification as a reciprocal relationship: "In empathy . . . my knowledge comes from the force of the object ('you,' the image, the representation), and my reciprocal sense that I recognize the feeling I perceive in your expression. 'You' move me to have feelings, but the feelings may not match your own" (2008, 24). Cartwright's definition of empathetic identification echoes Dominick LaCapra's notion of empa-thetic unsettlement. LaCapra argues that unlike a stance of full identifi-cation, wherein the self and the other are construed as fused, empathetic unsettlement recognizes and respects the alterity of the other (2001, 27; see also chapters 1 and 2 of this book). Kelly Oliver likewise addresses the ethi-cal and political significance of the symbolic violence of identification as a substitution of the other for the self, and she rejects the notion that the oppressed must embrace their oppressors' identification and recognition in order to have a sense of self-worth (2001, 27–29). In *Otherwise Than Being* (1981), to which Oliver is indebted, Emmanuel Lévinas grounds his philoso-phy in the ethics of a face-to-face encounter, which brings responsibilities with it. For Lévinas, as Oliver notes, "communication can take place only beyond recognition" (2001, 206). Lévinas puts it this way: "To communi-cate is indeed to open oneself, but the openness is not complete if it is on the watch for recognition. It is complete not in the opening to the spectacle of or the recognition of the other, but in becoming a responsibility for him" (1981, 119). Gayatri Spivak likewise calls for an ethics based not on recogni-tion or benevolent identifications, but on an understanding of ethics as "the experience of the impossible" (1995, xxv). She argues: "This understanding only sharpens the sense of the crucial and continuing need for collective struggle, . . . a collective struggle supplemented by the impossibility of full ethical engagement.... [T]he future is always around the corner, there is no victory, but only victories that are also warnings" (ibid.).

Despite the many differences among the aforementioned theorists, their emphasis on intersubjectivity, performativity, and language mesh with my emphasis on the politics of recognition and the progressive forces of, and ruptures in, identification and witnessing. Although I use *identification* to refer to rhetorical relations between texts and audiences (both imagined and real), I also uphold the view that identification practices are intimately tied to identity formations (Fuss 1995, 2). Links between these practices and formations are perhaps most visible in chapter 4, when I discuss the rhetorical dynamics of women's accounts of violation in antitrafficking video campaigns, campaigns that reveal the contrasting ways in which feminists mobilize victim identities to structure the rhetorical appeal of their subjects' stories.

Each rhetorical case study featured in *Spectacular Rhetorics* draws attention to the visual politics of recognition, and to the formation of ethical engagements that do not reside in an ethics of identification alone. I am not making an argument against identification, however. I am contesting the hierarchy of idealized identifications and recognitions. Kaja Silverman suggests that "we need to learn how to idealize oppositionally and provisionally, ... we need visual texts which activate in us the capacity to idealize bodies which diverge as wildly as possible both from ourselves and from the cultural norm" (1996, 37). Yet, as Oprah Winfrey's unveiling of Zoya, a feminist activist from Afghanistan, at a performance of Eve Ensler's *The Vagina Monologues* reminds us (see the introduction), those in positions of privilege need to be careful not simply to celebrate difference in a way that recenters themselves. Although Silverman recognizes the "limits and boundaries within which identification may occur," recalling Lacan's mirror stage essay, she believes in the radical potential of identification—namely, cinematic identification (88).

Silverman argues that the visual paradigm of psychoanalytic theory "confers visual authority not on the look but the gaze" (1996, 19). This distinction is crucial to her understanding of the potential identificatory lure of the cinema as a political asset, as a means toward "spectatorial self-estrangement" (85).

Self-recognition and identification are not purely imaginary transactions; they involve the gaze—metaphorized by the camera—which Silverman defines "as the inscription of Otherness within the field of vision" (56). Her view of the gaze as a field of vision shaped by technological apparatuses is consonant with my view, though I use the phrases *visual economy* and *structures of visibility and invisibility* instead of *gaze*, since my study is materially inflected rather than psychoanalytically derived. Silverman promotes heteropathic identifications that resist incorporative (idiopathic) identifications that result in the affirmation of self-sameness (88). She praises representations that "invest the other with the ability to return the look" (95), that enable viewers to arrive "at a conscious perception of [their] unconscious idealizing activities," and that facilitate "identity-at-distance"—an estrangement from one's "habitual bodily parameters" (90). She argues that "it can only be through the creation and circulation of alternative images and words that he or she can be given access to new identicatory coordinates" (81). But, as I demonstrate throughout this book, these "alternative images and words" and "new identicatory coordinates" do not exist outside the discourses they contest, or at a vantage point outside the visual field.

Rhetorical intercontextuality affords us a method to understand the dynamics of identification practices and recognition at the cultural and political level. The difficulty of these negotiations and their potential for revictimization is perhaps most clearly seen in the documentary *Calling the Ghosts: A Story about Rape, War, and Women* (Jacobson and Jelincic 1996), which alludes to the tension between witnessing and spectacle in its portrayal of female victims of rape warfare, who inevitably fed the media's insatiable voyeurism when they gave evidence (chapter 3). Human rights representations solicit an embodied spectatorship—an eye or I whose actions have been subjected to the normative frameworks of human rights law. Seeing ourselves as projected witnesses of human rights internationalism and its staging of the spectacle of suffering therefore requires that we attend to how human rights law and culture work together, and how human rights and humanitarianism converge to sustain normative frameworks of inclusion and exclusion and to legitimize certain identities, subjectivities, and social and economic relations. The spectacular rhetorics of identification, recognition, and witnessing are implicated in the performance of social and legal productivity. Therefore, instead of consolidating the regulatory effects of human rights, we need to expose their normativity, especially as these norms set the terms of public engagement and delimit possible forms of response to social injustices, systemic inequalities, and violence produced by both state and nonstate actors.

The transformation from passive spectator to active witness—a narrative trajectory at the heart of human rights advocacy and the engaged public it imagines—is not wed to or dependent on genre. Indeed, as this book has shown, this transformation narrative is deployed across various human rights media and truth-telling genres. To unsettle passive spectatorship and to facilitate greater critical reflexivity, artists and activists often appropriate and inscribe dominant symbols and symbolic practices, as did the street muralists in Tehran and the public protesters who reproduced and commented on the abuse of detainees at Abu Ghraib (see chapter 2). To facilitate a less spectacular dependency on visualization, human rights advocates and scholars also turn to the testimonies of victims—which are, however, no less encumbered in the ocular epistemology of modernity (recognition versus misrecognition, absence versus presence, and so on). As I discuss in chapter 5, notions of agency and voice that are associated with the transformation from passive spectatorship to active witnessing often reflect an idealized, humanist version of cultural cosmopolitanism, itself a narrative trajectory at the core of emerging models of human rights education (see Tibbitts 2002). In the Academy Award–winning documentary *Born into Brothels*, for example, freedom of expression and the right to voice (civil and political rights) are predicated on a process of self-recognition, which is sponsored by a privileged outsider, Zana Briski. Briski's rhetorical positioning contrasts with the model of ethical engagement put forward by Heather Montgomery in her ethnographic study *Modern Babylon?* (2001) and by Tareque and Catherine Masud in their documentary *A Kind of Childhood* (2007), both of which present children as complex moral and political agents who must negotiate contradictory cultural and familial expectations. Montgomery and the Masuds work against reductive representations by offering a differentiated politics of recognition (see chapters 1 and 5)—rather than the politics typified in human rights and humanitarian representations of distant others targeted at Western audiences—through their representation of the local as a locality, foregrounding the relationality of contexts and subjectivities.[1] Montgomery emphasizes the infusion of local, national, and international discourses in children's identity negotiations and their roles as sex workers, and thus her study exposes the limitations of the local-global binary, including its use as a symbolic marker. *A Kind of Childhood* similarly reorients this binary through its adjustment of the scale of the gaze of the documentarian and, by extension, that of the viewer. Aligned as they are with truth-telling genres—ethnography and observant documentary, respectively—both works risk voyeurism. But this risk is reallocated through each work's turn from moral superiority and the urgencies of humanitarian rhetoric, associated with American inflections of human rights internationalism, and their focus on economic exploitations and the injustices of poverty that sustain child labor.

Strategic configurations of silence and absence likewise elaborate a less spectacular aesthetic. As I discuss in chapter 3, Melanie Friend's evocative exhibition *Homes and Gardens*, which displays ordinary photographs of middle-class living quarters in Kosovo (or Kosova) accompanied by recordings of oral testimonies about the trauma of ethnic violence, suspends the spectacle of mass atrocity and human suffering and thereby prompts viewers to contemplate how they are positioned by the media to see themselves. In its coupling of the testimonies of victimization and trauma and images of the ordinary, *Homes and Gardens* exemplifies the simultaneous reinscription and deconstruction of spectacular human rights rhetorics. The visual dissemination of human rights norms and violations through cultural forms requires that we reject a mimetic understanding of human rights representations (the view that seeing is believing) and opt instead for a rhetorical view, which focuses on scenes of address through which the evidence of human rights violations is fashioned.

Ethical visions imply reflexive, rhetorical engagements. Images of human rights violations run risks, can be commodified, and do not, in and of themselves, generate social change. Yet spectacular representations are pervasive, if not always persuasive, sites of cultural and political engagement that keep the human rights agenda in the public eye. Throughout *Spectacular Rhetorics*, I have examined how the human rights spectacle incorporates the body and its pain into the discourse of human rights internationalism—

particularly as human rights appeals are framed for Western, and primarily American, audiences—and how spectacular rhetorics are mobilized by human rights media, governments, activist artists, and academics to serve a range of cultural, national, and political agendas. I am not convinced, however, that self-reflexivity or the process of empathetic unsettlement (LaCapra 2001) are enough to counter historically invasive and persistent objectifications of the other and the struggles for recognition that underlie the philosophical universalism of human rights law. But these are key components of ethical engagements. Finally, human rights are never pure, or culturally and politically unencumbered; therefore, instead of trying to purify (or abandon) them, those of us on the cultural left ought to work with their complexities and paradoxes as we move toward a future justice. Because controversies over visual representations of human suffering will perpetually resurface, especially given the prominence of visual technologies of interaction in human rights advocacy and international politics, and because ethical questions will necessarily arise from these interactions, this study has no definitive point of closure. I return then to several of the questions that set this project in motion. How do human rights images beckon us as scholars, activists, and citizens? What demands do human rights spectacles place on us? Who are we becoming in this spectacular discourse?

## Introduction

1. As part of its initial two-year campaign, AIUSA created a series of aesthetically eloquent and attention-grabbing posters showing populations vulnerable to state-sanctioned human rights violations, several of which, like the brochure cover, feature individual victims in tightly framed scenes. On 10 December 2005, AIUSA unveiled a new global initiative, which included a compact disc of international artists performing other iconic John Lennon songs.

2. The legal definition of a refugee or internally displaced person can be found in Article 1 of the UN's 1951 Refugee Convention: a person who, "owing to a well-founded fear of being persecuted for reasons of race, religion, nationality, membership of a particular social group, or political opinion, is outside the country of his nationality, and is unable or, owing to such fear, is unwilling to avail himself of the protection of that country."

3. At one time, over a hundred refugee camps in Pakistan held Afghan refugees from the Soviet occupation of Afghanistan during the 1980s and the wars that followed. Jalozai, Old Shamshatoo, and Panian are the largest refugee camps in Pakistan. For security reasons and to facilitate the repatriation process, all three have been slated for closure. In July 2007, after two years of negotiations, Kacha Garhi, then one of the oldest and largest camps, closed. Nearly 3.2 million Afghans returned to their homeland after the 2001 collapse of the Taliban; 2 million Afghans are still registered as being in Pakistan today (UNHCR 2007, 1).

4. *National Geographic* is one of the most widely circulated American magazines and has played a powerful role in representing non-Western cultures for its American audiences (see Lutz and Collins 1993). Additionally, the 1984 image appears repeatedly, hanging on shop walls in Kabul, in the 2002 movie *The Search for the Afghan Girl*, suggesting the dissemination of the image throughout the world. A card company in Kabul, called Breshna, produced a poster version of the image titled "Afghanistan." The image has been reproduced in numerous publications, including *National Geographic: The Photographs* (Bendavid-Val 2008) and McCurry's *Portraits* (1999). McCurry's images of Afghan girl refugees were also featured in the 2006 photo exhibition *Afghanistan's Children—the Next Generation* at the UN headquarters in New York. The more recent image of the Afghan girl (fig. 1) was reproduced on the cover of McCurry and Purcell 2007.

5. By *icon*, photojournalists mean a photographic image that is reproduced across a range of media (print, electronic, or digital) and genres, that is "widely recognized and remembered," and that "activate[s] strong emotional identification or response" (Hariman and Lucaites 2007, 27).

6. Asia and Africa, for instance, have taken many more refugees than North America and Western Europe, a pattern that Anthony Richmond has characterized as a "form of

global apartheid" (quoted in Grewal 2005, 168). Scholars have identified what they see as the inherent racism of refugee laws and treaties (Tuitt 1996), and others (for example, Malkki 1994 and Richmond 1994) have problematized the category of the refugee as one that does not account for "multiple, shifting identities" of those given that label (Grewal 2005, 169).

7. I would like to thank Joseph Slaughter for this observation.

8. Steve Ruhl, email message to author.

9. *National Geographic*'s documentary *The Search for the Afghan Girl*, released in March 2002, is a paradigmatic case of Western liberal representations of the Muslim other that structured the post-9/11 relationship between Afghanistan and the United States in terms that were reassuring for U.S. audiences. The film focuses on the photojournalist Steve McCurry's return to the Nasir Bagh refugee camp in Peshawar, Pakistan, seventeen years after the initial photograph (fig. 2) was taken, to find the Afghan girl. McCurry and his team of FBI examiners and forensic technicians, with the use of high-tech iris recognition tests, identified as the "missing" Afghan girl Sharbat Gula, then married with three daughters and living in a remote ethnic Pashtun region of Afghanistan. Like the caption that accompanied the 1985 *National Geographic* cover—"Haunted eyes tell of a young Afghan refugee's fears"—the film imagines a specular relationship between its Western audience and the older Gula; she is subject to "the public eye of the lens, the eyes that authenticate her identity" (Whitlock 2007, 71). At Nasir Bagh, McCurry came across and photographed the young girl pictured on AIUSA's "Imagine" brochure (fig. 1), whose arresting eyes reminded him of the other girl from his past. See Hesford and Kozol (2005) for a fuller analysis of this film and its construal of Gula in terms of the Western imaginary. For more on the link between human rights advocacy, humanitarianism, and empire building see Armitage 2000, Harlow 1996, Haskell 1985, Mertus 2003, Rieff 2003, Robbins 1999, and Weiss and Collins 1996.

10. Afghan feminists have used the burqa as a symbol of nationalist unity and feminist resistance. Under the Taliban regime, for instance, women used the burqa to conceal weapons and banned publications they were transporting, and video equipment they were using to film the Taliban's oppressive acts. The video footage taken by Afghan women includes the widely circulated 1999 public execution of a woman in Kabul, identified only as Zarmeena, who was found guilty of beating her husband to death. The footage was distributed to the international media by the Revolutionary Association of Women of Afghanistan. The burqa has also been used by male militants. For example, at a highway checkpoint in Afghanistan in 2007, Afghan police discovered a Siberian man covered in a burqa, who was attempting to transport a truckload of explosives. The man was later identified by Afghan and American officials as an intended suicide bomber (Rohde 2007). For further discussions of the veil as trope in Western representations of East-West colonial relations, see Harlow 1986 and, for example, L. Ahmed 1993, Eisenstein 2004a, Hesford and Kozol 2005, Said 1981, Shohat 2006, and Whitlock 2007.

11. Laura Bush's address was titled "The Taliban's War against Women." It is available through the U.S. Department of State's website.

12. Human rights law gives the state power and makes it responsible for reducing struc-tural violence in society, protecting individuals from abuse, and facilitating corrective justice. In contrast, humanitarianism embedded in relief and development agendas focuses on alleviating the symptoms of suffering. In the post–cold war era, humanitar-ian actors have increasingly invoked human rights principles. Human rights may give greater legal footing to the so-called new humanitarianism, but, as critics have argued, a human rights approach raises issues of conditionality at odds with the traditional humanitarian ethic of political neutrality (Chandler 2001).

13. I would like to thank Steven Mailloux (e-mail message to author, 1 May 2009) for sug-gesting the need to emphasize the different ways in which intertextuality works as an explanatory concept. I have chosen to use the phrase *rhetorical intercontextuality* to foreground the persuasive power of intertextuality and its mobilization in certain contexts. My approach to rhetorical criticism has been influenced by transnational feminists and postcolonial rhetorical theorists (Bahir 2008, Hesford 2006, Hesford and Schell 2008, Jarratt 2000, Schell 2006, Shome 1999, and Spurr 1993) and social theorists who focus on the materiality of discourse, such as Hennessy 1993, and Laclau and Mouffe 1985, among others.

14. My definition of rhetoric builds on both DeLuca's construal of rhetoric in *Image Politics* as "the mobilization of signs for the articulation of identities, ideologies, conscious-ness, communities, publics, and cultures" (1999, 17) and Riedner and Mahoney's (2008) conceptualization of rhetoric as an activating force.

15. Scholarly investigations of narrative are broad in scope. The following list is meant to highlight some of the works that have been particularly helpful to this project and its articulation of the relation among narrative, rhetoric, and human rights (Kapur 2005 and 2006, Mutua 2001, Phelan 1966, Schaffer and Smith 2004, Slaughter 1997, 2006, 2007, and Shuman 2005).

16. *Kairos* is a multidimensional rhetorical term that refers to a situational understand-ing of space and time and to the material circumstances—namely, the cultural climate—of rhetorical situations (Crowley and Hawhee 2004, 37). Social theorists use the term *opportunity structures* in ways that parallel rhetoricians' use of the term *kairos*. My emphasis on social, cultural, and political frames shares the concerns of construc-tionists in international relations theory and social movement theory. Petruzzi (2001) understands *kairos* not as a transformation of contentious discourse into a harmonious situation, but as an analytical method that breaks down oppositions in order to enable new knowledge.

17. In *The Dialogic Imagination*, Bakhtin writes: "At any given moment of its historical existence, language is heteroglot from top to bottom: it represents the co-existence of socio-ideological contradictions between the present and the past, between differing epochs of the past, between different social-ideological groups in the present, between tendencies, schools, circles and so forth, all given a bodily form. These 'languages of heteroglossia intersect each other in a variety of ways, forming new socially typifying 'languages'" (1981, 291). According to Bazerman (2004), the concept of intertextuality does not originate with Bakhtin: Kristeva first coined the term in *Desire in Language: A Semiotic Approach to Literature and Art* (first published in English in 1980). Theories

of intertextuality trouble modernist notions of authorship. In *S/Z*, Barthes characterizes the author as orchestrating the "already written" (1974, 21), and in *Image-Music-
Text*, he describes the text as "a multidimensional space in which a variety of writings,
none of them original, blend and clash" (1977, 146). Similarly, with regard to the reader,
Jameson argues that "texts come before us as the always-already-read; we apprehend
them through the sedimented layers of previous interpretations, or—if the text is
brand-new—through the sedimented reading habits and categories developed by
those inherited interpretive traditions" (1981, 9).

18. Scholars from various fields have applied a methodology that emphasizes intertextuality. Scholars in literary theory deploy intertextuality to complicate the status of
the author and to elucidate how intertextuality works in specific texts (Bakhtin 1981,
Barthes 1974 and 1977, Kristeva 1980, Volosinov 1973, Gennett 1997). In composition
and rhetorical studies, see Bazerman 2004, Porter 1986, Seltzer 1993. In visual culture
studies, Chouliaraki employs a multimodal analytic that shares several characteristics
with my approach, namely her emphasis on the multifunctionality of the verbal and
visual, though her study focuses on the mediated environment of television (2006, 78).

19. Here Puar invokes Deleuze and Guattari's claim that "[t]he assemblage, as a series of
dispersed but mutually implicated and messy networks, draws together enunciation
and dissolution, causality and effect, organic and nonorganic forces [and that] assemblages are collections of multiplicities" (Deleuze and Guattari 1983, 211).

20. My view of the imaginary as a social and rhetorical phenomena is influenced by
Castoriadis's (1987) concept of a social imaginary to refer to "the final articulations the
society in question has imposed on the world, on itself, and on its needs, the organizing
patterns that are the conditions for the representability of everything that the society
can give to itself" (as quoted in Poovey 2002, 130).

21. My view of the ideological status of the imaginary shares some of the properties of
Burke's configuration of the terministic screen. Burke writes: "Not only does the nature of our terms affect the nature of our observations, in the sense that the terms
direct the attention to one field rather than another. Also, many of the 'observations'
are but implications of the particular terminology in terms of which the observations
are made" (1966, 46).

22. Although the SI conceptualized the spectacle as an all-inclusive phenomenon, their
writings reflect a deep nostalgia for the "real" beyond representation, for the authentic
experience lurking beyond the spectacle. The SI's nostalgia for the authentic can be
seen in their idealization of the working class, in relation to whom they "displayed a
telling mixture of anthropological distance . . . and fond attachment" (Bonnett 2006,
28). Debord writes: "In the demand to live the historical time which it makes, the pro-
letariat finds the simple unforgettable centre of its revolutionary project" (1994, 143).

23. Significant works on the spectacle include Baudrillard 1981, Best 1994, Best and Kellner
1999, Debord 1994, Erickson 1992, Foucault 1975, Kellner 2005, Plant 1992, and Retort
2005. There is also a vast literature on the disciplinary and disciplining functions of
visuality and the reproduction of social hierarchies through visual technologies. I include only a cursory list here: Bal 2007; Benjamin 1986; Bronfen 1992; Cartwright 1995;

Chow 2006; Fabian 1983; Garland-Thomson 2002; Gilman 2001; Grewal 2005; James 1998; Kapsalis 1997; Kozol 2010; Lutz and Collins 1993; Mirzoeff 1998, 2005, and 2006; Mitchell 1994, 2002; Petro 1995; Sekula 1986; Shohat and Stam 1994, 1999; Silverman 1996; Spurr 1993; and Tagg 1993. Still others—Boltanski 1999; Feldman 2004b; Giroux 2007; Hirsch 1997, 2002a, and 2002b; Sontag 2003; D. Taylor 1997; J. Young 2000; and Zelizer 2000, 2001, and 2003 in particular—have examined the spectacular role of images of mass atrocity in popular culture and in the construction of historical memory. Scholarly works about human rights, media, and the spectacle of suffering that have been particularly useful to my project include L. Allen 2009, Bob 2002, Chouliaraki 2006, Goldberg 2001 and 2007, Kleinman and Kleinman 1996, Moeller 2002, and Reinhardt and Edwards 2007.

24. These links are discernible in Plato's allegory of the cave, described in *The Republic*. Although the point of the allegory is to direct the men bound in the cave toward enlightenment—out of the darkness of the hidden truth—this process involves pain and coercion (Plato 2003, 121). The shackled prisoners are also spellbound by illusions; they stare at shadows on the wall and mistake them for real objects. Socrates describes the prisoners' ascent from disillusionment and their acclimation to the light as a process that, in Blumenberg's words, both "diminishes [the light's] dazzling effects" and becomes a "source of deception about one's own standpoint vis-à-vis Being" (Blumenberg 1993, 45). Plato's myth of the cave would be used two millennia later by French philosophers, who linked the hegemonic tradition of Western philosophy and science to the privileging of vision. In his critique of the ocular focus of Western metaphysics, Derrida (1987) deconstructs the opposition between truth and illusion that structures Plato's allegory. In *Speculum of the Other Woman* (1985), Irigaray re-envisions the allegory of the cave from a psychoanalytic perspective as a phantasmic primal scene that represses feminine desire "in favor of the father, the solar origin of Ideas, the specular fount of sameness" (quoted in Jay 1994, 536–37).

25. This quote is from Amnesty International's web campaign, http://www.tearitdown .org.

## One. Human Rights Visions and Recognitions

1. The visual connotations of recognition are most explicit in the verb from which the term is derived: "to recognize means to look over again, to acknowledge by omission or confession or avowal, to treat as valid or having existence or as entitled to consideration, to take notice in some way, to know again" (Oliver 2001, 170).

2. Kapur observes that the "modernist narrative of human progress [is] based on the idea that the world has emerged from a darker, more uncivilized era" (2005, 21). Modernity's thesis of history as progressive is inextricably linked to the colonial enterprise (Kapur 2005, 21). Colonial power structures, likewise, were reinforced through the use of visualization techniques and empirical methodologies, which enabled the definition and evaluation, if not the possession, of the "other" (Mirzoeff 1998, 282). See also Kapur 2006.

3. The postwar juridical revolution included the United Nations Charter of 1945, the

constitutional basis for all UN human rights texts; the 1948 Universal Declaration of Human Rights; the genocide convention (Convention on the Prevention and Punishment of the Crime of Genocide), which protected religious, racial, and ethnic groups against extermination; the 1949 Geneva Conventions, which were later revised to strengthen noncombatant immunity; and the 1951 Convention Relating to the Status of Refugees.

4. In highlighting the paradoxes of the interwar period, for example, Afshari explains how nationalist movements undercut the evolution of the concept of universal human rights: "The paradox of considering nationalism as a human-rights-based paradigm, or the nationalistically motivated right to self-determination as a human right, lies in the nature of nationalism itself, i.e., its inability, by its own inherent logic, to show any tolerance toward an outside intervention, on behalf of international human rights laws or anything else" (2007, 51). Nationalist fervor, such as we have seen articulated through the post-9/11 policies of the Bush administration, has proven, once again, to be antithetical to human rights visions and should give us pause as we consider how to approach human rights, past and future. Afshari also exposes the contradictions in the discourses and actions of prominent individuals in various single-issue struggles in order to further demonstrate the unfeasibility of an unencumbered progress narrative.

5. Joseph Slaughter uses "(self)recognition scene" to refer to representations of "the moment of personification (or incorporation) when the individual becomes conscious of being a subject to and for the rules of law and narrative . . . [it] is also a moment when the abstract symmetricalness of the law reveals itself" (2007, 254). My use of the term picks up on Slaughter's emphasis on the narrative (rhetorical) incorporation of the subject and the incorporation of the subject into the plot of human rights history.

6. Mutua is rightly sensitive to the "irony of brutalizing colonial powers pushing for . . . the adoption of the UDHR [the Universal Declaration of Human Rights]" (2001, 210). For Mutua, it is important to acknowledge that it was "genocidal extermination of Jews in Europe that started the process of the codification and universalization of human rights norms," not the enslavement of Africans or the colonial conquests of Asia, Africa, and Latin America, with their atrocities and genocidal dimensions (ibid.).

7. Forty-eight members of the UN voted for the UDHR, and none voted against it. Eight —six Communist states, Saudi Arabia, and South Africa—abstained.

8. UN GA Resolution 421, Fifth Session, 4 December 1959.

9. Article 2 of the UDHR states that "no distinction shall be made on the basis of the political, jurisdictional or international status of the country or territory to which a person belongs, whether it be independent, trust, non-self-governing or under any other limitation of sovereignty."

10. One of the few human rights documents to address abuses suffered by migrants, such as forced labor and debt bondage, is the 1990 International Convention on the Protection of the Rights of All Migrant Workers and Members of Their Families, which only entered into force on 1 July 2003 and has not been ratified by any of the industrial countries. But this convention cannot address the transnationalization of labor and migration within its immigration framework (Kapur 2005, 152).

11. For more on both media and legal representations of refugees, see Bohmer and Shuman 2007, and Grewal 2005.

12. The establishment of the International Criminal Court in 2002, which can prosecute on behalf of individuals if the states in which human rights violations were committed do not perform this legal function, has challenged the role of state sovereignty in the domain of human rights (Cubilié 2005, 22).

13. Available at http://www2.ohchr.org/english/law/crc.htm.

14. Ricoeur notes between these phrases a shift in usage from the active verb form (to recognize something) to the passive form (to be recognized), the latter of which requires institutions and political and legal processes for its realization and therefore represents an increasing liberation of the concept from epistemology (2005, 21).

15. Honneth writes: "The motives for rebellion, protest and resistance have generally been transformed into categories of 'interest' and those interests are supposed to emerge from the objective inequalities in the distribution of material opportunities without ever being linked . . . to the everyday web of moral feelings" (1995, 161).

16. Scholarship in autobiography studies likewise draws attention to the performative dimensions of self-representation. See especially Leigh Gilmore 1994, S. Smith and Watson 1992, and Whitlock 2007.

17. In *Giving an Account of Oneself*, Butler problematizes her earlier embrace of the Hegelian dyadic and its view of subjection as the foundation of subject formation and sociability. She writes: "In *The Psychic Life of Power*, I perhaps too quickly accepted this punitive scene of inauguration for the subject" (2005, 15). In developing a post-Hegelian model, Butler seems to align herself with Foucault's refusal to "generalize the scene of punishment to account for how a reflexive subject comes about" (ibid.). She also revises the Hegelian concept of reciprocal recognition in its desire for self-sameness (seeing the other in oneself) by proposing an ethics "based on our shared, invariable, and partial blindness about ourselves," and "reading the scene of recognition in which precisely my own opacity to myself occasions my capacity to confer a certain kind of recognition on others" (41).

18. There are historical precedents in rights campaigns for such troubling identifications, most notably the nineteenth-century campaigns of white women suffragists, which linked the plight of white women to that of slaves and appropriated antislavery discourse as a weapon in the fight for women's voting rights. The question then and now, as Spelman (1997) reminds us, is whether such appropriations subvert or help to sustain power structures and thereby mask our participation in the struggles of others.

19. Butler makes a similar point: "It is not just that some humans are treated as humans, and others are dehumanized; it is rather that dehumanization becomes the condition for the production of the human to the extent that a 'Western' civilization defines itself over and against a population understood as, by definition, illegitimate, if not dubiously human" (2004, 91).

20. See "Read Obama's Comments In The Yad Vashem Holocaust Memorial Visitors' Book," *Huffington Post*, 24 July 2008 (http://www.huffingtonpost.com/2008/07/24/read-obamas-comments-in-t_n_114665.html).

21. Eichmann was indicted on fifteen criminal charges, including crimes against human-ity; sentenced to death on December 15, 1961; and, after several failed appeals, executed on May 31, 1962.

22. Media depictions of more recent atrocities often recall the Holocaust, which further reveals the fundamental intercontextuality of human rights representations. The tele-vised coverage of violence and the plight of civilians in the context of the Vietnam War, for instance, renewed interest in the atrocity photographs of the Second World War. In 1978, at a time of increased soul searching in the United States over the country's involvement in the Vietnam War, the American miniseries *Holocaust* drew millions of viewers. The surge of Holocaust memory projects in the late 1970s in the United States, and later in Britain, occurred across a wide range of cultural settings. Atrocity photographs have played a major role in the cultural production of Holocaust memory; photographs of the camps have been used in films, cultural exhibits, official commem-orations, and media retrospectives (Zelizer 2000, 173).

23. *Testimony* is indebted to psychoanalytic frameworks and de Manian deconstruction. Indeed, Felman was criticized for her seeming exoneration of de Man and her appro-priation of the survivor identity to describe his suicide. See Tal 1996, LaCapra 2001, and Hungerford 2001, especially 77–78.

24. Likewise, in the "Rhetoric of Temporality," de Man claims: "The translator can never do what the original text did. Any translation is always second in relation to the origi-nal. . . . They disarticulate, they undo the original, and they reveal that the original was always already disarticulated. They reveal that their failure . . . reveals an essential failure. . . . They kill the original, by discovering that the original was already dead" (quoted in Felman and Laub 1992, 158). In other words, what the "translator fails to do is to . . . erase the murder of the original" (158).

25. In *When the Moon Waxes Red*, Minh-ha engages the rhetorical politics of what she de-fines as "all-owning spectatorship," which champions dominant forms of expression, or literal and linear readings that level out differences; the "fetishistic language of the spectacle," or the denial of spectators' subjectivity as meaning makers (1991, 93); and "normalized filmic codes," or moralizing information and objective explanations (88).

26. Human rights advocacy training programs are proliferating in Europe and the United States. For instance, the Center for the Study of Human Rights at Columbia University offers a four-month training program for human rights activists to use human rights laws and skills such as media advocacy and fundraising. Other sites include the Univer-sity of Connecticut's Human Rights Institute (http://humanrights.uconn.edu/) and the University of California at Berkeley's Human Rights Center (http://hrc.berkeley .edu/). See Gregory et al. 2005 for explication of how WITNESS, a nongovernmental human rights organization, uses visual technologies in their advocacy work.

27. Bill Nichols has written incisively on expository documentary, which he characterizes as works that make an "argument about the world, or representation in the sense of placing evidence before others, in order to convey a particular viewpoint" (1992, 125). Other works in documentary and ethnographic film include Minh-ha 1991, Renov 1993, and Zimmerman 2000.

28. Five Serbian men, former members of the paramilitary group known as the Scorpions, who murdered six Muslim teenagers from Srebrenica on 17 July 1995, were identified through video footage and arrested. The video, taken by a sixth Serbian man involved in the actions, documents only one of many massacres that took place in the UN-protected enclave of Srebrenica in 1995, when the region was overrun by Bosnian Serbs and Serbian police units—backed by the regime of Slobodan Milošević—who killed more than 8,000 Muslim men and boys ("Conversation: War Crimes," *Online NewsHour*, PBS, 14 June 2005).

29. Website can be found at http://www.serbianna.com/features/srebrenica.

30. In a speech at the 2005 fiftieth anniversary of World Press Photo, Jan Pronk, former special representative of the UN secretary-general and head of the UN mission in Sudan, linked the absence of photographic witnesses in Darfur to the world's inattention and lack of concern. He urged reporters and photographers to go to Darfur to document the atrocities for the world to see (2005, 2). According to the Center for American Progress, "during June 2005, CNN, Fox News, NBC/MSNBC, ABC, and CBS ran 50 times as many stories about Michael Jackson and 12 times as many stories about Tom Cruise as they did about the genocide in Darfur" (http://SaveDarfur.org). Despite reports by human rights organizations in 2003 and early 2004, media coverage of Darfur was practically nonexistent (366). Important reports from various groups (Human Rights Watch, Amnesty International, Refugees International, Physicians for Human Rights, International Crisis Group, and the Sudan Organization against Torture), as well as belated UN reports from the Office for the Coordination of Humanitarian Affairs document the atrocities that have occurred in the western Sudan since the conflict erupted (Reeves 2006).

31. U.S. showcases for human rights documentaries include the Public Broadcasting System's P.O.V series, the annual Human Rights Watch Film Festival (New York and London), the Human Rights Watch Traveling Film Festival, Amnesty International Film Festival (Seattle), Media That Matters Film Festival (online only), and human rights centers and programs at major universities across the country. The International Human Rights Watch Film Festival, sponsored by a division of Human Rights Watch (HRW), is one of the major venues for human rights cinema in the United States. The annual budget for the festival is $20,000, which HRW uses to license films for it (Andrea Holley, interview with author). Among the most prominent human rights centers and programs in the United States are the Center for the Study of Human Rights at Columbia University, the Center for Human Rights at Duke University, the Human Rights Program at Harvard Law School, the Human Rights Institute at the University of Connecticut, the Human Rights Center at the University of California at Berkeley, the University of Chicago Human Rights Program, and the Orville H. Schell, Jr. Center for International Rights at Yale Law School. Among the major distributors of human rights video and film are Third World Newsreel, Witness, and Women Make Movies. There are also smaller distributors such as the Human Rights Video Project, which distributes films free of charge to public libraries across the United States. U.S. funding sources for documentary videos and films that focus on human rights include:

the Independent Television Service (which is supported in part by the Corporation for Public Broadcasting), National Endowment for the Humanities, Sundance Documentary Fund, Witness, John D. and Catherine T. MacArthur Foundation, and the Ford Foundation.

32. See McLagen for a discussion of how powerful NGOs, such as AI, provide "scaffolding for the production and distribution of these media," and the advantage for local activists of having links to these powerful NGOs (2007, 311). See Gregory 2006 for further discussion of the concept of transnational witnessing and human rights video advocacy.

## Two. Staging Terror Spectacles

1. My use of the term *terror spectacle* combines Henry Giroux's articulation of two overlapping and coexistent expressions of the spectacle post-9/11: *the spectacle of terrorism*, which refers to spectacularized violence, and the *terror of the spectacle*, which refers to the politics of exhibitionism, pageantry, and mythological nationalism. The latter is also associated with the *spectacle of fascism* and the *spectacle of consumerism* (2007, 18).

2. In November 2003, Major General Donald J. Ryder filed a report that concluded there were potential systematic human rights abuses at Abu Ghraib. Two months later, Major General Taguba's report (though not meant to be released to the public) found numerous instances of abuses there. See Hersh 2004 and Danner 2004 for more on the debates over interrogation, and Danner 2004 for reproductions of government memos and other key investigative reports, including the Taguba report.

3. There are many available editorials and critical analyses of the Abu Ghraib photographs. For general discussions of Abu Ghraib torture photography, see Boxer 2004, Brison 2004, Danner 2004, Feldman 2004b, Willis 2005, and Žižek 2004.

4. The exhibit ran from 17 September through 28 November 2004 in New York and at the Andy Warhol Museum, in Pittsburgh, from 11 September through 28 November 2004. For reviews of the exhibit, see Awad 2004, S. Shapiro 2004, and Strauss 2004.

5. See also Baudrillard's *The Spirit of Terrorism*, in which he articulates how terrorist acts that aim to "destabilize the global order" risk reinforcing it instead (2002, 55). "But perhaps," he suggests, "that is the terrorists' dream: the dream of an immortal enemy. For, if the enemy no longer exists, it becomes difficult to destroy it. A tautology, admittedly, but terrorism is tautological" (55–56).

6. As Puar notes, drawing on the work of Darius Rejali (1998), this pose is based on the forced standing technique used by torturers in the British army (where it was known as "the crucifixion") and the French army (where it was known as "the Silo"), armies in the early twentieth century, U.S. police, Stalin's People's Commissariat for Internal Affairs (NKVD), the Gestapo in the 1930s, and South African and Brazilian police (who added the electrical supplement) in the 1970s" (2007, 102).

7. To keep public pressure on the Bush administration and to make U.S. torture policy an issue in the 2008 national election, Kennedy launched a campaign with the same name as the documentary on 17 October 2007, one year after the passage of the Military Commissions Act, which authorized a new system of military trials for noncitizens

determined to be "unlawful enemy combatants" (Human Rights Watch 2006). The campaign involved screening the film in thousands of key districts and congregations across the United States.

8. Fantasy-theme rhetorical criticism is associated with Ernest G. Bormann and symbolic convergence theory, which highlighted the epistemological properties of rhetoric —namely, that "rhetoric creates knowledge" (Foss 1996, 122). The criticism is useful precisely because it helps us to understand the rhetorical identifications and differences that structure the War on Terror.

9. "The Bush administration's narrower definition, unrecognized anywhere else, defined torture as 'severe physical or mental pain or suffering' that results in significant harm of significant duration, lasting 'months or even years'" (Kennedy, "This Government Does Not Torture People," Huffingtonpost.com, 8 October 2007).

10. The concept originates with Susan Sontag's "The Pornographic Imagination" (1967).

11. The subtitle of the play, "honor bound to defend freedom," ironically refers to a sign in the prison.

12. The play also appeared in Chicago at the Theatre Company, 11 February to 26 March 2005; in San Francisco at the Brava Theater Center, 23 March to 17 April 2005; and in Washington at the Studio Theatre, 2 November to 11 December 2005.

13. According to Gary Fisher Dawson, documentary theater dates back to 1835, with Georg Büchner's play *Danton's Death* (1999, 1). Many scholars, however, locate the roots of contemporary documentary theater in the work of Bertolt Brecht and Erwin Piscator, who used a wide range of techniques—including the immediacy of news coverage— in the 1920s to persuade audiences toward social action.

14. Interrogators claimed that the Tipton Three—Ruhel Ahmed, Asif Iqbal, and Shafiq Rasul—were at a training camp with Osama bin Laden, and that they had a video as proof. The three men initially denied their involvement but later confessed; however, it was subsequently discovered that they had been in the United Kingdom when the video was made, and were therefore presumed not guilty.

15. *Rasul v. Bush*, challenged the Bush administration's policy of indefinitely holding detainees at Guantánamo Bay without judicial review. On 28 June 2004, the Supreme Court ruled that prisoners at Guantánamo Bay are entitled to military trials or to hearings to determine the validity of the charges against them.

16. Definitions of torture are contained in numerous human rights conventions, including four of the Geneva Conventions of 1949.

17. On 23 June 2005, Vice President Dick Cheney (who is not a character in the play) declared that detainees at Guantánamo Bay were well treated. "They're living in the tropics," he said. "They've got everything they could possibly want. There isn't any other nation in the world that would treat people who were determined to kill Americans the way we're treating these people" (Agence France-Presse 2005, A16).

18. There were numerous opportunities for political acts suggested in the lobby of the Culture Project production of Guantánamo. Among those present were representatives from the Center for Constitutional Rights, the Guantánamo Human Rights Commission, and the Guantánamo Reading Project.

### Three. Witnessing Rape Warfare

1. As one of several lawyers representing a group of Bosnian Muslim and Croatian women survivors, MacKinnon brought Radovan Karadžić, the leader of the Bosnian Serbs, to trial in the United States under the Alien Tort Claims Act of 1789 (1993). MacKinnon approached the issue of rape warfare through a civil lawsuit. Although the suit was successful in awarding the plaintiffs $745 million in compensatory and punitive damages, several of her critics have argued that MacKinnon failed to address the foundational role that human rights law played in the case. As Serena Parekh aptly puts it: "If it were not for the fact that genocide is a human rights violation, there would be no ground for a civil lawsuit. The moral force behind these civil suits comes from the language of human rights" (2007, 136).

2. The complete official title of this judicial body, established in 1991, is the International Tribunal for the Prosecution of Persons Responsible for Serious Violations of International Humanitarian Law Committed in the Territory of the Former Yugoslavia.

3. Several concerns may help to explain MacKinnon's insistence on the particularity of experiences of violation, despite its spectacular functions. These include her validation of the experiential and her disdain for the postmodern feminist emphasis on the discursive. MacKinnon claims that postmodernists, in their focus on the discursive, have "vault[ed] themselves out of power methodologically" (reprinted in 2006a, 56). She argues that postmodernism "erects itself on its lack of relation to the realities of the subordinated because it is only in social reality that human violation takes place, can be known, and can be stopped" (62). Though I share her concern about the need to attend to the materiality of power and agency, I would argue that it is MacKinnon who has slammed the vault shut in terms of the recognition of key theoretical and pragmatic considerations of the importance of the rhetoric-material dyad in shaping human experience and human rights claims. MacKinnon offers a more nuanced analysis of the power of language (and, more broadly, discourse) in her discussion of particular cases, as in her essay "Defining Rape Internationally: A Comment on Akayesu" (reprinted in 2006c). But her recognition of interdependence of the material and rhetorical is not carried over to her theoretical considerations.

4. The war heightened conflicts among Zagreb feminist groups. Four women's groups retained MacKinnon as their attorney: Kareta (a radical feminist group), Bedem Ljubavi (Wall of Love, a Croatian women's group), Zene BiH (a Bosnian refugee women's group), and Biser (International Initiative of Women of Bosnia-Herzegovina). Their stand, as Benderly characterizes it, "is that rape is a distinctly Serbian weapon for which all Serbians—even feminists who oppose the war—are culpable" (1997, 66–67).

5. The accounts in MacKinnon 1993, for instance, are based on original research conducted by Natalie Nenadic and Asia Armanda, and their translations.

6. On 27 June 1996, based on the historical evidence and eyewitness accounts that Jadranka Cigeli and others had gathered, as represented in the film *Calling the Ghosts* (Jacobson and Jelincic 1996), the ICTY indicted eight male Bosnian Serbs for the rapes of Bosnian Muslim women. Efforts to indict and prosecute war crimes suspects have remained limited, primarily because of the difficulty of taking suspects into custody.

The ICTY cannot compel suspects to appear but can only hope they will be arrested if they leave the protection of officials in their country.

According to Amnesty International's 2003 annual report, which covers events between January and December 2002, ten trials were held before the tribunal, involving a total of thirteen people accused of war crimes. Twenty-four publicly indicted suspects remain at large; most reportedly are in the Federal Republic of Yugoslavia. Some 10,000 potential suspects were listed in local investigation files of domestic prosecutions for war crimes, of which 2,500 had been reviewed by the ICTY prosecutor. Thousands of cases of disappearances remain unsolved. (See Amnesty International 2009 for an overview of those indicted since the ICTY was established.)

7. Gender violence emerged as a major focus of human rights in the early 1990s, when feminist activists began to make arguments like: "A state's failure to protect women from violence is itself a human rights violation" (Merry 2001, 87). Although the Convention on the Elimination of All Forms of Discrimination Against Women entered into force in 1981, the United States has yet to ratify it. In 1989 the CEDAW Committee reintroduced gender violence within a human rights framework, with a general recommendation, and in 1993 the UN General Assembly adopted the Declaration on the Elimination of Violence Against Women. The declaration says that "states should condemn violence against women, and should not invoke any custom, tradition, or religion or other consideration to avoid their obligation with respect to its elimination" (Article 4).

8. In contrast to MacKinnon, for example, the feminist scholar and activist Beverly Allen employs rhetorical specificity but does not reproduce actual testimonies of rape warfare. Allen tells her readers why she decided not to represent the spectacle of genocidal rape by storytelling: to attempt to avoid reordering the disorder of war into a linear narrative of traditional historiography (1996, 32), and to avoid recreating the "interpersonal dynamics of the crime" that position readers as voyeurs (33). As she puts it: "A repetitive serial form may easily hook even a reader disgusted by the events the text relates into wondering at least what comes next. This scene was so horrible, can the next one possibly be worse? And so the reader may keep turning the pages, caught in spite of her or his revulsion in the formal pleasure of repetitive linear narrative" (32). Although she does not reproduce women's testimonies, Allen nevertheless argues that the particularities of genocidal rape need to be understood to avoid the universalizing tendencies that dismiss rape as an inevitable outcome of war. She asks: What are the political and ethical implications of turning genocidal rape into something incredulous, beyond what we know or think? Allen therefore forgoes storytelling, except when the stories are her own, and instead opts for a historical chronology of the conflicts, and an expository excursion followed by an analysis of reports and memorandums to document the atrocities (38).

9. Similarly, in her discussion of the challenges of representing the Holocaust, Felman and Laub note that "the need to testify to history as Holocaust repeatedly comes up against the impossibility of witnessing the original event; and yet, in the acknowledgement —in the historical translation—of this impossibility, *there is a witness*" (1992, 160).

10. See, for example, critical works by Behar 1993, Beverley 1992, Carr 1994, Sánchez-Casal 2001, Sommer 1988, and Yudice 1991.

11. See, for example, Bose and Varghese 2001, Bow 2001, Chow 1993, Fernandes 2001, Hesford and Kozol 2001 and 2005, Jarratt 2000, A. Kaplan 1994, Roof and Wiegman 1995, and Spivak 1988.

12. Susan Jarratt (2000) argues that the rhetorical moves of diasporic postcolonial intellectuals create a sense of disidentification with the audience. This deidentificatory rhetoric tends to disperse subjectivity and representativeness, thereby challenging assumptions of social similarity and presumed identification—the coming together of rhetor and audience—of traditional rhetorical theory.

13. Notably, it is the bodies of women of color that are visualized in *The Sky*. At the level of individual motive, invisibility may be read as a protective visual rhetoric; however, at the larger cultural level, absence might be read as a "power-concealing rhetoric" (Joyce Middleton quoted in Glenn 2002, 285). While the category "women of color" is itself a generalization not particularly conducive to a transnational feminist analysis—which would attempt to delineate intersecting identifications of gender, race, ethnicity, class, sexuality, and nationality—one might argue that the visualization of certain bodies and not others in *The Sky* plays into the politics of racial representation that renders whiteness invisible. One might also argue that the United States is imaged in *The Sky* as the "normative interlocutor" (Shohat 1998, 31) through the figure of Eleanor Roosevelt, who—as the delegate from the United States and chair of the United Nations commission—helped write the Universal Declaration of Human Rights.

14. Moreover, there were severe attacks on feminists who opposed nationalism. For example, five Croatian women writers who opposed Croatian nationalism became targets of an intense hate campaign orchestrated by Zagreb's yellow press. Among the "five witches" were the well-known feminist writer Slavenka Drakulić, the feminist philosopher Rada Iveković, and the feminist editor and journalist Vesna Kesić, whose photographs appeared on the front pages of newspapers under headlines indicating that they were feminist Communists who "rape Croatia" (Benderly 1997, 68). In addition, as Jill Benderly notes, nationalism took its toll on feminists in Serbia, as articulated by Lepa Mladjenovic and Vera Litričin, activists in Women in Black: "When the war started, nationalist hatred increased dramatically and the Serbian government began to produce propaganda and the notion of the Enemy. All of a sudden Slovenians became an enemy, then Croats, then Muslims, then Americans, Albanians, and so on. . . . Can a feminist be a nationalist chauvinist? Can a pacifist be a nationalist? Should the groups take clear attitudes toward nationalist questions (and therefore the war) and in that way lose some women? Should the groups avoid the issue of nationalism altogether? . . . So nationalism made some women split within themselves" (quoted in ibid.).

15. For example, Hozic argues that the "portrayal of Sarajevo's multicultural *ethos* stood in sharp contrast with the images (or, better, with the absolute lack thereof) of the ethnic hatred that was flaring throughout Bosnia" (2000, 230). For instance, journalists were often surprised by the absence of physical difference between Serbs and Croats, and

Muslims" (230). Sarajevo, Hozic argues, became a museum: "The showcased destruction constituted the city as an exhibit of ironic survival and of transformation" (231). She continues: "Consumed as an image but rejected as a territory, [the] ethnic war zone emerges as a new kind of colony—*unwanted, un-desired, un-called* for, and thus, as a playground for a new type of capitalism" (229).

16. Bosniak is the Balkan term for Bosnians who are Muslim (Boose 2002, 72).

17. Serbian national mythology, Boose notes, constructs the Slavic conversion to Christianity after the Serbs' sixth-century arrival in the Balkans as valid, but depicts the Slavs' conversion to Islam after the late-fourteenth-century Ottoman invasion as a "race betrayal" (2002, 76).

18. Boose notes the infamous testimony about an incident at the Omarska Camp, where it was reported that Serb guards forced two Muslim prisoners to hold down a third male prisoner in the position of crucified Christ while a fourth prisoner was forced to bite off the third man's testicles (2002, 90). On a related note, there is some testimonial evidence that suggests that the rape of Muslim men may have been much more frequent than recorded. As Boose observes (91–92), the Montenegrin journalist Seada Vranić interviewed six men who admitted they had been raped. According to a footnote in David Campbell, "accounts can be found in 'Thousands of Men Raped in Bosnia: A Taboo on War Reporting' in *BosNews* (Digest 211), 13 March 1995; and a Reuters report in *Tribunal Watch*, 3 July 1996" (1998, 274).

19. Davidson gives the following example: "Unlike their parents, or even their grandparents, many of the people who came to be described as 'ethnic Muslims' in Bosnia-Hercegovina had never been inside a mosque in their lives[,] at least not until they began to be identified in this way for the purposes of persecution, when religion took on a new significance for them. As this example suggests, the distinction between 'imposed' and 'chosen' ethnic identities is not one which can be sustained, since there are many cases where groups which have been identified as possessing a particular attribute and discriminated against on that basis have subsequently chosen to militantly assert that identity in response to their oppressors" (1999). On the issue of ethnic and national identity with an emphasis on women's experience in the region, see Korać 1996.

20. For further exploration of the economic conditions that facilitated the conflicts in the former Yugoslavia, see Michael Brown 1997, Chomsky 1999, Davidson 1999, German 2000, Haynes 1999, Magas 1997, and Power 2002, among others.

21. *Homes and Gardens* has been exhibited at Camerawork, London, 1996; the Houston Center for Photography, Texas, 1998; and Hasselblad Centre, Goteborg, Sweden, 2001. It also toured the United Kingdom in 1997 and that country and elsewhere in Europe in 1998–2000.

22. For example, Kosovo is the name most used and recognized by the international media. Albanians use Kosova.

23. *Calling the Ghosts* was Jacobson's debut documentary. A South African–born New York filmmaker, Jacobson got in touch with the Macedonian director Milcho Manshevski, whose feature film *Before the Rain* (1995) won numerous awards. Apparently,

Manshevski put Jacobson in touch with Jelincic. Jacobson notes in an interview on 26 July 1996 that the film's title refers to an interview she and Jelincic had with four women who had been in Omarska with Jadranka Cigelj, and who told a story about "calling the ghosts." One woman said: "Dika and I were sitting around and we were calling the ghosts. We only wanted to cheer ourselves up a little but it wasn't working. So we were calling the ghosts to come. All was silent. And the next thing, a Chetnik soldier came in. And I quickly gathered all the candles and pieces of paper and hid them in my skirt. The Chetnik said 'Are you calling the ghosts?' To which we said, 'No, sir, we do nothing of the sort.' Then he said 'What's burning?' And the only skirt I had was in flames." The interview is available at http://www.arsenal-berlin.de.

24. Although the numbers are still in dispute because of the difficulty of gathering evidence, there is little question about the magnitude of these crimes. Enloe writes: "The European Union's investigators calculated that in 1992 alone, 20,000 Muslim Bosnian women and girls had been raped by Bosnian Serb combatants. By the time of the ceasefire in 1995, the number of women from all communities who endured wartime rape was estimated to be between 30,000–50,000. The numerical uncertainty reflected the ongoing gendered politics of silence and denial" (2000, 140). For further discussion in English of rape and the Bosnian war, see B. Allen 1996, Bernard 1994, Drakulić 2001, Ramet 1999, Rejali 1998, Stiglmayer 1994, and Vranić 1996. See also Nikolić-Ristanović 1999 and Power 2002 for a brief historical account of the positions adopted by the United States during the Bosnian war.

25. It is important to note the common assumption among North Americans that Yugoslavia was an Eastern bloc country, which contrasts with the perception in the Eastern bloc of Yugoslavia as Western. Since Yugoslavia severed its ties with the Soviet Union in 1948, in the words of Vida Penezić, it has been "precariously balanced between the blocs and a founding member of the nonaligned movement" (1995, 59). Penezić further notes that these perceptions reflect and emerge from a dominant American cold war paradigm, which configured the Western bloc as a free world, progressive and enlightened, and the Eastern bloc as Communist and bad. Cold war discourse has therefore reinforced perceptions of Yugoslavia as an Eastern bloc country.

26. I use the term *ethnic cleansing* in this sentence to highlight the metaphor of purification. However, throughout the essay I have chosen to use the term *ethnic genocide* instead of the term *ethnic cleansing*. Controversy lingers over the use of the term *genocide* to describe atrocities of the wars in the Balkans. The conclusion that Bosnia has suffered genocide has been reached by many nongovernmental organizations, such as Amnesty International, Helsinki Watch, and United Nations commissions. These agencies and commissions concluded that 90 percent of the "ethnic cleansing" has been committed by Serbs, and they have provided concrete evidence of a systematic Serbian policy to get rid of Muslims. But as Power notes in her discussion of the controversy surrounding the term, the Bush administration avoided the word because a "genocide finding would create a moral imperative" (2002, 288).

As Davidson notes, the term *ethnic cleansing* is an English translation of the Serbo-Croat phrase *etnicko ciscenje*. The term was first used in Yugoslavia by the Croatian

Ustaša during the Second World War to "describe its policy of killing or expelling Serbs, Jews, Gypsies and Muslims from the fascist state the Ustashe briefly set up with Nazi support" (1999). Davidson continues: "The first use during the current events was by the Croatian Supreme Council in 1991, after the Croatian declaration of independence from Yugoslavia, to describe the actions of Serb guerillas who were attempting to drive Croats out of areas where Serbs were in the majority. . . . The phrase only began to appear in the British press—and thereafter in the popular usage—during the war which began in Bosnia-Hercegovina the following year, when Bosnian Serb forces, initially backed by the Milosević regime in Belgrade, started expelling Muslims and Croats from those parts of the state territory that the Bosnian Serbs considered to be Serbian."

27. Marsha Freeman (1999) discusses the dilemma of double victimization—that is, legal efforts to prosecute war criminals confront the difficulties of finding victims willing to testify while needing to protect those witnesses from possible community retaliation. Critics of the ICTY charge that not enough attention has been paid to the physical and emotional needs of witnesses, making it difficult and often dangerous for women to testify. For instance, the statute creating the ICTY does not provide for either compensation or rehabilitation for survivors. For more on this point, see Copelon (1988, 72). For further analysis of the politics of representing rape, see Hesford 2001, Sharpe 1991, and Tanner 1994.

28. Weine argues that the Tito regime's suppression of histories of violent conflict during the Second World War led to conditions in which the rise of ethnic nationalism met no counterdiscourse able to resist its powerful force (1999, 29–31).

29. K. Stiles, response to author, American Studies Association Annual Conference, October 2000.

30. The phrase "wounded attachments" is taken from Wendy Brown (1995a and 1995b), in which she critiques the limitations of identity politics and argues that identity has become overly attached to woundedness. For my purposes here, I would simply point out that Brown's critique does not address the internationalization of identity politics: how trauma marks and reshapes identity in ways that affect communities, and how the reclamation or reconfiguration of identity may foster social change, justice, and healing. In other words, injury and identity may not be as productively separated as Brown seems to suggest. I share her skepticism about the potential of identity and rights claims to address historical inequities at the structural level. However, what Brown doesn't account for, which is crucial to my argument, is how rights claims and identities are combined in new ways in human rights contexts.

31. According to Amnesty International's 1999 annual report, efforts to facilitate the return of Balkan refugees who had fled the armed conflicts of 1992–95 were expedited by intergovernmental organizations in 1998. This effort, however, met with limited success because of persistent human rights abuses and bureaucratic opposition by local and national administrators. At the same time, pressure from host countries has forced approximately 88,000 to return to the region, despite the fact that the refugees are unable to go back to their homes. As of 1999, approximately 1.2 million people were still either refugees in other countries or displaced within their country of origin.

## Four. Global Sex Work

1. Nicholas Kristof admits that "buying sex slaves and freeing them is not a long-term solution. It helps individuals but risks creating incentives for other girls to be kidnapped into servitude" ("Stopping the Traffickers," *New York Times*, 31 January 2004). To his credit, in an e-mail correspondence to his readers on 20 January 2004, he recognizes that a broad solution to the problem is needed, one that involves "a mix of economic development, literacy programs for girls, improved police and judicial systems, and constant crackdowns on the brothels that confine girls against their will. It's critical that governments do more to raise the status of girls and women so that they are not second-class citizens, for so many of these problems arise from power disparities between males and females in poor countries."

2. Human rights groups estimate that between 600,000 and 800,000 people each year are sold into the sex trade worldwide, with a sizable portion of those coming from South Asia, Central and South America, and Eastern Europe. Between 14,500 and 17,500 are trafficked each year into the United States (2004 Department of Health and Human Services, "Human Trafficking Fact Sheet," www.acf.hhs.gov/trafficking/about/factsheets.html). Reliable statistics are not available, however, due to covert channels of human trafficking.

3. Nicholas D. Kristof, "Girls for Sale." *New York Times*, 17 January 2004. The other articles in this series include "Bargaining for Freedom" (21 January 2004), "Going Home, with Hope" (24 January 2004), "Loss of Innocence" (28 January 2004), and "Stopping the Traffickers" (31 January 2004).

4. Melanie Simmons generalizes the position of Feminists against Systems of Prostitution (FASP), a movement inspired by Catharine MacKinnon and others, which construes sex workers as "economically compelled, lured by false claims, or duped into prostitution" (1999, 129) and therefore in need of rescue and rehabilitation. Simmons states that "FASP activists see prostitution as little more than rape and celebrate prostitutes for simply surviving the situation" (129), as well as seeing "women's sexual desires and expression as constructed by a patriarchal society and thus not of their own making" (131). She notes that FASP, which seems to be reconsidering depenalization of prostitutes, does not have a clear position on depenalization versus decriminalization. Simmons cites the example of PROMISE in San Francisco, a program that women arrested for prostitution can attend as an alternative to incarceration (http://www.prostitutionresearch.com/services.html) (133). CATW is also included as an organization that has begun to support depenalization (http://www.catwinternational.org).

Simmons argues that the prostitutes' rights movement is congruent with a rights discourse. Similarly, Shannon Bell argues: "A discourse premised on the extension of basic human and civil rights . . . as far as it may go in changing the identity and status of the claimant group and even in undoing the traditional concept of rights, can only act as an intervention. It is an act of micropolitics concerned with its specific struggle, . . . and not with a change in any totality" (Bell quoted in Simmons 1999, 132). Kamala Kempadoo and Jo Doezema are critical of Bell on the ground that her work contributes, indirectly, to hegemonic Western scripts about prostitution. Building on

Shannon Bell's *Rewriting the Prostitute Body* (1994), they argue that her act of locating the prostitute "at the heart of Western thought" (Bell quoted in Kempadoo and Doezema 1998, 12) homogenizes the origins of prostitution and erases contextual differences, resulting in an essentialist definition of the prostitute (Kempadoo and Doezema 1998, 13).

5. For example, the danger of campaigns against sexual victimization when focused exclusively on non-Western women is that they can—as happened in the campaign against gender apartheid in Afghanistan led by Western feminist groups like the Feminist Majority—reproduce anti-Arab sentiment and reinforce the view that Muslim women are "victims of Islamic faith" (Basu 2000, 82).

6. In the early part of the twentieth century, the League of Nations (the forerunner of the United Nations) recognized trafficking of women and children. The emphasis at this time was on white women forced into prostitution, which was known as the "white slave trade." In 1951 the UN Convention for the Suppression of the Traffic in Persons and of the Exploitation of the Prostitution of Others (which replaced earlier international conventions of 1904, 1919, 1921, and 1933), which focused on trafficking for prostitution entered into force (Skrobanek, Boonpakdee, and Jantateero 1997, 7). As Siriporn Skrobanek, Nataya Boonpakdee, and Chutima Jantateero importantly note, national antiprostitution laws have been based on the 1951 UN convention, which calls for the abolition of prostitution and the prosecution of those involved, regardless of whether or not their participation was forced. The 1981 Convention on the Elimination of All Forms of Discrimination against Women calls on governments to suppress all forms of traffic in women and the exploitation of the prostitution of others (article 6). The 1990 Convention on the Rights of the Child also demands that governments prevent the traffic in children (article 35) (Skrobanek, Boonpakdee, and Jantateero 1997, 27).

In terms of the relation between trafficking and migration, it is important to note that the Universal Declaration of Human Rights states: "Everyone has the right to leave any country including his [*sic*] own" (article 13). Article 12 of the 1976 International Covenant on Civil and Political Rights set limits on the UDHR by subjecting migration to legal restrictions, when issues of national security and public health and morals, as well as the rights of others, are involved (Skrobanek, Boonpakdee, and Jantateero 1997, 7).

In 2000, the UN General Assembly adopted a new instrument on trafficking, the Protocol to Prevent, Suppress and Punish Trafficking in Persons, Especially Women and Children. And the U.S. Victims of Trafficking and Violence Protection Act of 2000 aims to assist and to protect trafficked persons and to increase the penalties for traffickers. It defines severe forms of trafficking as sex trafficking in which a commercial sex act is induced by force, fraud, or coercion; or in which the person induced to perform such an act is not eighteen; or the recruitment, harboring, or transportation of a person for labor or services, through the use of force, fraud, or coercion, for the purposes of subjection to involuntary servitude, peonage, debt bondage, or slavery.

7. See Kelly Oliver (2001) for a critical review of seminal works in psychoanalytical theory, postcolonial theory, and feminist theory in which identification and recognition

224 NOTES TO CHAPTER FOUR

(and misrecognition) play a foundational role. See chapter 1 of this book for an overview of Oliver's alternative to the Hegelian understanding of subject formation.

8. In my use of the term *sympathetic visibility*, I follow Ann Van Sant's (1993) incisive study
of sensibility and representations of suffering in the novel and philanthropic practices
of the eighteenth century.

9. CATW defines sexual exploitation as practices "by which persons achieve sexual grati-
fication or financial gain or advancement through the abuse of a person's sexuality by
abrogating that person's human right to dignity, equality, autonomy, and physical and
mental well-being" (Crago 2003).

10. See Wendy Brown (1995) for an important critique of the relationship between identity, injury, and rights discourse.

11. Given Doezema's recognition of the power of rhetorical appeals and pervasive cultural
myths, I find her claim that the "image of the 'trafficking' victim . . . [is] a figment of
neo-Victorian imaginations" (1998, 44) a bit puzzling. At the macro level, her claim at
first appears more or less reasonable, but it ignores the micro-level politics of particular
rhetorical situations. For example, though she does allude to this dynamic elsewhere
(2000), in "Forced to Choose," she doesn't address the limitations of geopolitical realities and the context that enables the proliferation of such myths (1998). We need
to make distinctions in terms of who or which groups invoke certain cultural myths,
and with what intent. In other words, claims of the agency of sex workers can become
overly romanticized just as easily as cultural myths of victimization.

12. Doezema refers to "The Human Rights Watch Global Report on Women's Human
Rights" from 1995 as an example of a recent publication that reproduces trafficking
stereotypes.

13. As Doezema notes, the anti-white-slavery campaigns in the early twentieth century
need to be seen within the context of nineteenth-century discourses on prostitution.
She notes two competing views held at the time: the regulationist view, which refers
to state systems of licensed brothels and forced medical examination of prostitutes
and restriction of their mobility; and abolitionist discourse, which arose as a response
to the Contagious Diseases Acts in England in the 1860s (2000, 26–27). Among the
recurring narrative motifs in the United States and Europe were the image of an "innocent country girl" lured to the corrupt city and the emphasis on disease (in particular,
syphilis) and degradation. In addition, drawing on racist conceptions of whiteness as
purity, white migrant prostitutes were construed as white slaves rather than as common prostitutes (29).

14. CATW's website refers to article 3 of the UN Protocol to Prevent, Suppress and Punish
Trafficking in Persons, Especially Women and Children, which supplements the UN
Convention against Transnational Organized Crime, in defense of the organization's
position that even consensual prostitution is exploitation. The protocol states: "The
consent of a victim of trafficking in persons to the intended exploitation set forth in
subparagraph (a) of this article shall be irrelevant where any of the means set forth in
subparagraph (a) have been used" (the report is available at http://www1.umn.edu/
humanrts/instree/trafficking.html). CATW calls for the decriminalization of women in

prostitution and the criminalization of men who buy women and children and anyone who promotes sexual exploitation; however, the organization does not position itself as an advocate for the decriminalization of prostitution as labor.

15. As Crago notes, this policy may affect the funding of groups such as Empower, a sex workers' group in Thailand that has expressed support for the legalization and political organizing of sex workers (2003).

16. Unlike many definitions of trafficking, as Doezema notes, Wijers and Lap-Chew's report "expands the scope of trafficking to include trafficking for domestic work and marriage" (Doezema 1999, 165). Wijers and Lap-Chew's position in their 1998 report resonates with that of the Global Alliance against Traffic in Women. Also see Wijers 1997.

17. In 1999, GAATW developed a document called "The Human Rights Standards for the Treatment of Trafficked Persons" with the International Human Rights Law Group and the Foundation against Trafficking in Women and in conjunction with other NGOS. These standards are included in Global Alliance against Traffic in Women (2001). GAATW also worked with human rights groups like the two mentioned above to lobby successfully for a broader definition of trafficking. The UN Protocol to Prevent, Suppress and Punish Trafficking in Persons, Especially Women and Children provides the first internationally agreed upon definition of trafficking. The protocol does not equate trafficking with prostitution and distinguishes between voluntary and forced prostitution. GAATW considered the Convention on the Elimination of All Forms of Discrimination against Women an ineffective human rights instrument because its conflation of trafficking and prostitution reproduced the victim stereotype, disregarded the agency of women, and left out those trafficked for purposes other than prostitution (http://www.gaatw.org). The protocol has a crime-control approach (a product of its negotiations at the UN Crime Commission in Vienna), but it now includes a human rights component, though its implementation remains at the discretion of individual states. For more recent articulations of these linkages see GAATW's 2010 multiyear program, also available on their website.

18. WITNESS is a not-for-profit human rights organization based in New York that uses video and technology to fight for human rights. See chapter 1.

19. See WITNESS's "International Trafficking of Women" (2000) on www.witness.org.

20. Documentary videos not discussed in this essay that focus on child prostitution and the global sex trade include Andrew Levine's *The Price of Youth* (2000) distributed by WITNESS; Brian Edwards and Kate Blewett's *Slavery: A Global Investigation* (2000); Justin Kerrigan's *Human Traffic* (1999), distributed by Miramax; Ellen Bruno's *Sacrifice: The Story of Child Prostitutes from Burma* (1998) available through The Film Library; and David Feingold's *Trading Women* (2003), available through Documentary Educational Resources. Another movie, Lukas Moodysson's *Lilya 4-ever* (2002) (distributed by Sonet film) is a drama about how trafficking works in the former Soviet Union.

21. Ursula Biemann, e-mail message to author.

22. For a further discussion of Biemann's construction of gender in transnational spaces, see Berelowitz 2001 and Biemann 2000. For information on *Writing Desire*'s screenings

see the Women Making Movies website: http://www.wmm.com/filmcatalog/pages/c537.shtml.

23. Biemann indicated that she is the narrator (e-mail message to author). But she also notes: "It's not one authorial voice, it's many theoretical voices that speak through me, not that I'm merely quoting, but it's all shared knowledge somehow."

24. Ursula Biemann, e-mail message to author.

25. For insightful critiques and a qualified embrace of cosmopolitanism, see Appiah 2006, Robbins 1999, and Cheah 2006.

26. Ursula Biemann, e-mail message to author.

27. Ibid.

28. Ibid.

## Five. Spectacular Childhoods

1. Article 3 of the 1990 UN Convention on the Rights of the Child speaks to this principle: "In all actions concerning children, whether undertaken by public or private social welfare institutions, courts of law, administrative authorities or legislative bodies, the best interests of the child shall be a primary consideration." Article 12 states: "States Parties shall assure to the child who is capable of forming his or her own views the rights to express those views freely in all matters affecting the child, the views of the child being given due weight in accordance with the age and maturity of the child."

2. Article 39 of the Convention on the Rights of the Child states: "State Parties shall take all appropriate measures to promote physical and psychological recovery and social reintegration of a child victim of: any form of neglect, exploitation, or abuse; torture or any other form of cruel, inhuman or degrading treatment or punishment; or armed conflict. Such recovery and reintegration shall take place in an environment which fosters the health, self-respect and dignity of the child."

3. In 2010, the International Labor Organization estimated that 215 million children work worldwide. Among these, nearly one-third are in what the UN designates as the "worst forms" of child labor: trafficking, forced labor, armed conflict, prostitution, and crime. (See the ILO's web page, http://ilo.org/ipec/ChildlabourstatisticsSIMPOC/lang—en/index.htm.)

4. India may have the largest number of children working in the world (estimates indicate 15 million), but wealthy countries are not immune to the problem. Estimates of working children in the United States and the United Kingdom have been as high as 2 million, with 230,000 children working in agriculture in the United States and 13,000 working in sweatshops (Arat 2002, 180).

5. Between 2004 and 2007 NBC's *Dateline* aired more than a dozen episodes devoted to online child sex predators in a series titled "To Catch a Predator." With the help of the vigilante justice group Perverted Justice, *Dateline* presented itself as a media watchdog, catching would-be child predators on camera as they entered private homes in affluent, middle-class neighborhoods. In a separate documentary, "Children for Sale," a *Dateline* producer, a cameraman, and a former police detective from New Zealand investigated child prostitution in Cambodia by going undercover as sex tourists. "Chil-

dren for Sale" focuses on an American doctor "prowling" Svay Pak, a village on the outskirts of Phnom Penh, and bragging about his sexual exploits. The documentary exposes the trafficking of children for sex work and the sexual exploitation of children as young as five by brothel owners, and it stages a spectacular rescue with the help of Gary Haugen, who runs the faith-based human rights group International Justice Mission, which received a million dollar grant from the U.S. government during President George W. Bush's administration. Not surprisingly, there has been criticism because the spectacular busts and rescues did not lead to significant prosecutions.

6. See Hauser 1999 and Lyotard 1984 for further details on those excluded from the public sphere imagined by Habermas 1989; Negt and Kluge 1993 for their focus on proletarian issues; Landes 1988, Felski 1989, and Fraser 1990, 2003, and 2005a for an explicit critique of the gendered dynamics of the public sphere; and Papacharissi 2002 for a discussion of the Internet as a public sphere.

7. Postcolonial and transnational feminist theorists have also raised key questions about who can speak, on whose behalf, and in what contexts. See, for instance, Chow 1993, Spivak 1998, and Roof and Wiegman 1995.

8. The debate between Ann Douglas and Jane Tompkins typifies the controversy over the cultural work of sentimentality in literary studies. In *The Feminization of American Culture*, Douglas claims that sentimental novels published by women in the mid-nineteenth century marked the embrace of "individualist emotionalism." In *Sensational Designs*, Tompkins argues that women's sentimental fiction affirmed women's power and propelled a grass-roots antipatriarchal politics (both quoted in Howard 2001, 215).

9. Nicholas D. Kristof, "Girls for Sale." *New York Times*, 17 January 2004.

10. Nicholas D. Kristof, "Fighting Brothels with Books." *New York Times*, 24 December 2006.

11. Middle-class perspectives and nationalist fears framed early-twentieth-century child-labor battles in the United States and United Kingdom. Middle-class children were "assured a fiction of agency and control, and the possession of subjectivity," whereas children represented by labor reformers in the early twentieth century seem to lack agency (Pace 2003, 341). These views of the "priceless child" represented a shift from mid-nineteenth-century conceptions of the child as an "economically valuable asset" (Barbie Zelizer quoted in Bhabha 2006, 1527). When children of the working classes were depicted as anything other than helpless victims in need of protection by the state, their agency was typically constrained by the gendered dangers, lure, and temptations of particular industries. For girls, the stage and theatrical life, which presumably would turn into a life of prostitution, was seen as the greatest danger, while serving as messengers exposed boys to such vices as drugs and alcohol (Novkov 2000, 377).

12. See, for example, this text used in the DVD's description on Amazon.com.

13. Harvey Graff has pointed out the limitations of the notion of education as empowerment in his articulation of the "literacy myth" (1979), which refers, in part, to the Enlightenment idea that education will lead to social empowerment. We can see the resonance of this idea in article 26 of the UDHR: "Everyone has a right to education. ... Education shall be directed to the full development of the human personality."

14. Melissa Block, "Interview: Zana Briski Discusses Her Documentary Film *Born into Brothels*," *All Things Considered*, 6 December 2004 (http://www.npr.org/templates/story/story.php?storyId=4205049).

15. Another critic similarly characterizes Briski "as a rather aggressive guardian angel from the West, who comes in and tries to save only a few children," though in the end, he finds that Briski's "quest makes sense" (Denby 2005, 46).

16. The Hindu Right, however, is not a monolithic entity. The BJP (Bharatiya Janata Party, or Indian People's Party), which depends on electoral politics, assumes a more moderate stance, whereas the VHP (Vishva Hindu Parishad, or World Hindu Council) is more militant in its appeals to traditional religion and anti-Muslim rhetoric (Kapur 2005, 43). Although the BJP was defeated in national elections in 2004, the Hindu Right remains strong; the VHP and RSS (Rashtriya Swayamsevak Sangh, or National Patriotism Organization) share a vision that places the ideology of Hindutva, or Hindu principles, at its center and consider Hinduism the supreme faith. See Kapur 2005, especially 43–50, for a discussion of the appropriation by the Hindu Right of issues of violence against women and the discourse of liberal rights.

17. Certain behaviors—adultery, sodomy, and most forms of rape—are criminalized, but the rape of a woman by her husband is not viewed as a criminal act. Kapur notes: "Marital rape is not recognized under current legal definitions of rape. Section 375 of the Indian Penal Code 1860 (IPC) provides that 'Sexual intercourse by a man with his own wife, the wife not being under 15 years of age, is not rape.' . . . The marital exemption has since been narrowed by the introduction of 376(a) of the IPC, which states that the rape of a woman by a husband from whom she is judicially separated constitutes rape, and is punishable by up to two years' imprisonment" (2005, 34–35). However, not all sexuality within the private sphere is considered by criminal law to be private; forms of sexuality that are considered to be against Indian cultural values, such as homosexuality and sodomy, are penalized under provisions of the Indian Penal Code.

18. Briski recognizes the potential risk to the women exposed through the documentary and apparently promised them that she will protect their identity. She also agreed not to show the film at film festivals in India, release it to any Indian television stations, or sell it in India. Reportedly, she did release the film to a few organizations in India to promote the work of Kids with Cameras. But because the DVD of the film is widely available, the protection of the women and children's identities is compromised (Curry 2005, 62).

19. Andrew Curry points out in his review of the film that critics in Calcutta "complain that Briski didn't sufficiently credit aid workers who helped her, and that her approach—taking the children out of their brothel homes and placing them in boarding schools—was presumptuous" (2005, 62). John Petrakis makes a similar point in his review: "It's disappointing that the stories of the prostitutes themselves get lost in the shuffle. I would have liked to know more about their lives and their histories, and their relationships with their seemingly disposable children" (2005, 64). However, he finds much to value in the film, including the children's photographs, which he describes as "nothing short of remarkable" (ibid.).

20. The organization has argued that under no circumstances should prostitution be viewed as work (Gangoli 2001, 11). Some feminists have argued, however, that Sanlaap's rhetoric infantilizes women and "homogenizes women and girls" as "undifferentiated and permanent victims" (13). Geetanjali Gangoli highlights which subject positions Sanlaap invests in and reproduces. Finally, Sanlaap is dependent on international funding, and therefore we also need to consider the extent to which the organization's platform is influenced by the dictates of funders and the prominence of the discourse of rehabilitation in children's human rights campaigns. Sanlaap has received funds from the U.S. government's International Anti-Trafficking Programs, USAID, and UN-sponsored programs.

21. For recent updates on the children, see Kids with Cameras's July 2010 newsletter, available through their e-mail subscriber service (see http://kids-with-cameras.org).

22. Rick Westhead reports that ThinkFilm paid $30,000 for rights to the movie (2005).

23. Brian Johnson, "Points of No Return," *Maclean's*, 21 February 2005, 47.

24. Kids with Cameras has projects in Jerusalem, Cairo, Haiti, and Calcutta. A cursory search on the Internet reveals numerous youth participatory photography projects in the United States, including Eyes Open Wide in Ohio, Literary through Photography in North Carolina, and the international online project Bridges to Understanding projects in Africa such as Through the Eyes of Children, in Rwanda; and others in places like London, Nepal, and on the border between Laos and Burma.

25. *Born into Brothels* may not consider how the children's rights and agency are mediated by "transnational connectivities"—to use Grewal's phrase (2005)—but it does identify the paternalist logic of citizenship and children's rights in its representation of the struggles involved in getting children registered and admitted to boarding schools. A customary practice in school admission procedures is that the father's name must be stated. Briski and the girls' parents learn that they need multiple copies of each child's photograph, the children's passports, paperwork and grades from previous schools, and medical certificates from doctors stating that they are not carrying the HIV virus. These requirements are represented as insurmountable obstacles for a few of the mothers and grandmothers, who cannot locate papers in their homes or pay for tests; only Briski, with her persistence, efficiency, and funds, can provide these things. Thus she takes the children to doctors and to get their passport photographs while their mothers work. These scenes also speak to children's official status or lack thereof as national subjects, as citizens with rights. In a barely noticed judgment issued by the Indian Supreme Court in January 1993, brought on by petition, the Bhartiya Patita Uddhar Sabha—an organization for the welfare of prostitutes and their children—permission was granted for children's admission to school based on their mother's identity (A. Dutt 1993).

26. Arat notes: "In the name of economic stability, these agencies require governments to implement measures of 'fiscal discipline' which involve freezing wages, reducing government spending, and privatizing government enterprises. . . . [L]ow income households in recipient countries find themselves tightening their belts more and more . . . [and] are likely to turn to child labor for additional income" (2002, 190–91). According

to Arat, the World Bank allocated only about 8 percent of its development assistance in 2000 to projects on health care and education. Globally, it devotes most of its money to population control policies, many of which are both coercive and ineffective (188).

27. Scholars across the disciplines have exposed the objectifying, colonial practices of both documentary and ethnography and have called for greater sensitivity to the power differentials in representational practices and in the research situation, as well as increased collaboration among researchers and their subjects (see, for example Clifford 1992; Goldberg 2001; and Lutz and Collins 1993).

28. Contemporary Western ideology presumes a fundamental link between sexuality and personality that is not widely adopted in Thailand, and that is particularly absent in representations of gay sexuality. In Thailand, unlike in the West, gay sexuality is not seen primarily as a threat to the social order (Montgomery 2001, 121). Moreover, a majority do not view themselves as exclusively gay (ibid.). However, to say that homosexuality is tolerated outside the structures of family and the traditional roles of father and son is not to imply that there are no intolerant undercurrents to separate homosexuality from those aspects of life. There are.

29. Abigail Bray highlights how the spectacle of the sexual child can become "a synecdoche for political freedom" and "normative technologies of neoliberal governmentality" (2009, 177, 173). Bray analyzes the debates in Australia among media, art critics, and civil liberties groups about an exhibition at a gallery in Sydney of Bill Henson's erotic images of naked children. Government officials in Australia declared the photographs "absolutely revolting," whereas civil liberties groups and art critics and intellectuals saw the exhibition as an expression of democratic and aesthetic resistance to the spectacle of and cultural anxieties about child sexual abuse. These debates, she argues, raised the political question of whether children's human rights become more marginalized if the sexually violated child is no longer construed as a victim. Bray admonishes feminist scholars and human rights advocates to consider the risks in representing children's sexual agency as a triumph over victim politics, moral panic, and the reactionary spectacle of child sexual abuse in mass media, and how such triumphs underpin the normative regulation of feminist critiques (181).

30. Montgomery notes that U.S. military personnel stationed in Thailand at the end of the 1960s—when the Vietnam War spilled over into Cambodia—fueled the sex industry in Thailand and left behind the infrastructure of the sex industry as well as stereotypes of docile Oriental women (2001, 47). But the history of prostitution in Thailand complicates portrayals of outsiders as perpetrators, including earlier Vietnamese soldiers and the waves of Chinese immigrants in the 1920s and 1930s. Prostitution has a long history in Thailand, with evidence of the practice dating back to the Ayudhaya period of 1350–1767, when prostitution was legal and taxed by the government (41). In Thai terms at that point, prostitutes would have been known as slave wives (*mia klang todd*). In 1805 the Law of Three Seals introduced the legal category of prostitution, "formalizing the social position of women who sold their bodies" (Truong quoted in Montgomery 1998, 42). This law also provided a framework to divide women into categories and "stigmatise women who did not belong to any man" (42). The Penal Code of 1908

imposed punishments for the seduction of children under twelve and for the adduction of those under ten. But the law did not apply if children aged ten to fourteen had consented to the abduction and that prostitution was legal if the sex was consensual (43). In 1960 prostitution was outlawed (42).

31. The film is produced by Trudie Styler and Susan Bissell.

32. Articles 23 and 24 of the constitution of Bangladesh and current legislative measures ensure the rights embodied in the CRC and prohibit all forms of forced labor and human trafficking. Government initiatives to reduce child labor include a memorandum of understanding between the Bangladesh Garment Manufacturers and Exporters Association (BGME), UNICEF, and the International Labour Organization (ILO). As a result of the U.S. Child Labor Deterrence Act of 1993 (introduced by Senator Tom Harkin) and other similar measures, 50,000 children in Bangladesh were dismissed from garment factories and later found work in more hazardous occupations (Rahman, Khanam, and Absar 1999). For most recent statistics on child labor in Bangladesh see the International Labor Organization's 2008 report Bangladesh Child Labor Data Country Brief, available on ILO's website (http://ilo.org/ipec/Childlabourstatistics SIMPOC/lang—en/index.htm).

33. In 2004, Senator Tom Harkin introduced new legislation in the Senate to address child labor in the United States. Some scholars have noted the unpredictable impact of flat bans such as Harkin's bill, which bans the import of goods produced by child labor: "Many children were forced to turn to more hazardous and exploitative work, such as stone crushing and prostitution. In efforts to remedy the situation, the U.S., UNICEF, and Bangladesh Garment Manufacturers reached an agreement to make alternative arrangements for children to compensate families for lost wages so that kids could attend school. This occurred at the same time that the U.S. and IMF enforced governments to reduce expenditures on health and education" (Rasheda Khanam, "Child Labour in Bangladesh: Trends, Patterns and Policy Options," MPRA paper, March 2005, http://mpra.ub.uni-muenchen.de/8008).

## Conclusion

1. Here I draw on Arjun Appadurai's notion of "locality" as a phenomenological quality, "primarily relational and contextual rather than as scalar or spatial. [It is] constituted by a series of links between the sense of social immediacy, the technologies of interactivity, and the relativity of contexts" (1996, 178).

Afshari, Reza. 2007. "On Historiography of Human Rights: Reflections on Paul Gordon Lauren's The Evolution of International Human Rights: Visions Seen." *Human Rights Quarterly* 29, no. 1: 1–67.

Agamben, Giorgio. 1998. *Homo Sacer: Sovereign Power and Bare Life*. Trans. Daniel Heller-Roazen. Stanford: Stanford University Press.

Agence France-Presse. 2005. "Cheney Says Detainees Are Well Treated." *New York Times*, 24 June, A16.

Ahmed, Leila. 1993. *Women and Gender in Islam: Historical Roots of a Modern Debate*. New Haven: Yale University Press.

Ahmed, Sara. 2004. "Affective Economies." *Social Text* 22, no. 2: 117–39.

Allen, Beverly. 1996. *Rape Warfare: The Hidden Genocide in Bosnia-Herzegovina and Croatia*. Minneapolis: University of Minnesota Press.

Allen, Lori A. 2009. "Martyr Bodies in the Media: Human Rights, Aesthetics, and the Politics of Immediation in the Palestinian Intifada." *American Ethnologist* 36, no. 1: 161–80.

Alloula, Malek. 1986. *The Colonial Harem*. Trans. Myrna Godzich and Wlad Godzich. Minneapolis: University of Minnesota Press.

Amnesty International. 2009. "Ending Impunity: Developing and Implementing a Global Action Plan." http://www.icty.org/sections/TheCases/KeyFigures.

Amoore, Louise. 2007. "Vigilant Visualities: The Watchful Politics of the War on Terror." *PRIO* 38, no. 2: 215–32.

An-Na'im, Abdullahi Ahmed. 1992. *Human Rights in Cross-Cultural Perspectives: A Quest for Consensus*. Philadelphia: University of Pennsylvania Press.

Appadurai, Arjun. 1996. *Modernity at Large: Cultural Dimensions of Globalizations*. Minneapolis: University of Minnesota Press.

Appiah, Kwame Anthony. 2006. *Cosmopolitanism: Ethics in a World of Strangers*. New York: W. W. Norton and Company.

Arat, Zehra F. 2002. "Analyzing Child Labor as a Human Rights Issue: Its Causes, Aggravating Policies, and Alternative Proposals." *Human Rights Quarterly* 24, no. 1:177–204.

Arendt, Hannah. 1958. *The Human Condition*. Chicago: University of Chicago Press.

———. 1978. *The Origins of Totalitarianism*. New York: Houghton Mifflin Harcourt.

Armitage, David. 2000. *The Idealized Origins of the British Empire*. Cambridge: Cambridge University Press.

Awad, Nadia. 2004. "Andy Warhol at Abu Ghraib." *Muslim Wakeup!* 27 July.

Baer, Ulrich. 2002. *Spectral Evidence: The Photography of Trauma*. Cambridge: MIT Press.

Bahir, Deepika. 2008. "Response: A World of Difference." *College English* 70, no. 5: 522–28.

Bakhtin, Mikhail. 1981. *The Dialogical Imagination: Four Essays*. Ed. Michael Holquist, trans. Caryl Emerson and Michael Holquist. Austin: University of Texas Press.

Bal, Mieke. 2007. "The Pain of Images." In *Beautiful Suffering: Photography and the Traffic in Pain*, ed. Mark Reinhardt, Holly Edwards, and Erina Dugganne, 93–115. Williamstown, Mass.: Williams College Museum of Art.

Banerjee, Partha. 2005. "Documentary *Born into Brothels*: An Insiders Point of View." Mukto-mona.com. http://www.mukto-mona.com/Articles/partha_ban/born_into_brothels.htm.

Barthes, Roland. 1974. *S/Z*. Trans. Richard Miller. New York: Hill and Wang.

———. 1977. *Image-Music-Text*. Trans. Stephen Heath. New York: Hill and Wang.

Bass, Alan. 1987. Introduction. In *The Post Card: From Socrates to Freud and Beyond*, by Jacques Derrida, ix–xx. Trans. Alan Bass. Chicago: University of Chicago Press.

Basu, Amrita. 2000. "Globalization of the Local/Localization of the Global: Mapping Transnational Women's Movements." *Meridians* 1, no. 1: 68–84.

Baudrillard, Jean. 1981. *Simulacra and Simulation*. Trans. Sheila Faria Glazer. Ann Arbor: University of Michigan Press.

———. 2002. *The Spirit of Terrorism*. 2nd ed. Trans. Chris Turner. London: Verso.

———. 2005. *The Conspiracy of Art: Manifestos, Interviews, Essays*. Ed. Sylvère Lotringer, trans. Ames Hodges. Cambridge: MIT Press.

Baxi, Upendra. 2006. *The Future of Human Rights*. 2nd ed. New Delhi: Oxford University Press.

Bazerman, Charles. 2004. "Intertextualities: Volosinov, Bakhtin, Literary Theory, and Literacy Studies." In *Bakhtinian Perspectives on Language, Literacy, and Learning*, ed. Arnetha F. Ball and Sarah Warshauer Freedman, 53–65. Cambridge: Cambridge University Press.

Behar, Ruth. 1993. *Translated Woman: Crossing the Border with Esperanza's Story*. Boston: Beacon.

Bendavid-Val, Lean. 2008. *National Geographic: The Photographs*. Washington: National Geographic Society.

Benderly, Jill. 1997. "Rape, Feminism, and Nationalism in the War in Yugoslav Successor States." In *Feminist Nationalism*, ed. Lois West, 59–72. New York: Routledge.

Benhabib, Seyla. 2004. *The Rights of Others: Aliens, Residents, and Citizens*. Cambridge: Cambridge University Press.

———. 2006. *Another Cosmopolitanism: Hospitality, Sovereignty, and Democratic Iterations*. New York: Oxford University Press,

Benjamin, Walter. 1986. *Illuminations*. Ed. Hannah Arendt, trans. Harry Zohn. New York: Schocken.

Bennett, Jill, and Rosanna Kennedy, eds. 2003. *World Memory: Personal Trajectories in Global Time*. London: Palgrave.

Berelowitz, Jo-Anne. 2001. "A Journey Shared: Ursula Biemann's *Been There and Back to Nowhere: Gender in Transnational Spaces*." *Genders* 33:1–7.

Berlant, Lauren. 1997. *The Queen of America Goes to Washington City: Essays on Sex and Citizenship*. Durham: Duke University Press.

———. 1998. "Poor Eliza." *American Literature* 70, no. 3: 635–68.

———. 1999. "The Subject of True Feeling: Pain, Privacy, and Politics." In *Cultural Plu-*

*ralism, Identity Politics, and the Law,* ed. Austin Sarat and Thomas R. Kearns, 48–84. Ann Arbor: University of Michigan Press.

———. 2001. "Trauma and Ineloquence." *Cultural Values* 5, no. 1: 41–58.

———, ed. 2004. *Compassion: The Culture and Politics of an Emotion.* New York: Routledge.

Bernard, Cheryl. 1994. "Rape as Terror: The Case of Bosnia." *Terrorism and Political Violence* 6 (spring): 24–43.

Bernstein, Mary, and Nancy Naples. 2010. "Sexual Citizenship and the Pursuit of Relationship-Recognition Policies in Australia and the United States." *Women's Studies Quarterly* 38, nos. 1 and 2: 132–56.

Best, Steven. 1994. *"The Commodification of Reality and the Reality of Commodification: Baudrillard, Debord, and Postmodern Theory."* In *Baudrillard: A Critical Reader,* ed. Douglas Kellner. Oxford: Blackwell.

Best, Steven, and Douglas Kellner. 1999. "Debord and the Postmodern Turn: New Stages of Spectacle." *Substance: A Review of Theory and Criticism* 90:129–56.

———. 2001. *The Postmodern Adventure: Science, Technology, and Cultural Studies at the Third Millennium.* New York: Guilford Press.

Beverley, John. 1992. "The Margin at the Center on Testimonio (Testimonial Narrative)." In *De/Colonizing the Subject: The Politics of Gender in Women's Autobiography,* ed. Sidonie Smith and Julia Watson, 91–114. Minneapolis: University of Minnesota Press.

Bhabha, Jacqueline. 2006. "The Child—What Sort of Human?" *PMLA* 121, no. 5: 1526–35.

Biemann, Ursula. 2000. *Been There and Back to Nowhere: Gender in Transnational Spaces, Postproduction Documents 1988–2000.* Berlin: b books.

———. 2001a. "Female Geobodies: Resignifying the Economic within Sexual Difference." *n. paradoxa* (July): 1–6.

———, director. 2001b. *Remote Sensing.* New York: Women Make Movies.

———, director. 2001c. *Writing Desire.* New York: Women Make Movies.

Blumenberg, Hans. 1993. "Light as a Metaphor for Truth." In *Modernity and the Hegemony of Vision.* ed. David Michael Levin, 30–62. Berkeley: University of California Press.

Bob, Clifford. 2002. "Merchants of Morality." *Foreign Policy* (March/April): 36–45.

Bohmer, Carol, and Amy Shuman. 2007. *Rejecting Refugees: Political Asylum in the 21st Century.* Abingdon, England: Routledge.

Boltanski, Luc. 1999. *Distant Suffering: Morality, Media, and Politics.* Trans. Graham Burchell. Cambridge: Cambridge University Press.

Bonnett, Alastair. 2006. "The Nostalgia of Situationist Subversion." *Theory, Culture & Society* 23, no. 5: 23–48.

Boose, Lynda E. 2002. "Crossing the River Drina: Bosnian Rape Camps, Turkish Impalement, and Serb Cultural Memory." *Signs* 28, no. 1: 71–96.

Bose, Purnima, and Linta Varghese. 2001. "Mississippi Masala, South African Activism, and Agency." In *Haunting Violations: Feminist Criticism and the Crisis of the "Real,"* ed. Wendy Hesford and Wendy Kozol, 137–68. Urbana: University of Illinois Press.

Bow, Leslie. 2001. "Third-World Testimony in the Era of Globalization: Vietnam, Sexual Trauma, and Le Ly Hayslip's Art of Neutrality." In *Haunting Violations: Feminist Criti-*

*cism and the Crisis of the "Real,"* ed. Wendy Hesford and Wendy Kozol, 169–94. Urbana: University of Illinois Press.

Boxer, Sarah. 2004. "Humiliating Photographs as Trophies of War." *New York Times*, 20 May.

Bray, Abigail. 2009. "Governing the Gaze: Child Sexual Abuse, Moral Panics, and the Post-Feminist Blind Spot." *Feminist Media Studies* 9, no. 2: 173–91.

Briski, Zana. 2004. "Born into Brothels Press Kit: Directors' Statements." Kids with Cameras. http://www.kids-with-cameras.org.

Briski, Zana, and Ross Kauffman. 2004. *Born into Brothels: Calcutta's Red Light Kids.* Red Lights Films in association with ThinkFilm. New York, and HBO/Cinemax Documentary Films.

Brison, Susan J. 2004. "Torture, or 'Good Old American Pornography'?" *Chronicle of Higher Education*, 4 June.

Brittain, Victoria, and Gillian Slovo. 2004. *Guantánamo: "Honor Bound to Protect Freedom."* London: Oberon.

Bronfen, Elisabeth. 1992. *Over Her Dead Body: Death, Femininity and the Aesthetic.* New York: Routledge.

Brown, Michael Barratt. 1997. "The Role of Economic Factors in Social Crisis: The Case of Yugoslavia." *New Political Economy* 2 (July): 299–316.

Brown, Michelle. 2005. "Setting the Conditions for Abu Ghraib: The Prison Nation Abroad." *American Quarterly* 57, no. 3: 973–97.

Brown, Wendy. 1995a. *States of Injury: Power and Freedom in Late Modernity.* Princeton: Princeton University Press.

———. 1995b. "Wounded Attachments: Late Modern Oppositional Political Formations." In *The Identity in Question.*, ed. John Rajchman, 199–228. New York: Routledge.

———. 2002. "Suffering the Paradoxes of Rights." In *Left Legalism/Left Critique*, ed. Janet E. Halley, 420–34. Durham: Duke University Press.

Bryst, Alison. 2004. "Children Across Borders: New Subjects." In *Human Rights and Private Wrongs: Constructing Global Civil Society*, 29–59. New York: Routledge.

Buell, Frederick. 1994. *National Culture and the New Global System.* Baltimore: Johns Hopkins University Press.

Bunch, Charlotte. 1990. "Women's Rights as Human Rights: Toward a Re-Vision of Human Rights." *Human Rights Quarterly* 12:489–98.

Burke, Kenneth, 1950. *A Rhetoric of Motives.* New York: Prentice-Hall.

———. 1966. *Language as Symbolic Action: Essays on Life, Literature, and Method.* Berkeley, University of California Press.

———. 1969. *A Grammar of Motives.* Berkeley: University of California Press.

Butler, Judith. 1990. *Gender Trouble: Feminism and the Subversion of Identity.* New York: Routledge.

———. 1993. *Bodies That Matter: On the Discursive Limits of "Sex."* New York: Routledge.

———. 1997. *The Psychic Life of Power: Theories in Subjection.* Stanford: Stanford University Press.

———. 2000. "Restaging the Universal: Hegemony and the Limits of Formalism." In *Contingency, Hegemony, Universality: Contemporary Dialogues on the Left*, ed. Judith Butler, Ernesto Laclau, and Slavoj Žižek, 11–43. London: Verso.

———. 2004. *Precarious Life: The Powers of Mourning and Violence*. London: Verso.

———. 2005. *Giving an Account of Oneself*. New York: Fordham University Press.

Cabezas, Amalia Lucia. 1998. "A World of People: Sex Workers in Mexico." In *Global Sex Workers: Rights, Resistance, and Redefinition*, ed. Kamala Kempadoo and Jo Doezema, 197–99. New York: Routledge.

Cadava, Eduardo. 1997. *Words of Light: Theses on the Photography of History*. Princeton: Princeton University Press.

Caldwell, Gillian, and Steven Galster, directors. 1997. *Bought and Sold: An Investigative Documentary about the International Trade in Women*. New York: WITNESS.

Campbell, David. 1998. *National Deconstruction: Violence, Identity, and Justice in Bosnia*. Minneapolis: University of Minnesota Press.

———. 2007. "Geopolitics and Visuality: Sighting the Darfur Conflict." *Political Geography* 26:357–82.

Carpenter, R. Charli. 2010. *Forgetting Children Born of War: Setting the Human Rights Agenda in Bosnia and Beyond*. New York: Columbia University Press.

Carr, Robert. 1994. "Crossing the First World/Third World Divides: Testimonial, Transnational Feminisms, and the Postmodern Condition." In *Scattered Hegemonies: Postmodernity and Transnational Feminist Practices*, ed. Inderpal Grewal and Caren Kaplan, 153–72. Minneapolis: University of Minnesota Press.

Cartwright, Lisa. 1995. *Screening the Body: Tracing Medicine's Visual Culture*. Minneapolis: University of Minnesota Press.

———. 2008. *Moral Spectatorship: Technologies of Voice and Affect in Postwar Representations of the Child*. Durham: Duke University Press.

Caruth, Cathy. 1996. *Unclaimed Experience: Trauma, Narrative, and History*. Baltimore: Johns Hopkins University Press.

Castoriadis, Cornelius. 1987. *The Imaginary Institution of Society*. Trans. Kathleen Blamey. Cambridge: MIT Press.

Chakravarti, Sonali. 2008. "More than 'Cheap Sentimentality': Victim Testimony at Nuremberg, the Eichmann Trial, and Truth Commissions." *Constellations* 15, no. 2: 223–35.

Chambers, Iain. 1996. "Signs of Silence, Lines of Listening." In *The Post-Colonial Question: Common Skies, Divided Horizons*, ed. Iain Chambers and Lidia Curti, 47–62. London: Routledge.

Chandler, David. 2001. "The Road to Military Humanitarianism: How the Human Rights NGOs Shaped a New Humanitarian Agenda." *Human Rights Quarterly* 23:678–700.

Chavez, Linda. 2004. "Sexual Tension in the Military." Townhall.com, 5 May.

Cheah, Pheng. 2006. *Inhuman Conditions: On Cosmopolitanism and Human Rights*. Cambridge: Harvard University Press.

Chomsky, Noam. 1999. "Crisis in the Balkans." *Z Magazine*, May.

Chouliaraki, Lilie. 2006. *The Spectatorship of Suffering*. Thousand Oaks, Calif.: Sage.

Chow, Rey. 1991. "Violence in the Other Country: China as Crisis, Spectacle, and Woman." In *Third World Women and the Politics of Feminism*, ed. Chandra Talpade Mohanty, Lourdes Torres, and Ann Russo, 81–100. Bloomington: Indiana University Press.

———. 1993. *Writing Diaspora: Tactics of Intervention in Contemporary Cultural Studies*. Bloomington: Indiana University Press.

———. 2006. *The Age of the World Target: Self-Referentiality in War, Theory, and Comparative Work*. Durham: Duke University Press.

Chun, Wendy Hui Kyong. 2002. "Unbearable Witness: Toward a Politics of Listening." In *Extremities: Trauma, Testimony, and Community*, ed. Nancy K. Miller and Jason Tougaw, 143–65. Urbana: University of Illinois Press.

Claycomb, Ryan M. 2007. "The Inscrutable Terrorist and the Righteous Rioter." *Politics and Culture* 1. www.politicsandculture.org.

Clifford, James. 1992. "Traveling Cultures." In *Cultural Studies*, ed. Lawrence Goldberg, Cary Nelson, and Paula A. Treichler, 96–116. New York: Routledge.

Coalition against Trafficking in Women [CATW]. 2000. *So Deep a Violence: Prostitution, Trafficking, and the Global Sex Industry*.

Cohen, Stanley, and Bruna Seu. 2002. "Knowing Enough Not to Feel Too Much: Emotional Thinking about Human Rights Appeals." In *Truth Claims: Representation and Human Rights*, ed. Mark Philip Bradley and Patrice Petro, 187–201. New Directions in International Studies. New Brunswick, N.J.: Rutgers University Press.

Collins, Lauren. 2005. "Passage to India." *Women's Wear Daily*. 3 February, 4.

Copelon, Rhonda. 1988. "Surfacing Gender: Reconceptualizing Crimes against Women in Times of War." In *The Women and War Reader*, ed. Lois Ann Lorentzen and Jennifer Turpin, 63–79. New York: New York University Press.

Crago, Anna-Louise. 2003. "Unholy Alliance." *Rabble*. May.

Crary, Jonathan. 1999. *Suspensions of Perception: Attention, Spectacle, and Modern Culture*. Cambridge: MIT Press.

Crowley, Sharon, and Debra Hawhee. 2004. *Ancient Rhetorics for Contemporary Students*. 3rd ed. New York: Pearson Longman.

Cubilié, Anne. 2005. *Women Witnessing Terror: Testimony and the Cultural Politics of Human Rights*. New York: Fordham University Press.

Cumbo, Lawrence. 2002. *The Search for the Afghan Girl*. Video. National Geographic Society.

Curry, Andrew. 2005. "Young Eyes on Calcutta." *Smithsonian*, May, 62–66.

Danner, Mark. 2004. *Torture and Truth: America, Abu Ghraib, and the War on Terror*. New York: New York Review Books.

Das, Veena. 2007. *Life and Words: Violence and the Descent into the Ordinary*. Berkeley: University of California Press.

Davidson, Neil. 1999. "The Trouble with 'Ethnicity.'" *International Socialism Journal* 84 (autumn). http://pubs.socialistreviewindex.org.uk/isj84/davidson.htm.

Dawes, James. 2007. *That the World May Know: Bearing Witness to Atrocity*. Cambridge: Harvard University Press.

Dawson, Gary Fisher. 1999. *Documentary Theatre in the United States.* Westport, Conn.: Greenwood.

Debord, Guy. 1994. *The Society of the Spectacle.* Trans. Donald Nicholson. New York: Zone.

———. 2007. *Comments on the Society of the Spectacle.* 2nd ed. Trans. Macolm Imrie. London: Verso.

Deleuze, Gilles, and Felix Guattari. 1983. *Anti-Oedipus: Capitalism and Schizophrenia.* Trans. Robert Hurly, Mark Seem, and Helen R. Lane. Minneapolis: University of Minnesota Press.

DeLuca, Kevin Michael. 1999. *Image Politics: The New Rhetoric of Environmental Activism.* New York: Guilford Press.

Denby, David. 2005. "Born into Brothels." *New Yorker,* 28 February, 24, 46.

Derrida, Jacques. 1987. *The Post Card: From Socrates to Freud and Beyond.* Trans. Alan Bass. Chicago: University of Chicago Press.

———. 1994. *Specters of Marx: The State of Debt, the Work of Mourning, and the New International.* Trans. Peggy Kamuf. New York: Routledge.

———. 1996. *Archive Fever: A Freudian Impression.* Trans. Eric Prenowitz. Chicago: University of Chicago Press.

Doezema, Jo. 1998. "Forced to Choose: Beyond the Voluntary v. Forced Prostitution Dichotomy." In *Global Sex Workers: Rights, Resistance, and Redefinition,* ed. Kamala Kempadoo and Jo Doezema, 34–50. New York: Routledge.

———. 1999. "Trafficking in Myths?" In *Sex Work and Sex Workers,* ed. Barry M. Dank and Roberto Refinetti, 165–68. New Brunswick, N.J.: Transaction.

———. 2000. "Loose Women or Lost Women? The Re-Emergence of the Myth of White Slavery in Contemporary Discourses of Trafficking in Women." *Gender Issues* 18, no. 1: 23–50.

Donnelly, Jack. 2003. *Universal Human Rights in Theory and Practice.* 2nd ed. Ithaca: Cornell University Press.

Douglass, Ana, and Thomas A. Vogler. 2003. *Witness and Memory: The Discourse of Trauma.* New York: Routledge.

Douzinas, Costas. 2002. "Identity, Recognition, Rights or What Can Hegel Teach Us About Human Rights?" *Journal of Law and Society* 29, no. 3: 379–405.

Dowd, Maureen. 2005. "Torture Chicks Gone Wild." *New York Times,* 30 January.

Drakulić, Slavenka. 2001. "Bosnian Women Witness." *Nation,* 19 March, 5–6.

Drinan, Robert F. 2001. *The Mobilization of Shame: A World View of Human Rights.* New Haven: Yale University Press.

DuBois, Page. 1991. *Torture and Truth.* New York: Routledge.

Dutt, Anuradha. 1993. "In the Name of the Mother: Education Rights for Prostitutes' Children." *Manushi* 79 (November–December): 23–26.

Dutt, Mallika. 1998. "Reclaiming a Human Rights Culture: Feminism of Difference and Alliance." In *Talking Visions: Multicultural Feminism in a Transnational Age,* ed. Ella Shohat, 225–46. New York: New Museum of Contemporary Art.

Edwards, Holly. 2007. "Cover to Cover: The Life Cycle of an Image in Contemporary Visual Culture." In *Beautiful Suffering: Photography and the Traffic in Pain,* ed. Mark

Reinhardt, Holly Edwards, and Erina Dugganne, 75–92. Williamstown, Mass.: Williams College Museum of Art.

Ehrenreich, Barbara. 2004. "Prison Abuse: Feminism's Assumptions Upended. A Uterus Is Not a Substitute for a Conscience." *Los Angeles Times*, 16 May, M1.

Eisenstein, Zillah. 2004a. *Against Empire: Feminisms, Racism, and the West*. New York: Zed.

———. 2004b. "Sexual Humiliation, Gender Confusion and the Horrors at Abu Ghraib." ZNet Activism. http://www.zcommunications.org.

Enloe, Cynthia. 2000. *Maneuvers: The International Politics of Militarizing Women's Lives*. Berkeley: University of California Press.

Ensler, Eve. 2006. *Insecure at Last: Losing It in Our Security-Obsessed World*. New York: Villard.

Erickson, Jon. 1992. "The Spectacle of the Anti-Spectacle: Happenings and the Situationist International." *Discourse* 14, no. 2: 36–58.

Esmeir, Samera. 2006. "On Making Dehumanization Possible." *PMLA* 121, no. 5: 1544–52.

Fabian, Johannes. 1983. *Time and the Other: How Anthropology Makes Its Object*. New York: Columbia University Press.

Fanon, Frantz. 1967. *Black Skin, White Masks*. Trans. Charles Lam Markmann. New York: Grove Press.

Federle, Kate. 1994. "Rights Flow Downhill." *International Journal of Children's Rights* 2:343–68.

Feldman, Allen. 2004a. "Abu Ghraib: Ceremonies of Nostalgia." *Open Democracy*, 17 October. www.opendemocracy.net.

———. 2004b. "Memory Theatres, Virtual Witnessing, and the Trauma-Aesthetic." *Biography* 21, no. 1: 163–202.

———. 2005. "The Actuarial Gaze: From 9/11 to Abu Ghraib." *Cultural Studies* 19, no. 2: 203–26.

Felman, Shoshana, and Dori Laub. 1992. *Testimony: Crises of Witnessing in Literature, Psychoanalysis, and History*. New York: Routledge.

Felski, Rita. 1989. *Beyond Feminist Aesthetics: Feminist Literature and Social Change*. Cambridge: Harvard University Press.

Fernandes, Leela. 2001. "Reading 'India's Bandit Queen': A Trans/National Feminist Perspective on the Discrepancies of Representation." In *Haunting Violations: Feminist Criticism and the Crisis of the "Real,"* ed. Wendy Hesford and Wendy Kozol, 47–75. Urbana: University of Illinois Press.

Foss, Sonja. 1996. *Rhetorical Criticism: Exploration and Practice*. 2nd ed. Prospect Heights, Ill.: Waveland.

Foucault, Michel. 1972. *The Archaeology of Knowledge and the Discourse on Language*. New York: Pantheon Books.

———. 1975. *Discipline and Punish: The Birth of the Prison*. Trans. Alan Sheridan. London: Allen Lane.

———. 1997. *Ethics: Subjectivity and Truth*. Ed. Paul Rabinow. New York: The New Press.

Fraser, Nancy. 1990. "Rethinking the Public Sphere: A Contribution to the Critique of Actually Existing Democracy." *Social Text* nos. 25 and 26:56–80.

———. 2003. "Social Justice in the Age of Identity Politics: Redistribution, Recognition, and Participation." In *Redistribution or Recognition: A Political-Philosophical Exchange*, ed. Nancy Frasher and Axel Honneth, 6–109. London: Verso.

———. 2005a. "Mapping the Feminist Imagination: From Redistribution to Recognition to Representation." *Constellations* 12, no. 3: 295–307.

———. 2005b. "Reframing Justice in a Globalizing World." *New Left Review* 36:1–19.

Freedman, Jane. 2007. "Women, Islam and Rights in Europe: Beyond a Universalist/Culturalist Dichotomy." *Review of International Studies* 33, no. 1: 29–44.

Freeman, Marsha. 1999. "International Institutions and Gendered Justice." *Journal of International Affairs* 52, no. 2: 513–33.

Friend, Melanie. 2001. *No Place Like Home: Echoes from Kosovo*. San Francisco: Midnight Editions.

Fuss, Diana. 1995. *Identification Papers*. New York: Routledge.

Gajicki, Marija. 2003. *Vivisect*. Novi Sad, Serbia: Vojvodanka-Regional Women's Initiative.

Gangoli, Geetanjali. 2001. "Prostitution as Livelihood: 'Work' or 'Crime.'" Paper presented at the Livelihoods and Poverty Reduction Conference, 25–27 September, Bhubaneswar, India.

Garland-Thomson, Rosemarie. 2002. "The Politics of Staring: Visual Rhetorics of Disability in Popular Photography." In *Disability Studies: Enabling the Humanities*, ed. Sharon L. Snyder, Brenda Jo Brueggemann, and Rosemarie Garland-Thomson, 56–75. New York: Modern Language Association.

Geisler, Cheryl. 2004. "How to Understand the Concept of Rhetorical Agency." *Rhetoric Society Quarterly*, 34, no. 3: 1–12.

Genette, Gerald. 1997. *Paratexts: Thresholds of Interpretation*. Trans. Jane E. Lewin. Cambridge: Cambridge University Press.

German, Lindsey. 2000. "Serbia's Spring in October." *International Socialism Journal* 89 (winter). http://pubs.socialistreviewindex.org.uk/isj89/german.htm.

Gilman, Sander. 2001. *Making the Body Beautiful: A Cultural History of Aesthetic Surgery*. Princeton: Princeton University Press.

Gilmore, Leigh. 1994. *Autobiographics: A Feminist Theory of Women's Self-Representation*. Ithaca: Cornell University Press.

———. 2001. *The Limits of Autobiography: Trauma and Testimony*. Ithaca: Cornell University Press.

Giroux, Henry. 1998. "Nymphet Fantasies: Child Beauty Pageants and the Politics of Innocence." *Social Text* 57 (winter): 31–53.

———. 2007. "Beyond the Spectacle of Terrorism." *Situations* 2, no. 1: 17–51.

Glenn, Cheryl. 2002. "Silence: A Rhetorical Art for Resisting Discipline(s)." *JAC* 22, no. 2: 261–91.

Global Alliance against Traffic in Women [GAATW]. 2001. "Human Rights in Practice: A Guide to Assist Trafficked Women and Children." Bangkok: GAATW.

Goldberg, Elizabeth Swanson. 2001. "Splitting Difference: Global Identity Politics and the Representation of Torture in the Counterhistorical Dramatic Film." In *Violence and American Cinema*, ed. J. David Slocum, 245–70. New York: Routledge.

———. 2007. *Beyond Terror: Gender, Narrative, Human Rights.* New Brunswick, N.J.: Rutgers University Press.

Gordon, Avery F. 1997. *Ghostly Matters: Haunting and the Sociological Imagination.* Minneapolis: University of Minnesota Press.

Graff, Harvey J. 1979. *The Literacy Myth: Literacy and Social Structure in the Nineteenth-Century City.* New York: Academic Press.

Gregory, Sam. 2006. "Transnational Storytelling: Human Rights WITNESS, and Video Advocacy." *American Anthropologist* 108, no. 1: 195–204.

Gregory, Sam, Gillian Caldwell, Ronit Avni, and Thomas Harding. eds. 2005. *Video for Change: A Guide for Advocacy and Activism.* London: Pluto Press.

Grewal, Inderpal. 1998. "On the New Global Feminism and the Family of Nations: Dilemmas of Transnational Feminist Practice." In *Talking Visions: Multicultural Feminism in a Transnational Age,* ed. Ella Shohat, 501–30. New York: New Museum of Contemporary Art.

———. 2005. *Transnational America: Feminisms, Diasporas, Neoliberalisms.* Durham: Duke University Press.

Grewal, Inderpal, and Caren Kaplan. 1996. "Warrior Marks: Global Womanism's Neo-Colonial Discourse in a Multicultural Context." *Camera Obscura* 39 (September): 5–33.

———. 2001. "Global Identities: Theorizing Transnational Studies of Sexuality." GLQ 7, no. 4: 663–79.

———. 2002. "Transnational Practices and Interdisciplinary Feminist Scholarship: Refiguring Women's and Gender Studies." In *Women's Studies on Its Own: A Next Wave Reader in Institutional Change,* ed. Robyn Wiegman, 66–81. Durham: Duke University Press.

Grigor, Talinn. 2002. "(Re)claiming Space: The Use/Misuse of Propaganda Murals in Republican Tehran." *Asian Arts and Cultures Newsletter,* August 37.

Gross, Daniel M. 2006. *The Secret History of Emotion: From Aristotle's Rhetoric to Modern Brain Science.* Chicago: University of Chicago Press.

Gunn, Joshua. 2006. "Review Essay: Mourning Humanism, or, the Idiom of Haunting." *Quarterly Journal of Speech* 92, no. 1: 77–102.

Gunning, Isabelle R. 1998. "Cutting Through the Obfuscation: Female Genital Surgeries in Neoimperial Culture." In *Talking Visions: Multicultural Feminism in a Transnational Age,* ed. Ella Shohat, 203–24. New York: New Museum of Contemporary Art.

Gurstein, Rochelle. 2005. "On the Triumph of the Pornographic Imagination." *New York Times,* 1 May.

Habermas, Jürgen. 1989. *The Structural Transformation of the Public Sphere: An Inquiry into a Category of Bourgeois Society.* Trans. Thomas Burger with the assistance of Frederick Lawrence. Cambridge: MIT Press.

Hannerz, Ulf. 1990. "Cosmopolitans and Locals in World Culture." *Theory, Culture & Society* 7:237–51.

Haraway, Donna J. 1991. *Simians, Cyborgs, and Women: The Reinvention of Nature.* New York: Routledge.

Hariman, Robert, and John Louis Lucaites. 2007. *No Caption Needed: Iconic Photographs, Public Culture, and Liberal Democracy.* Chicago: University of Chicago Press.

Harlow, Barbara. 1986. Introduction. In *The Colonial Harem*, by Malek Alloula, trans. Myrna Godzich and Wlad Godzich, ix–xx. Minneapolis: University of Minnesota Press.

———. 1996. "From the 'Civilizing Mission' to 'Humanitarian Intervention': Postmodernism, Writing, and Human Rights." In *Text and Nation: Cross-Disciplinary Essays on Cultural and National Identities*, ed. Laura García-Moreno and Peter C. Pfeffer, 31–47. Columbia, S.C.: Camden House.

Haskell, Thomas J. 1985. "Capitalism and the Origins of the Humanitarian Sensibility, Part 1." *American Historical Review* 90 (April): 339–61.

Hauser, Gerard A. 1999. *Vernacular Voices: The Rhetorics of Publics and Public Spheres.* Columbia: University of South Carolina Press.

Haviv, Ron. 2000. *Blood and Honey: A Balkan War Journal*. New York: Umbrage.

Hayles, Katherine. 1999. *How We Became Posthuman: Virtual Bodies in Cybernetics, Literature, and Informatics*. Chicago: University of Chicago Press.

Haynes, Mike. 1999. "Theses on the Balkan War." *International Socialism Journal* 83 (summer). http://www.isj1text.ble.org.uk/pubs/isj83/haynes.htm.

Hegel, G. W. F. [1830] 1971. *Hegel's Philosophy of Mind*. Trans. W. Wallace. Ed. J. N. Findlay. Oxford: Clarendon Press.

———. [1807] 1994. *Hegel's Phenomenology of Spirit*. Trans. Howard P. Kainz. University Park: Pennsylvania State University Press.

Heidegger, Martin. [1938] 1997. *The Question Concerning Technology and Other Essays*. Trans with an introduction by William Lovitt. New York: Harper Colophon Books.

———. [1947] 1993. "Letter on Humanism." In *Martin Heidegger: Basic Writings*, rev. ed., ed. David Farrell Krell, 217–65. San Francisco: Harper SanFrancisco.

Hennessy, Rosemary. 1993. *Materialist Feminism and the Politics of Discourse*. New York: Routledge.

Herndl, Carl G., and Adela C. Licona. 2007. "Shifting Agency: Agency, Kairos, and the Possibilities of Social Action." In *Communicative Practices in Workplaces and the Professions: Cultural Perspectives on the Regulation of Discourse and Organizations*, ed. Mark Zachry and Charlotte Thralls, 133–53. Amityville, N.Y.: Baywood.

Herscher, Andrew. 2010. *Violence Taking Place: The Architecture of the Kosovo Conflict*. Stanford: Stanford University Press.

Hersh, Seymour M. 2004. "Torture at Abu Ghraib." *New Yorker*, 10 May, 42–47.

Hesford, Wendy S. 2001. "Reading Rape Stories: Material Rhetoric and the Trauma of Representation." In *Haunting Violations: Feminist Criticism and the Crisis of the "Real,"* ed. Wendy Hesford and Wendy Kozol, 13–46. Urbana: University of Illinois Press.

———. 2010. "Cosmopolitanism and Feminist Geopolitical Rhetorics." In *Rhetorica in Motion*, ed. Eileen Schell and Kelly Rawson, 53–70. Pittsburgh: University of Pittsburgh Press.

Hesford, Wendy S., and Wendy Kozol, eds. 2001. *Haunting Violations: Feminist Criticism and the Crisis of the "Real."* Urbana: University of Illinois Press.

———. 2005. Introduction. In *Just Advocacy? Women's Human Rights, Transnational Feminisms, and the Politics of Representation*, 1–29. New Brunswick, N.J.: Rutgers University Press.

———. 2006. "Global Turns and Cautions in Rhetoric and Composition." *PMLA* 121, no. 3: 787–801.

Hesford, Wendy, and Eileen Schell. 2008. "Configurations of Transnationality: Locating Feminist Rhetorics." *College English* 70, no. 5: 461–70.

Hirsch, Marianne. 1997. *Family Frames: Photography, Narrative, and Postmemory*. Cambridge: Harvard University Press.

———. 2002a. "Marked by Memory: Feminist Reflections on Trauma and Transmission." In *Extremities: Trauma, Testimony, and Community*, ed. Nancy K. Miller and Jason Tougaw, 71–91. Urbana: University of Illinois Press.

———. 2002b. "Surviving Images: Holocaust Photographs and the Work of Postmemory." *Yale Journal of Criticism* 14, no. 1: 5–37.

Holquist, Michael. 1990. *Dialogism: Bakhtin and His World*. London: Routledge.

Honneth, Axel. 1995. *The Struggle for Recognition: The Moral Grammar of Social Conflicts*. Cambridge: Polity.

Horkheimer, M., and T. W. Adorno. [1947] 1972. *Dialectic of Enlightenment: Philosophical Fragments*. Trans. John Cumming. New York: Herder and Herder.

Howard, June. 2001. *Publishing the Family*. Durham: Duke University Press.

Howell, Peter. 2005. *"Born into Brothels* Shines a Light." *Toronto Star*, 18 February.

Hozic, Aida A. 2000. "Making of the Unwanted Colonies: (Un)imagining Desire." In *Political Theory and Cultural Studies*, ed. Jodi Dean, 228–40. Ithaca: Cornell University Press.

Human Rights Watch. 1995. "The Human Rights Watch Global Report on Women's Human Rights." 1 August. www.hrw.org.

———. 2006. "Military Commission." 23 June. www.hrw.org.

Hungerford, Amy. 2001. "Memorializing Memory." *Yale Journal of Criticism* 14, no. 1: 67–93.

Hunt, Lynn. 2007. *Inventing Human Rights: A History*. New York: W. W. Norton and Company.

Ignatieff, Michael. 2001. "Human Rights as Politics." In *Human Rights as Politics and Idolatry*, by Michael Ignatieff, 3–52. Edited and introduced by Amy Gutmann. Princeton: Princeton University Press.

Irigaray, Luce. 1985. *Speculum of the Other Woman*. Trans. Gillian G. Gill. Ithaca: Cornell University Press.

Jacobson, Mandy, and Karmen Jelincic. 1996. *Calling the Ghosts: A Story about Rape, War, and Women*. New York: Women Make Movies.

James, Joy. 1998. *Resisting State Violence: Radicalism, Gender, and Race in U.S. Culture*. Minneapolis: University of Minnesota Press.

Jameson, Fredric. 1981. *The Political Unconscious: Narrative as a Socially Symbolic Act*. Ithaca: Cornell University Press.

———. 1992. *Signatures of the Visible*. New York: Routledge.

Jarratt, Susan. 2000. "Besides Ourselves: Rhetoric and Representation in Postcolonial Feminist Writing." In *The Kinneavy Papers: Theory and the Study of Discourse*, ed. Lynn Worsham, Sidney I. Dobrin, and Gary A. Olson, 327–52. Albany: State University of New York Press.

Johnson, Nan. 2002. *Gender and Rhetorical Space in American Life, 1866–1910*. Carbondale: Southern Illinois University Press.

Kaplan, Amy. 2004. "Violent Belongings and the Question of Empire Today: Presidential Address to the American Studies Association, October 17, 2003." *American Quarterly* 56, no. 1: 1–18.

Kaplan, Caren. 1994. "The Politics of Location as Transnational Feminist Practice." In *Scattered Hegemonies: Postmodernity and Transnational Feminist Practices*, ed. Inderpal Grewal and Caren Kaplan, 137–52. Minneapolis: University of Minnesota Press.

———. 1996. *Questions of Travel: Postmodern Discourses of Displacement*. Durham: Duke University Press.

———. 2001. "Hillary Rodham Clinton's Orient: Cosmopolitan Travel and Global Feminist Subjects." *Meridians* 2, no. 1: 219–40.

Kapsalis, Terri. 1997. *Public Privates: Performing Gynecology from Both Ends of the Speculum*. Durham: Duke University Press.

Kapur, Ratna. 2005. *Erotic Justice: Law and the New Politics of Postcolonialism*. Permanent Black: New Delhi.

———. 2006. "Human Rights in the 21st Century: Take a Walk on the Dark Side." *Sydney Law Review* 28:665–87.

Keck, Margaret E., and Kathryn Sikkink. 1998. *Activists beyond Borders: Advocacy Networks in International Politics*. Ithaca: Cornell University Press.

Keenan, Thomas. 2002. "Publicity and Indifference (Sarajevo on Television)." PMLA 117, no. 1: 104–16.

———. 2004. "Mobilizing Shame." *South Atlantic Quarterly* 103:435–49.

Kellner, Douglas. 2005. *Media Spectacle and the Crisis of Democracy*. Boulder, Colo.: Paradigm.

Kennedy, David. 2004. *The Dark Sides of Virtue: Reassessing International Humanitarianism*. Princeton: Princeton University Press.

Kennedy, Rory. 2007. *Ghosts of Abu Ghraib*. HBO Documentary Films.

Kershaw, Baz. 2003. "Curiosity or Contempt: On Spectacle, the Human, and Activism." *Theatre Journal* 55, no. 4: 591–611.

Kirin, Renata Jambresic. 1996. "Narrating War and Exile Experiences." In *War, Exile, Everyday Life: Cultural Perspectives*, ed. Renata Jambresic Kirin and Maja Povrzanovic, 63–82. Zagreb, Croatia: Institute of Ethnology and Folklore Research.

Kleinman, Arthur, and Joan Kleinman. 1996. "The Appeal of Experience; the Dismay of Images: Cultural Appropriations of Suffering in Our Times." *Daedalus* 125, no. 1: 1–23.

Knabb, Ken, ed. and trans. 1981. "Definitions." In *Situationist International Anthology*, 44–46. Berkeley, Calif.: Bureau of Public Secrets.

Korać, Maja. 1996. "Understanding Ethnic-National Identity and Its Meaning: Questions from Women's Experience." *Women's Studies International Forum* 19:133–43.

Koshy, Susan. 1999. "From Cold War to Trade War: Neocolonialism and Human Rights." *Social Text* 17, no. 1: 1–32.

Kozol, Wendy. 2004. "Documenting NATO's War in Kosovo/a: (In)Visible Bodies and the Dilemma of Photojournalism." *Meridians* 4, no. 2: 1–38.

———. n.d. *"Visible Wars and the Ambivalences of Witnessing."* Unpublished manuscript.

Kramer, Lloyd. 1989. "Literature, Criticism, and Historical Imagination: The Literary Challenge of Hayden White and Dominick LaCapra." In *The New Cultural History: Essays,* ed. with an introduction by Lynn Hunt, 97–128. Berkeley: University of California Press.

Kristeva, Julia. 1980. *Desire in Language: A Semiotic Approach to Literature and Art.* Ed. Leon S. Roudiez, trans. Thomas Gora, Alice Jardin, and Leon S. Roudiez. New York: Columbia University Press.

Kristof, Nicholas, and Sheryl WuDunn. 2009. *Half the Sky: Turning Oppression into Opportunity for Women Worldwide.* New York: Alfred A. Knopf.

Kubiak, Anthony. 1991. *Stages of Terror: Terrorism, Ideology, and Coercion as Theatre History.* Bloomington: Indiana University Press.

Kulnych, Jessica. 2001. "No Playing in the Public Sphere: Democratic Theory and the Exclusion of Children." *Social Theory and Practice* 27, no. 2: 231–64.

LaCapra, Dominick. 1983. *Rethinking Intellectual History: Texts, Contexts, and Language.* Ithaca: Cornell University Press.

———. 2001. *Writing History, Writing Trauma.* Baltimore: Johns Hopkins University Press.

Laclau, Ernesto, and Chantel Mouffe. 1985. *Hegemony and Socialist Strategy: Towards a Radical Democratic Politics.* London: Verso.

Landes, Joan. 1988. *Women and the Public Sphere in the Age of the French Revolution.* Ithaca: Cornell University Press.

Lévinas, Emmanuel. 1981. *Otherwise Than Being: or, Beyond Essence.* Trans. Alphonso Lingis. Hague: Nijhoff.

———. 1969. *Totality and Infinity.* Trans. Alphonso Lingis. Pittsburgh: Duquesne University Press.

Levin, David Michael. 2003. *The Philosopher's Gaze: Modernity in the Shadows of Enlightenment.* Pittsburgh: Duquense University Press.

Levy, Daniel, Natea Sznaider, and Assenka Oksiloff. 2005. *Holocaust and Memory in the Global Age.* Philadelphia: Temple University Press, 2005.

Li, Juan. 2009. "Intertextuality and National Identity." *Discourse and Society* 20, no. 1: 85–121.

Lister, Ruth. 2003. *Citizenship: Feminist Perspectives.* 2nd ed. New York: New York University Press.

Lutz, Catherine A., and Jane L. Collins. 1993. *Reading National Geographic.* Chicago: University of Chicago Press.

Lyotard, Jean-Francois. 1984. *The Postmodern Condition.* Trans. Geoff Bennington and Brian Massumi. Minneapolis: University of Minnesota Press.

Mackenzie, Midge. 1995. *The Sky: A Silent Witness.* New York: Women Make Movies.

MacKinnon, Catharine A. 1993. "Turning Rape into Pornography: Postmodern Genocide." *Ms.,* July–August, 24–30.

———. 2006a. "Postmodernism and Human Rights." In *Are Women Human? and Other International Dialogues,* 44–63. Cambridge: Harvard University Press.

————. 2006b. "Crimes of War, Crimes of Peace." In *Are Women Human? and Other International Dialogues*, 141–59. Cambridge: Harvard University Press.

————. 2006c. "Defining Rape Internationally: A Comment on Akayesu." In *Are Women Human? and Other International Dialogues*, 237–46. Cambridge: Harvard University Press.

Maclear, Kyo. 1999. *Beclouded Visions: Hiroshima-Nagasaki and the Art of Witness*. Albany: State University of New York Press.

Magas, Branka. 1997. "Unforgettable Yugoslavia: A Reply to Barratt Brown." *New Political Economy* 2, no. 3: 465–69.

Mahila Samanwaya Committee [Minu Pal, Sadhana Mukherji, Madhabi Jaiswal, and Bachhy Dutta]. 1998. "The Wind of Change Is Whispering at Your Door." In *Global Sex Workers: Rights, Resistance, and Redefinition*, ed. Kamala Kempadoo and Jo Doezema, 200–202. New York: Routledge.

Mahmood, Saba. 2004. *Politics of Piety: The Islamic Revival and the Feminist Subject*. Princeton: Princeton University Press.

Mailloux, Steven. 2006. *Disciplinary Identities: Rhetorical Paths of English, Speech, and Composition*. New York: Modern Language Association.

Malkki, Liisa. 1994. "Citizens of Humanity: Internationalism and the Imagined Community of Nations." *Diaspora* 3, no. 1: 41–68.

Mandel, Naomi. 2001. "Rethinking 'After Auschwitz': Against a Rhetoric of the Unspeakable in Holocaust Writing." *boundary 2* 28, no. 2: 203–28.

Mann, Emily. 1997. *Testimonies: Four Plays*. New York: Theatre Communications Group.

Marcuse, Herbert. 1964. *One Dimensional Man*. Boston: Beacon Press.

Marks, Laura U. 2000. *The Skin of the Film: Intercultural Cinema, Embodiment, and the Senses*. Durham: Duke University Press.

Martin, Carol. 2006. "Bodies of Evidence. *TDR* 50, no. 3: 8–15.

Masud, Tareque, and Catherine Masud. 2007. *A Kind of Childhood: A Film About Child Labor in the Third World*. Santa Monica, Calif.: Direct Cinema Limited.

Mazumdar, Sudip. 1999. "Red-light Revolution." *Newsweek*, 15 February, 40.

McCarthy, Todd. 2004. "Born into Brothels: Calcutta's Red Light Kids." *Variety*, 8 March, 41.

McClennen, Sophia A. 2008. "The Humanities, Human Rights, and the Comparative Imagination." In CLC *Web: Comparative Literature and Culture* 9, no. 1: 1–19.

McCurry, Steve. 1999. *Portraits*. London: Phaidon Press.

McCurry, Steve, and Kerry William Purcell, 2007. In *The Shadow of Mountains*. London: Phaidon Press.

McGrew, Anthony G. 1998. "Human Rights in a Global Age: Coming to Terms with Globalization." In *Human Rights Fifty Years On: A Reappraisal*, ed. Tony Evans, 188–210. Manchester, UK: Manchester University Press.

McLagen, Megan. 2007. "Human Rights, Testimony, and Transnational Publicity." In *Nongovernmental Politics*, ed. Michel Feher, with Gaelle Krikorian and Yates McKee, 304–17. New York: Zone.

McNay, Lois. 2008. "The Trouble with Recognition: Subjectivity, Suffering, and Agency." *Sociological Theory* 26, no. 3: 271–96.

Merleau-Ponty, Maurice. 1962. *Phenomenology of Perception*. Trans. Colin Smith. London: Humanities Press.

———. 1968. *The Visible and the Invisible*. Trans. Alphonso Lingis. Evanston, Ill.: Northwestern University Press.

Merry, Sally Engle. 2001. "Women, Violence, and the Human Rights System." In *Women, Gender, and Human Rights: A Global Perspective*, ed. Marjorie Agosin, 83–97. New Brunswick, N.J.: Rutgers University Press.

———. 2006. *Human Rights and Gender Violence: Translating International Law into Local Justice*. Chicago: University of Chicago Press.

Mertus, Julie. 2003. "The New U.S. Human Rights Policy: A Radical Departure." *International Studies Perspectives* 4, no. 4: 371–84.

———. 2004. "Shouting from the Bottom of the Well: The Impact of International Trials for Wartime Rape on Women's Agency." *International Feminist Journal of Politics* 6, no. 1: 110–28.

Miller, Carolyn R. 2007. "What Can Automation Tell Us about Agency?" *Rhetoric Society Quarterly* 37, no. 2: 137–57.

Miller, David. 1995. *On Nationality*. Oxford: Clarendon Press.

Minh-ha, Trinh T. 1989. *Woman, Native, Other: Writing Postcoloniality and Feminism*. Bloomington: Indiana University Press.

———. 1991. *When the Moon Waxes Red: Representation, Gender, and Cultural Politics*. New York: Routledge.

———. 2005. *The Digital Film Event*. New York: Routledge.

Mirzoeff, Nicholas, ed. 1998. "Introduction to Part Four." *The Visual Culture Reader*, 281–90. London: Routledge.

———. 2005. *Watching Babylon*. New York: Routledge.

———. 2006. "Invisible Empire: Visual Culture, Embodied Spectacle, and Abu Ghraib." *Radical History Review* 95 (spring): 21–44.

Mitchell, W. J. T. 1994. *Picture Theory: Essays on Verbal and Visual Representation*. Chicago: University of Chicago Press.

———. 2002. "Showing Seeing: A Critique of Visual Culture." *Journal of Visual Culture* 1, no. 2: 165–81.

Moeller, Susan. 1998. *Compassion Fatigue: How the Media Sell Disease, Famine, War, and Death*. London: Routledge.

———. 2002. "A Hierarchy of Innocence: The Media's Use of Children in the Telling of International News." *Press/Politics* 7, no. 1: 36–56.

Mohanty, Chandra Talpade. 1991. "Under Western Eyes: Feminist Scholarship and Colonial Discourses." In *Third World Women and the Politics of Feminism*, ed. Chandra Talpade Mohanty, Ann Russo, and Lourdes Torres, 51–80. Bloomington: Indiana University Press.

Montgomery, Heather. 1998. "Children, Prostitution, and Identity: A Case Study from a Tourist Resort in Thailand." In *Global Sex Workers: Rights, Resistance, and Redefinition*, ed. Kamala Kempadoo and Jo Doezema, 139–50. New York: Routledge.

———. 2001. *Modern Babylon? Prostituting Children in Thailand*. New York: Berghahn.

Mutua, Makau. 2001. "Savages, Victims, and Saviors: The Metaphor of Human Rights." *Harvard International Law Journal* 42:201–45.

Narayan, Uma. 1998. "Essence of Culture and a Sense of History: A Feminist Critique of Cultural Essentialism." *Hypatia* 13, no. 2: 86–106.

Negt, Oskar, and Alexander Kluge. 1993. *Public Sphere and Experience: Toward an Analysis of the Bourgeois and Proletarian Public Sphere*. Trans. Peter Labanyi, Jamie Owen Daniel, and Assenka Oksiloff. Minneapolis: University of Minnesota Press.

Neumayr, George. 2004. "Thelma and Louise in Iraq." *American Spectator*, 5 May.

Nichols, Bill. 1992. *Representing Reality: Images and Concepts in Documentary*. Bloomington: Indiana University Press.

Nikolić-Ristanović, Vesna. 1999. "Living without Democracy and Peace: Violence against Women in the Former Yugoslavia." *Violence against Women* 51, no. 1: 63–81.

Norton, Anne. 1988. *Reflections on Political Identity*. Baltimore: Johns Hopkins University Press.

Novkov, Julie. 2000. "Historicizing the Figure of the Child in Legal Discourse: The Battle over the Regulation of Child Labor." *American Journal of Legal History* 90, no. 4: 369–404.

Nussbaum, Martha. 1998. *Cultivating Humanity: A Classical Defense of Reform in Liberal Education*. Cambridge: Harvard University Press.

Oliver, Kelly. 2001. *Witnessing beyond Recognition*. Minneapolis: University of Minnesota Press.

Ong, Aihwa. 1999. *Flexible Citizenship: The Cultural Logics of Transnationality*. Durham: Duke University Press.

Pace, Patricia. 2002. "Staging Childhood: Lewis Hine's Photographs of Child Labor." *Lion and the Unicorn* 26:324–52.

Pal, Minu, Sadhana Mukherji, Madhabi Jaisal, and Bachhu Dutta. 1998. "The Wind of Change is Whispering at Your Door: The Mahila Samanwaya Committee." In *Global Sex Workers: Rights, Resistance, and Redefinition*, ed. Kamala Kempadoo and Jo Doezema, 200–203. New York: Routledge.

Papacharissi, Zizi. 2002. "The Virtual Sphere: The Internet as a Public Sphere." *New Media and Society* 4, no. 1: 9–27.

Parekh, Serena. 2007. "Can a Violent Husband Violate Human Rights?" *Journal of Human Rights* 6, no. 1: 131–41.

Parks, Lisa. 2007. "Digging into Google Earth: An Analysis of 'Crisis in Darfur.'" Paper presented as part of the University of Michigan Rackham Human Rights Lecture Series, 30 November.

Penezić, Vida. 1995. "Women in Yugoslavia." In *Postcommunism and the Body Politic*, ed. Ellen E. Berry, 57–77. New York: New York University Press.

Perucci, Toni. 2005. "Performance Complexes: Abu Ghraib and the Culture of Neoliberalism." Paper presented at the National Communication Association Annual Convention.

Petrakis, John. 2005. "Kids with Cameras." *Christian Century*, 22 February, 64.

Petro, Patrice, ed. 1995. *Fugitive Images: From Photography to Video*. Bloomington: Indiana University Press.

Petruzzi, Anthony P. 2001. "Kairotic Rhetoric in Freire's Liberatory Pedagogy." JAC 21, no. 2: 349–81.

Phelan, James. 1996. *Narrative as Rhetoric: Technique, Audiences, Ethics, Ideology*. Columbus: Ohio University Press.

Plant, Sadie. 1992. *The Most Radical Gesture: The Situationist International in a Postmodern Age*. New York: Routledge.

Plato. 2003. *The Republic*. Trans. Desmond Less. 2nd ed. London: Penguin.

Poovey, Mary. 2002. "The Liberal Civil Subject and the Social in 18th Century British Moral Philosophy." *Public Culture* 14, no. 1: 125–45.

Porter, James. 1986. "Intertextuality and the Discourse Community." *Rhetoric Review* 5:34–47.

Power, Samantha. 2002. *"A Problem from Hell": America and the Age of Genocide*. New York: Harper Collins.

Price, Joshua M. 2001. "Violence against Prostitutes and a Re-evaluation of the Counterpublic Sphere." *Genders* 34:1–38.

Pronk, Jan. 2005. "We Need More Stories and More Pictures." Address to World Press Photo, 8 October, Amsterdam.

Puar, Jasbir. 2007. *Terrorist Assemblages: Homonationalism in Queer Times*. Durham: Duke University Press.

Pupavac, Vanessa. 2001. "Misanthropy without Borders: The International Children's Rights Regime." *Disasters* 25, no. 2: 95–112.

Rahman, Mohammad Mafizur, Rasheda Khanam, and Nur Uddin Absar. 1999. "Child Labor in Bangladesh: A Critical Appraisal of Harkin's Bill and the MOU-Type Schooling Program." *Journal of Economic Issues* 3, no. 4.

Ramet, Sabrina P., ed. 1999. *Gender Politics in the Western Balkans: Women and Society in Yugoslavia and the Yugoslavia Successor States*. University Park: Pennsylvania State University Press.

Rancière, Jacques. 2004. "Who Is the Subject of the Rights of Man?" *South Atlantic Quarterly* 103, nos. 2 and 3: 297–310.

———. 2007a. Reprint. *The Politics of Aesthetics: The Distribution of the Sensible*. Trans. Gabriel Rockhill. London: Continuum.

———. 2007b. "The Emancipated Spectator." *Art Forum*, March, 270–77.

———. 2007c. *The Future of the Image*. Trans. Gregory Elliott. London: Verso.

Rasmussen, Mikkel Bolt. 2006. "Counterrevolution, the Spectacle, and the Situationist Avant-Garde." *Social Justice* 33, no. 2: 5–15.

Ratcliffe, Krista. 1999. "Rhetorical Listening: A Trope for Interpretive Invention and a Code of Cross-Cultural Conduct." *College Composition and Communication* 51, no. 2: 195–224.

———. 2005. *Rhetorical Listening: Indentification, Gender, Whiteness*. Carbondale: Southern Illinois University Press.

Reeves, Eric. 2006. "Watching Genocide, Doing Nothing: The Final Betrayal of Darfur." *Dissent* (fall): 5–9.

Reinelt, Janell. 1998. "Notes for a Radical Democratic Theater: Productive Crises and the Challenge of Indeterminacy." In *Staging Resistance: Essays on Political Theater*, ed. Jeanne Colleran and Jenny S. Spencer, 283–300. Ann Arbor: University of Michigan Press.

Reinhardt, Mark, and Holly Edwards. 2007. "Traffic in Pain." In *Beautiful Suffering: Photography and the Traffic in Pain*, ed. Mark Reinhardt, Holly Edwards, and Erina Dugganne, 7–12. Williamstown, Mass.: Williams College Museum of Art.

Rejali, Darius M. 1998. "After Feminist Analyses of Bosnian Violence." In *The Women and War Reader*, ed. Lois Ann Lorentzen and Jennifer Turpin, 26–32. New York: New York University Press.

Renov, Michael. 1993. *Theorizing Documentary*. New York: Routledge.

Rentschler, Carrie A. 2004. "Witnessing: U.S. Citizenship and the Vicarious Experience of Suffering." *Media, Culture, and Society* 26, no. 2: 296–304.

Retort [Iain Boal, T. I. Clark, Joseph Matthews, and Michael Watts]. 2005. *Afflicted Powers: Capital and Spectacle in a New Age of War*. London: Verso.

Richmond, Anthony H. 1994. *Global Apartheid: Refugees, Racism, and the New World Order*. Toronto: Oxford University Press.

Richter-Montpetit, Melanie. 2007. "A Queer Transnational Feminist Reading of the Prisoner 'Abuse' in Abu Ghraib and the Question of 'Gender Equality.'" *International Feminist Journal of Politics* 9, no. 1: 38–59.

Ricoeur, Paul. 2005. *The Course of Recognition*. Trans. David Pellauer. Cambridge: Harvard University Press.

Riding, Alan. 2004. "On a London Stage: A Hearing for Guantanamo Detainees." *New York Times*, 15 June.

Riedner, Rachel, and Kevin Mahoney. 2008. *Democracies to Come: Rhetorical Action, Neoliberalism, and Communities of Resistance*. Lanham, Md.: Lexington.

Rieff, David. 2003. *A Bed for the Night: Humanitarianism in Crisis*. New York: Simon and Schuster.

Robbins, Bruce. 1998a. "Actually Existing Cosmopolitanism." In *Cosmopolitics: Thinking and Feeling beyond the Nation*, ed. Pheng Cheah and Bruce Robbins, 1–19. Minneapolis: University of Minnesota Press.

———. 1998b. "Comparative Cosmopolitanisms." In *Cosmopolitics: Thinking and Feeling beyond the Nation*, ed. Pheng Cheah and Bruce Robbins, 246–64. Minneapolis: University of Minnesota Press.

———. 1999. *Feeling Global: Internationalism in Distress*. New York: New York University Press.

Rodowick, D. N. 2002. Introduction. In "Special Topic: Mobile Citizens, Media States," coordinated by Emily Apter, Anton Kaes, and D. N. Rodowick. Special issue, PMLA 117, no. 1: 13–23.

Rogoff, Irit. 2000. *Terra Infirma: Geography's Visual Culture*. London: Routledge.

Rohde, David. 2007. "Foreign Fighters of Violent Bent Bolster Taliban." *New York Times*, 30 October.

Roof, Judith, and Robyn Wiegman. 1995. *Who Can Speak? Authority and Critical Identity*. Urbana: University of Illinois Press.

Rorty, Richard. 1993. "Human Rights, Rationality, and Sentimentality." In *On Human Rights: The Oxford Amnesty Lectures,* eds. Stephen Shute and Susan Hurley, 111–34. New York: Basic Books.

Rose, Gillian. 2001. *Visual Methodologies.* London: Sage.

Rothberg, Michael. 2000. *Traumatic Realism: The Demands of Holocaust Representation.* Minneapolis: University of Minnesota Press.

Said, Edward W. 1978. *Orientalism.* New York: Random House.

———. 1981. *Covering Islam: How the Media and the Experts Determine How We See the Rest of the World.* New York: Pantheon.

———. 2001. "The Essential Terrorist." In *Blaming the Victim: Spurious Scholarship and the Palestinian Question,* ed. Edward W. Said and Christopher Hitchens, 149–58. London: Verso.

Sánchez-Casal, Susan. 2001. "I Am [Not] Like You: Ideologies of Selfhood in *I, Rigoberta Menchu: An Indian Woman in Guatemala.*" In *Haunting Violations: Feminist Criticism and the Crisis of the "Real,"* ed. Wendy Hesford and Wendy Kozol, 76–110. Urbana: University of Illinois Press.

Sánchez-Eppler, Karen. 2005. *Dependent States: The Child's Part in Nineteenth Century American Culture.* Chicago: University of Chicago Press.

Scarry, Elaine. 1985. *The Body in Pain: The Making and Unmaking of the World.* New York: Oxford University Press.

Schaffer, Kay, and Sidonie Smith. 2004. *Human Rights and Narrated Lives: The Ethics of Recognition.* New York: Palgrave Macmillan.

Schell, Eileen E. 2006. "Gender, Rhetorics, and Globalization: Rethinking the Spaces and Locations of Feminist Rhetorics and Women's Rhetorics in Our Field." In *Rhetorica Redefines Theory and Practice,* ed. Joy Ritchie and Kate Ronald, 160–74. Portsmouth: Heinemann.

Schickel, Richard. 2005. "The Sins of the Mothers." *Time,* 7 February, 77.

Sekula, Allan. 1986. "The Body and the Archive." *October* 36 (winter): 3–64.

Selzer, Jack. 1993. "Intertextuality and the Writing Process." In *Writing in the Workplace,* ed. Rachel Spilka. Carbondale: Southern Illinois University Press.

Shah, Svati P. 2005. "Born into Saving Brothel Children." *Samar: South Asian Magazine for Action and Reflection* 19 (spring). www.samarmagazine.org/archive/article.php?id=190.

Shapiro, Bruce. 2007. "The Saddam Spectacle." *Nation,* 22 January, 4–5.

Shapiro, Stephanie. 2004. "Abu Ghraib Photos Are in Exhibits." *Baltimore Sun,* 17 September.

Sharpe, Jenny. 1991. "The Unspeakable Limits of Rape: Colonial Violence and Counter-Insurgency." *Genders* 10:25–46.

Shohat, Ella. 1998. Introduction. In *Talking Visions: Multicultural Feminism in a Transnational Age,* ed. Ella Shohat, 1–62. New York: New Museum of Contemporary Art.

———. 2006. *Taboo Memories, Diasporic Voices.* Durham: Duke University Press.

Shohat, Ella, and Robert Stam. 1994. *Unthinking Eurocentrism: Multiculturalism and the Media.* New York: Routledge.

———. 1999. "From the Imperial Family to the Transnational Imaginary: Media Spectatorship in the Age of Globalization." In *Global Local: Cultural Production and the Transnational Imaginary*, ed. Rob Wilson and Wimal Dissanayake, 145–70. Durham: Duke University Press.

Shome, Raka. 1999. "Postcolonial Interventions in the Rhetorical Canon: An 'Other' View." In *Contemporary Rhetorical Theory: A Reader*, ed. John Louis Lucaites, Celeste Michelle Condit, and Sally Caudill. New York: Guilford Press.

Shuman, Amy. 2005. *Other People's Stories*. Urbana: University of Illinois Press.

Silverman, Kaja. 1996. *The Threshold of the Visible World*. New York: Routledge.

Simmons, Melanie. 1999. "Theorizing Prostitution: The Question of Agency." In *Sex Work and Sex Workers*, ed. Barry M. Dank and Roberto Refinetti, 125–46. New Brunswick, N.J.: Transaction.

Simon, Roger I. 2000. "The Paradoxical Practice of Zakhor: Memories of 'What Has Never Been My Fault or My Deed.'" In *Between Hope and Despair: Pedagogy and the Remembrance of Historical Trauma*, ed. Roger I. Simon, Sharon Rosenberg, and Claudia Eppert, 9–26. Lanham, Md.: Rowman and Littlefield.

Skrobanek, Siriporn, Nataya Boonpakdee, and Chutima Jantateero. 1997. *The Traffic in Women: Human Realities of the International Sex Trade*. London: Zed.

Slaughter, Joseph R. 1997. "A Question of Narration: The Voice in International Human Rights Law." *Human Rights Quarterly* 19:406–30.

———. 2006. "Enabling Fictions and Novel Subjects: The *Bildungs-roman* and International Human Rights Law." *PMLA* 121, no. 5: 1405–24.

———. 2007. *Human Rights, Inc.: The World Novel, Narrative Form, and International Law*. New York: Fordham University Press.

Smith, Adam. [1759] 2000. *The Theory of Moral Sentiments*. Amherst: Prometheus Books.

Smith, Roberta. 2005. "From Children Raised in Brothels, Glimpses of Life's Possibilities." *New York Times*, 12 August.

Smith, Sidonie, and Julia Watson, eds. 1992. *De/Colonizing the Subject: The Politics of Gender in Women's Autobiography*. Minneapolis: University of Minnesota Press.

Solomon-Godeau, Abigail. 1991. *Photography at the Dock: Essays on Photographic History, Institutions, and Practices*. Minneapolis: University of Minnesota Press.

Sommer, Doris. 1988. "'Not Just a Personal Story': Women's *Testimonios* and the Plural Self." In *Life/Lines: Theorizing Women's Autobiography*, ed. Bella Brodzki and Celeste Schenck, 107–30. Ithaca: Cornell University Press.

Sontag, Susan. 1967. "The Pornographic Imagination." *Partisan Review* (spring).

———. 2003. *Regarding the Pain of Others*. New York: Farrar, Straus and Giroux.

———. 2004. "Regarding the Torture of Others." *New York Times Magazine*, 23 May, 24–29, 42.

Spelman, Elizabeth. 1997. *Fruits of Sorrow: Framing Our Attention to Suffering*. Boston: Beacon.

Spivak, Gayatri Chakravorty. 1988. "Can the Subaltern Speak?" In *Marxism and the Interpretation of Culture*, ed. Cary Nelson and Lawrence Grossberg, 271–313. Urbana: University of Illinois Press.

———. 1995. Introduction. *Imaginary Maps: Three Stories*, by Mahasweta Devi, xxiii–xxxi. Trans. Gayatri Spivak. New York: Routledge.

————. 2003. "Righting Wrongs." In *Human Rights, Human Wrongs: The Oxford Amnesty Lectures, 2001*, ed. Nicholas Owen, 164–227. Oxford: Oxford University Press.

Spurr, David. 1993. *Rhetoric of Empire*. Durham: Duke University Press.

Stanton, Donna. 2006. "The Humanities in Human Rights: Critique, Language, Politics." *PMLA* 121, no. 5: 1518–25.

Stiglmayer, Alexandra, ed. 1994. *Mass Rape: The War against Women in Bosnia-Herzegovina*. Lincoln: University of Nebraska Press.

Strauss, David Levi. 2004. "Breakdown in the Gray Room: Recent Turns in the Image War." In *Abu Ghraib: The Politics of Torture*, 87–101. Berkeley, Calif.: North Atlantic Books.

Swami, Praveen. 2005. "A Missionary Enterprise." *Frontline*, 12 March.

Tagg, John. 1993. *The Burden of Representation: Essays on Photographies and Histories*. Minneapolis: University of Minnesota Press.

Tal, Kali. 1996. *Worlds of Hurt: Reading the Literatures of Trauma*. New York: Cambridge University Press.

Tanner, Laura E. 1994. *Intimate Violence: Reading Rape and Torture in Twentieth-Century Fiction*. Bloomington: Indiana University Press.

Taylor, Charles. 2002. "Modern Social Imaginaries." *Public Culture* 14, no. 1: 91–124.

Taylor, Diana. 1997. *Disappearing Acts: Spectacles of Gender and Nationalism in Argentina's "Dirty War."* Durham: Duke University Press.

————. 2003. *The Archive and the Repertoire: Performing Cultural Memory in the Americas*. Durham: Duke University Press.

Tétreault, Mary Ann. 2006. "The Sexual Politics of Abu Ghraib: Hegemony, Spectacle, and the Global War on Terror." *NWSA Journal* 18, no. 3: 33–50.

Thayer, Millie. 2000. "Traveling Feminism: From Embodied Women to Gendered Citizenship." In *Global Ethnography: Forces, Connections, and Imaginations in a Postmodern World*, ed. Michael Burawoy et al., 203–34. Berkeley: University of California Press.

Thomas, Dorothy Q., and Michele E. Beasley. 1993. "Domestic Violence as a Human Rights Issue." *Human Rights Quarterly* 15:36–62.

Tibbetts, Felisa. 2002. "Understanding What We Do: Emerging Models of Human Rights Education." *International Review of Education* 43, no. 3/4: 159–71.

Tuitt, Patrica. 1996. *False Images: Law's Construction of the Refugee*. London: Pluto.

United Nations. 1994. "Commission of Experts' Final Report. Annex IX: Rape and Sexual Assault." Security Council, S/1994/674/Add.2 (vol. 5), 28, December.

United Nations High Commissioner for Refugees [UNHCR]. 2007. "Karcha Garhi Refugee Camp Closes in Pakistan after 27 Years." 27 July. http://www.reliefweb.int/rw/RWB.NSF/db900SID/EGUA-75HNLY?Open.

Van Sant, Ann Jessie. 1993. *Eighteenth Century Sensibility and the Novel: The Senses in Social Context*. New York: Cambridge University Press.

Volosinov, V. N. 1973. *Marxism and the Philosophy of Language*. Trans. Ladislaw Matejka and I. R. Titunik. New York: Seminar Press.

Volpp, Leti. 2006. "Disappearing Acts: On Gendered Violence, Pathological Cultures, and Civil Society." *PMLA* 121, no. 5: 1631–38.

Vranić, Seada. 1996. *Breaking the Wall of Silence: The Voice of Raped Bosnia.* Zagreb: Isdanja Antibarbarus.

Wallis, Brian. 2004. "Remember Abu Ghraib." In *Inconvenient Evidence: Iraqi Prison Photographs from Abu Ghraib. Exhibition catalogue*, 3–5. New York: International Center for Photography.

Wanzo, Rebecca. 2009. *The Suffering Will Not Be Televised.* Albany: State University of New York Press.

Warner, Marina. 2005. "Disembodied Eyes, or the Culture of Apocalypse." *Open Democracy*, 17 April. www.OpenDemocracy.net.

Weine, Stevan M. 1999. *When History Is a Nightmare: Lives and Memories of Ethnic Cleansing in Bosnia-Herzegovina.* New Brunswick, N.J.: Rutgers University Press.

Weinstock, Jeffrey A. 2004. *Spectral America: Phantoms and the National Imagination.* Madison: University of Wisconsin Press.

Weiss, Thomas G., and Cindy Collins. 1996. *Humanitarian Challenges and Intervention: World Politics and the Dilemmas of Help.* Boulder, Colo.: Westview Press.

Wells, Susan. 2003. "Rhetoric and Agency." Paper presented at Annual Rhetorical Society Conference, September.

Westhead, Rick. 2005. "Oscar's Midas Touch." *Toronto Star*, 8 March, C01.

Whitlock, Gillian. 2007. *Soft Weapons: Autobiography in Transit.* Chicago: University of Chicago Press.

Wiegman, Robyn. 1995. *American Anatomies: Theorizing Race and Gender.* Durham: Duke University Press.

Wijers, Marjan, and Lin Lap-Chew. 1997. "Trafficking in Women, Forced Labour and Slavery-Like Practices in Marriage, Domestic Labour, and Prostitution." Utrecht, Netherlands: STV.

Williams, Raymond. 1997. *Marxism and Literature.* Oxford: Oxford University Press.

Willis, Susan. 2005. *Portents of the Real: A Primer for Post-9/11 America.* London: Verso.

Wilson, Ara. 2004. "Remapping Trafficking: Conceptualizing Customer Demand." Paper presented at the Dark Side of Globalization: Trafficking in People conference, Ohio State University, Columbus, 15 May.

Wilson, Richard A., and Richard D. Brown, eds. 2009. *Humanitarianism and Suffering: The Mobilization of Empathy.* New York: Cambridge University Press.

Wilson, Rob. 1998. "A New Cosmopolitanism Is in the Air: Some Dialectical Twists and Turns." *Cosmopolitics: Thinking and Feeling beyond the Nation*, ed. Pheng Cheah and Bruce Robbins, 351–61. Minneapolis: University of Minnesota Press.

Woodward, Kathleen. 2004. "Calculating Compassion." In *Compassion: The Culture and Politics of an Emotion*, ed. Lauren Berlant, 59–86. New York: Routledge.

Woodward, Susan L. 2000. "Violence-Prone Area or International Transition? Addressing the Role of Outsiders in Balkan Violence." In *Violence and Subjectivity*, ed. Veena Das, Arthur Kleinman, Mamphela Ramphele, and Pamela Reynolds, 19–45. Berkeley: University of California Press.

Yaeger, Patricia. 2006. "Testimony without Intimacy." *Poetics Today* 27, no. 2: 399–423.

Young, Iris Marion. 1997. *Intersecting Voices: Dilemmas of Gender, Political Philosophy and Policy*. Princeton: Princeton University Press.

Young, James. 2000. *At Memory's Edge: After-Images of the Holocaust in Contemporary Art and Architecture*. New Haven: Yale University Press.

Yudice, George. 1991. "Testimonio and Postmodernism: Whom Does Testimonial Writing Represent?" In "Voices and the Voiceless in Testimonial Literature," ed. Georg Gugelberger and Michael Kearney. Special issue, *Latin American Perspectives* 18, no. 70: 15–31.

Žarkov, Dubravka. 2007. *The Body of War: Media, Ethnicity, and Gender in the Break-Up of Yugoslavia*. Durham: Duke University Press.

Zelizer, Barbie. 2000. *Remembering to Forget: Holocaust Memory through the Camera's Eye*. Chicago: University of Chicago Press.

———, ed. 2001. *Visual Culture and the Holocaust*. New Brunswick, N.J.: Rutgers University Press.

———. 2003. "Photography, Journalism, and Trauma." In *Journalism after September 11*, ed. Barbie Zelizer and Stuart Allan, 48–68. London: Routledge.

Zimmerman, Patricia R. 2000. *States of Emergency: Documentaries, Wars, Democracies*. Minneapolis: University of Minnesota Press.

Žižek, Slavoj. 1993. *Tarrying with the Negative: Kant, Hegel, and the Critique of Ideology*. Durham: Duke University Press.

———. 2000. *The Fragile Absolute, or, Why Is the Christian Legacy Worth Fighting For?* New York: Verso.

———. 2002. *Welcome to the Desert of the Real*. New York: Verson.

———. 2004. "Between Two Deaths." *London Review of Books*, 3 June, 19.

———. 2005. "The Obscenity of Human Rights: Violence as Symptom." http://www.lacan.com/zizviol.htm.

Zoya, with John Follain and Rita Cristofari. 2002. *Zoya's Story: An Afghan Woman's Struggle for Freedom*. New York: Harper Collins.

Wendy S. Hesford is professor of English, Ohio State University.

Library of Congress Cataloging-in-Publication Data

Hesford, Wendy S.

Spectacular rhetorics : human rights visions, recognitions,

feminisms / Wendy Hesford.

p. cm.—(Next wave)

Includes bibliographical references and index.

ISBN 978-0-8223-4933-4 (cloth : alk. paper)

ISBN 978-0-8223-4951-8 (pbk. : alk. paper)

1. Human rights.    2. Human rights advocacy.

3. Women's rights.    I. Title.    II. Series: Next wave.

JC571.H474    2011

323—dc22                        2010049649